Of Precariousness

CDE Studies

Edited by
Martin Middeke

Volume 28

Of Precariousness

Vulnerabilities, Responsibilities, Communities
in 21st-Century British Drama and Theatre

Edited by
Mireia Aragay and Martin Middeke

DE GRUYTER

ISBN 978-3-11-065159-1
e-ISBN (PDF) 978-3-11-054871-6
e-ISBN (EPUB) 978-3-11-054677-4
ISSN 2194-9069

Library of Congress Cataloging-in-Publication Data
A CIP catalog record for this book has been applied for at the Library of Congress.

Bibliographic information published by the Deutsche Nationalbibliothek
The Deutsche Nationalbibliothek lists this publication in the Deutsche Nationalbibliografie;
detailed bibliographic data are available on the Internet at http://dnb.dnb.de.

© 2019 Walter de Gruyter GmbH, Berlin/Boston
This volume is text- and page-identical with the hardback published in 2017.
Printing and binding: CPI books GmbH, Leck
♾ Printed on acid-free paper
Printed in Germany

www.degruyter.com

Acknowledgements

First and foremost, the editors wish to thank the contributors to this volume for their enthusiasm and commitment to the project, their scholarly rigour, their critically receptive engagement with ideas, and their human warmth and friendliness. We are also grateful to the student and research assistants at the University of Augsburg, Korbinian Stöckl, Julia Rössler, Christina Schönberger, Elisabeth Schmitt, Despina Repa, Alexander Lehner, Sarah Auer, Leonie Müller, and Eva-Maria Toth for their help during the proofreading stage, a task they performed under Martin Riedelsheimer's expert guidance.

This project would not have been possible without the financial support provided by the German Academic Exchange Service (DAAD) and the Spanish Ministry of Economy and Competitiveness (MINECO) via, respectively, the research projects "Representations of the Precarious in Contemporary British Theatre since 1989" (Projekt-ID 57049392) and "Ethical Issues in Contemporary British Theatre since 1989: Globalisation, Theatricality, Spectatorship" (project reference FFI2012–31842). The editors also wish to acknowledge the support given by the University of Augsburg and the recognition and funding granted by the Catalan government's research agency AGAUR to the research group Contemporary British Theatre Barcelona (CBTBarcelona), based at the University of Barcelona (http://www.ub.edu/cbtbarcelona). On a final note, we would like to thank all the students participating in several masterclasses on the precarious and literary/performative ethics in Augsburg, Barcelona, and Johannesburg for their enthusiasm and willingness to engage with our questions.

Mireia Aragay and Martin Middeke
Barcelona and Augsburg, May 2017

Table of Contents

Mireia Aragay/Martin Middeke
Precariousness in Drama and Theatre: An Introduction —— 1

Mireia Aragay
On the Threshold: Precarious Hospitalities as Utopian Imaginings in *Pornography*, *Fewer Emergencies* **and** *The American Pilot* —— 15

Enric Monforte
Staging Terror and Precariousness in Simon Stephens's *Pornography* **and Mark Ravenhill's** *Shoot/Get Treasure/Repeat* —— 31

Christian Attinger
Staging Hobbes, or: Theseus Goes to the Theatre. Precariousness, Cultural Memory and Dystopia in Philip Ridley's *Mercury Fur* —— 47

David Kerler
Jez Butterworth's *Jerusalem* **and Postmodern Precariousness** —— 63

Christoph Henke
Precarious Virtuality in Participatory Theatre: Tim Crouch's *The Author* —— 77

Cristina Delgado-García
"We're All in This Together": Reality, Vulnerability and Democratic Representation in Tim Crouch's *The Author* —— 91

Bettina Auerswald
Promises of the Real? The Precariousness of Verbatim Theatre and Robin Soans's *Talking to Terrorists* —— 109

José R. Prado
Spaces for the Construction of Community: The Theatre Uncut Phenomenon —— 125

Adina Sorian
Living in Liquid Times: Precariousness and Plasticity in Forced Entertainment's *Tomorrow's Parties* —— 141

Verónica Rodríguez
Bridging Precariousness and Precarity: Ecstasy and Bleeding Across in the Work of David Greig and Suspect Culture —— 155

Elżbieta Baraniecka
Precariousness of Love and Shattered Subjects in Dennis Kelly's *Love and Money* **—— 171**

Clara Escoda
Ethics, Precariousness and the 'Inclination' towards the Other in debbie tucker green's *dirty butterfly*, **Laura Wade's** *Posh* **and Martin Crimp's** *In the Republic of Happiness* **—— 187**

Martin Riedelsheimer
Vulnerability and the Community of the Precarious in David Greig's *The Events* **—— 203**

Martin Middeke
The Inoperative Community and Death: Ontological Aspects of the Precarious in David Greig's *The Events* **and Caryl Churchill's** *Here We Go* **—— 217**

Notes on Contributors —— 235

Index —— 237

Mireia Aragay/Martin Middeke
Precariousness in Drama and Theatre: An Introduction

The essays collected in this volume emerge out of a desire to examine the various ways in which contemporary British drama and theatre engage with 'precariousness'. Within the framework of two research projects – "Representations of the Precarious in Contemporary British Theatre since 1989", funded by the German Academic Exchange Service (DAAD), and "Ethical Issues in Contemporary British Theatre since 1989: Globalisation, Theatricality, Spectatorship", funded by the Spanish Ministry of Economy and Competitiveness (MINECO) – two groups of researchers, based at the Universities of Augsburg, Germany, and Barcelona, Spain, and led by the editors, took as their methodological starting point four core theoretical positions: Emmanuel Levinas's "Ethics as First Philosophy" (1989 [1984]); Judith Butler's *Precarious Life: The Powers of Mourning and Violence* (2004) and her later essay "Precarious Life, Vulnerability, and the Ethics of Cohabitation", delivered first as a lecture at the Centre de Cultura Contemporània (CCCB) in Barcelona in July 2011 and subsequently published, with minor revisions, in *Journal of Speculative Philosophy* (2012); Jacques Derrida's reflections on 'hos(ti)pitality' (2000); and, finally, Jean-Luc Nancy's study *The Inoperative Community*, originally published in 1986 (English translation, 1991).

The two groups of researchers met in Augsburg (April 2014) and Barcelona (September 2014), and in the convivial and intellectually stimulating atmosphere of two research seminars, key points were debated, significant threads identified and ideas began to expand in diverse directions and were subsequently shaped by each researcher into their individual contribution to the present collection.[1]

* * *

---

[1] Katharina Pewny's *Das Drama des Prekären: Über die Wiederkehr der Ethik in Theater und Performance* (2011) shares a concern with 'the precarious'. It is impossible to do justice to every detail in the dense and complex argumentation of Pewny's monograph. Although, inevitably, many of her arguments resurface in our analyses, her focus on performance, dance and film in German-speaking countries (Austria, Germany and Switzerland) and her positing of certain features – the central role of the performing body; relational and participatory modes of audience engagement – as distinctive of an alleged theatrical aesthetic of the precarious distinguish her approach from ours. Nevertheless, her thoroughly learned, painstaking analysis of the relevance of the precarious for a contemporary aesthetics of both stage and performance is groundbreaking and is taken up again at various points in our study.

When, in his *Dictionary of the English Language*, Samuel Johnson defines 'precarious' as meaning "[d]ependent; uncertain, because depending on the will of another; changeable or alienable at the pleasure of another", and goes on to add that although the word "is used for uncertain in all its senses [...] it only means uncertain, as dependent on others", he seems to be coupling the adjective primarily with the noun 'precarity' (Johnson 1968). Butler, one of the contemporary thinkers who has devoted most sustained attention to thinking the precarious in a post-9/11 globalised world, points out that 'precarity' in its current acceptation designates "that dimension of politics that addresses the organization and protection of bodily needs. Precarity exposes our sociality, the fragile and necessary dimensions of our interdependency" (Butler 2012: 148). The editors of the 2012 special issue of *The Drama Review* devoted to precarity go one step further when they describe it as "a byword for life in late and later capitalism" (Ridout and Schneider 2012: 7) – or, according to some, "life in capitalism *as usual*" (Ridout and Schneider 2012: 7) – that underlines "economic precarity, neoliberal precarity" (Ridout and Schneider 2012: 6).

It seems important to recall, however, that 'the precarious' may also make "a broad existential claim, namely, that everyone is precarious", given our "existence as bodily beings who depend upon one another for shelter and sustenance" (Butler 2012: 148), i.e. our ontological 'precariousness' (see also Korte and Regard 2014: 9). In this connection, Isabell Lorey suggests that "the term 'precarity' (*Prekarität*)" be used to designate "social positionings of insecurity and hierarchization", while "precariousness (*Prekärsein*)" be kept for the "relational condition of social being that cannot be avoided" (Puar 2012: 165).[2] Importantly, however, she adds that these two dimensions are "[i]ntertwined" (Puar 2012: 165). Indeed, in her 2012 article Butler concludes that since "the existential claim" must always "be articulated in its specificity", "it ceases to be existential" – "our precarity is *to a large extent* dependent upon the organization of econom-

---

[2] Korte and Regard quote the following pertinent definition of 'precarity' from Butler's *Frames of War: When Is Life Grievable?*: "[T]hat politically induced condition in which certain populations suffer from failing social and economic networks of support and become differentially exposed to injury, violence, and death. Such populations are at heightened risk of disease, poverty, starvation, displacement, and of exposure to violence without protection. Precarity also characterizes that politically induced condition of maximized precariousness for populations exposed to arbitrary state violence who often have no other option than to appeal to the very state from which they need protection" (Butler 2009: 26, qtd. in Korte and Regard 2014: 9). For further differentiation, see also Claviez 2016.

ic and social relationships, the presence or absence of sustaining infrastructures and social and political institutions" (2012: 148; emphasis added).³

We would suggest, however, the need to qualify Butler's conclusion somewhat – as she herself does, in fact, when she inserts the caveat "to a large extent" above. In a world where specific manifestations of precarity seem to be ceaselessly redoubling in intensity and becoming more widespread, it is certainly inexcusable not to address the political, social and economic managements of precariousness and examine the ways in which they produce and/or heighten forms of precarity. Since the start of 2015, the European migrant crisis has continued to escalate, with more than two million migrants, refugees and asylum seekers having crossed into Europe according to the UNHCR (numbers differ depending on the source). Although the topic does not currently dominate the news headlines as it did at the peak of the crisis in late 2015/early 2016, it continues to impact on the lives of thousands of people who, having escaped war zones or precarious lives in their home countries, find themselves in new conditions of precarity. News reports and visual records of the massive influx and of living conditions in the refugee camps remind us constantly that although we may indeed all share the same ontological condition known as precariousness, precarity on the other hand is not equally distributed. (At the same time, the presence of the European migration crisis in the media often foregrounds the problematics of representation when it comes to the precarious, a question to which we return in due course).

And yet, it seems equally urgent in such a context to underline the ethical and even political significance of (ontological) precariousness. As is well known, to a large extent Butler's explorations of precariousness/precarity emanate from her (critical) reading of Levinasian ethics. Levinas's much-discussed turn to 'the face of the Other' involves a two-pronged demand – namely, that the Self's existence (Being) is only justified in so far as it is open *both* to the absolute, irreducible alterity or difference of the Other *and* to their "nakedness and destitution", to their "extreme exposure, defencelessness, vulnerability", which ultimately amounts to an "exposure to invisible death" (Levinas 1989: 83). In other words, both to the political realm of difference and to the ethical realm of sameness, where our *shared* vulnerability, exposure and mortality are, in Butler's words, "the joint of our nonfoundation" (Butler 2012: 148), the indispensable basis, in her view, for a global ethics and a radically renewed humanism. Pertinently in relation to the European migration crisis, it is only if Levinas's re-

---

3 Butler's reflections on precariousness/precarity have evolved from what was perhaps a more binary position in, for example, *Frames of War* (2009: 25–26).

minder that we are all "stranger[s] or 'sojourner[s] on earth'" (Levinas 1989: 81) and its political implication – "[t]he unchosen character of earthly co-habitation [that] is [...] the condition of our very existence as ethical and political beings" (Butler 2012: 143) – were taken to heart that it might begin to be possible, perhaps, to fulfill our ethical and political obligation "to make mixed community [...] among those whose existence implies a right to exist and to lead a liveable life" (Butler 2012: 146) by managing our common condition – precariousness – in ways that produce more equitable distributions of precarity. After all, peace, defined by Levinas as "awakeness to the precariousness of the other" (qtd. in Butler 2004: 134), may well depend on our capacity to do so.

Such 'awakeness' requires, in Levinas's terms, an "ego (*moi*) which has got rid of self (*soi*) and instead fears for the Other" (1989: 85). "It is in the laying down by the ego of its sovereignty", Levinas continues, "that we find ethics" (1989: 85). Similarly, in the course of the conversation that makes up *Dispossession: The Performative in the Political*, Butler and Athena Athanasiou address "the fraught question of relational ethics" (2013: 92) but give it a political accent when they suggest that "the self-sufficient 'I' as a form of possession" (2013: 93) needs to be displaced, dispossessed, before it may enter into any kind of collective action that opposes existing forms of dispossession and precarity.

The question of the problematic nature of the I, or 'ego', underlies two other theoretical frames which have had a great impact on our understanding of precariousness. The poststructuralist ethics of Jacques Derrida have focused on equivocal issues such as undecidability, the – truly precarious – responsibility to the Other, and indeed on the aporias which are inherent to such concepts as 'the gift', 'forgiveness' or 'mourning'. In our context of explaining and further differentiating precariousness, the aporia of (im)possible 'hospitality' has proved extremely productive.[4] Many of the plays discussed in our volume depict communication with the Other (both within their diegetic frameworks as well as in their performative settings and their respective configurations of spectatorship) as a precarious act of hospitality. For Derrida, as for many of these plays, there can be no genuine, unconditional hospitality towards others or the Other, as it would entail giving up everything we call our own – an absolute surrender of mastery on the part of the 'I'. At the same time, however, Derrida insists on the necessity to keep the ideas of altruism and hospitality alive. In fact, hospitality exists in a precarious field of tension between its possibility and its impossi-

---

[4] Importantly, see also Thomas Claviez's collection *The Conditions of Hospitality: Ethics, Politcs and Aesthetics on the Threshold of the Possible* (2013).

bility (see Derrida 2000; Derrida and Dufourmantelle 2000; see also, earlier even, Derrida 1995: 70).

Finally, Jean-Luc Nancy's concept of what he calls an 'inoperative community' resonates significantly with Derrida's aporetic understanding of 'hospitality'. In tune with Derrida's deconstructive stance, Nancy is extremely suspicious of both a romanticised view of community and also of a retrospectively idealising ideology/consciousness that would proceed from the assumption of a formerly intact community and an ensuing sense of identity and belonging that we seem to have lost in times of 'liquid modernity' (see Bauman 2000 and 2006):

> [I]t is here that we should become suspicious of the retrospective consciousness of the lost community and its identity (whether this consciousness conceives of itself as effectively retrospective or whether, disregarding the realities of the past, it constructs images of this past for the sake of an ideal or prospective vision). We should be suspicious of this consciousness first of all because it seems to have accompanied the Western world from its very beginning: at every moment in its history, the Occident has given itself over to the nostalgia for a more archaic community that has disappeared, and to deploring a loss of familiarity, fraternity and conviviality. Our history begins with the departure of Ulysses and with the onset of rivalry, dissension, and conspiracy in his palace. Around Penelope, who reweaves the fabric of intimacy without ever managing to complete it, pretenders set up the warring and political scene of society – pure exteriority. (Nancy 1991: 10)

Instead of further pursuing a traditional conception of community based on its immanence and the myth of its loss in modern society, Nancy turns to Heidegger's ontological concept of Being and even radicalises it as he equals Being and Being-with. For Nancy, we are determined by our being in the world with others. The Other, as it were, precedes individuality. In this ontological community of Being-with, its members no longer share traditional values based on their immanence such as their nation, their nationality, their religion, their gender, their race, or even their individuality. Rather than that, Nancy considers human beings as singularities. What human beings ultimately share is their mortality, their finitude, their temporality, their transitoriness in time. Here lie the fundamental precariousness and the fundamental vulnerability of being and existence, but also the fundamental ethical responsibility for the Other that is inscribed into community as Being-with. For human beings, Being-with, aporetically, means to be singular and plural at the same time (see Nancy 2000). If being singular plural entails sharing one's finitude with others, then the community based on such finitude can neither be fully immanent to nor fully identical with itself, as it continuously progresses in time. The community of Being-with can, therefore, never be completed, can never be worked and will, accordingly, always be 'inoperative', as Nancy puts it – or, in Giorgio Agamben's phrasing, consistently 'coming' (see Agamben 1993). Many essays in this volume reveal how productive it is to view drama, the theatrical space and the concept of spectatorship through the lens of such an aporetic understanding of both hospitality and an inoperative community.[5] In brief, the aporia of hospitality and the inoperative community complement each other and become ciphers of precarious being.

* * *

In the context of a discussion of the post-9/11 war on terror in *Precarious Life: The Powers of Mourning and Violence,* Butler addresses the extent to which the face of the Other may be represented without either erasing or appropriating what is different or what is precarious about them. The "schemas of intelligibility" that underpin the mainstream media tend to use either a strategy of "effacement through occlusion" – "certain lives and deaths", certain forms of precariousness/precarity, simply remain unrepresented, excluded, obliterated, so that "there never was a human, there never was a life, and no murder has, therefore, ever taken place" (Butler 2004: 147) – or a strategy of "effacement through representation itself" – the precarious is represented in ways that produce "a symbolic identification of the face with the inhuman" (2004: 147) or render it a consumable object, thus suspending its precariousness and reinscribing it into a pre-given, normative representational order of things.

Following Levinas, Butler claims that the precariousness of the face can only be "indirectly affirmed in [the] very injunction that makes representation impossible" (2004: 144); it cannot be fully exhausted in representation, but neither is it to be identified with the unrepresentable:

> For representation to convey the human, representation must not only fail, but it must *show* its failure. There is something unrepresentable that we nevertheless seek to represent, and that paradox must be retained in the representation we give. [...] The face is not 'effaced' in this failure of representation, but is constituted in that very possibility. (2004: 144)

This is where representations beyond the media have a crucial role to play. The essays included in this volume engage with representations of precariousness/precarity in contemporary British drama and theatre. We resolved to use both terms, 'drama' and 'theatre', to indicate and emphasise that a play is a plurimedial form of representation that consists of a text or script (no matter if it is print-

---

[5] For a more general theoretical discussion see also J. Hillis Miller's reflections on the "conflagration" of community in fiction (Miller 2011), Martin Middeke's remarks on "The Art of Compearance: Ethics, (Reading) Literature, and the Coming Community" (2016) and the section in Claviez's compilation *The Common Growl* on "The Poetics of Community" (2016: 17–92).

ed, sketched, or only exists in/as the process of being constantly rewritten) and also of its performance. We contend, thus, that while the literary aspects of the text should not be discussed without carefully taking into account the performative aspects, the latter should also acknowledge the former. The fact that contemporary drama and theatre have for decades been deviating in all possible ways from the ancient Aristotelean form – to the point where drama has often become post-drama(tic) – does not mean that a postdramatic play is no longer drama, but *just* theatre. By and large, the plays we examine in this volume work exceptionally well both as literature and in performance. They make for excellent, complex reads as much as for outstanding, multifaceted shows on stage.

A brief survey of the individual chapters reveals a wide range of thematic and aesthetic engagements with the issue of precariousness/precarity. Focusing on Simon Stephens's *Pornography*, Martin Crimp's *Fewer Emergencies* and David Greig's *The American Pilot*, Mireia Aragay relates the figure of the neighbour to Derrida's reflections on the potential and the limits of unconditional hospitality. These plays precariously oscillate between the utopia of enriching coexistence with the Other and a more pessimistic vision of danger and violence. All three plays capture this oscillating movement in the conceptual metaphor of the 'threshold', which highlights utopian performatives on the one hand and eventual gaps and dead ends on the other. In Enric Monforte's essay on Stephens's *Pornography* and Mark Ravenhill's *Shoot/Get Treasure/Repeat* hospitality is viewed politically in relation to the concerns of precarity in a post-9/11 world characterised by the war on terror, neoliberalism and globalisation. Both plays, Monforte argues, can be interpreted in terms of the Levinasian address to the face of the Other, which not only lays bare ethical questions of obligation and responsibility, but also goes hand in hand with aesthetic solutions such as the subversion of conventionally realist modes of representation.

Christian Attinger reads Philip Ridley's notorious *Mercury Fur* as a dystopian adaptation of the myth of Theseus pregnant with Hobbesian resonances. By presenting his readers and audiences with a bleak, nightmarish world of consumerism and a dysfunctional social and political order, Ridley enters into a precarious renegotiation of ethical norms and limits. Not dissimilarly, Jez Butterworth's *Jerusalem* can be looked upon, as David Kerler states in his essay, as negotiating a decisively postmodernist variant of precariousness. The play is centred on the dissolution of such binary oppositions as nature/civilisation, individual/society, host/guest, or pleasure principle/reality principle. These oppositions, paradoxically, seem interrelated, yet at the same time incommensurable. *Jerusalem* is a highly intertextual play in which cultural memory and collective identity and their deconstruction are presented in an ambiguous aesthetic framework that underlines vulnerability.

Christoph Henke and Cristina Delgado-García centre their essays on Tim Crouch's *The Author*. Henke argues that the ethical agency of Crouch's play is generated by its opening up of a precarious virtual space for spectators. By focusing on 'virtuality', Henke thus introduces another aesthetic level beyond the fictional to the analysis of drama. In *The Author* Crouch produces seductive invitations to participate in rather disconcerting experiences while spectators are made to feel that they are being restricted and manipulated. Spectators being hosts or their being held as hostages, thus, constitutes an ambiguous aesthetic/theatrical strategy that often has satirical overtones and, hence, serves as a questioning of the (ethical) limits of the postmodernist subject. On its part, Delgado's analysis of the play corroborates the presence of a complex network of fictional, autofictional and real layers. Delgado carefully analyses how an initial sense of immediacy and intimacy is gradually deconstructed through narratives of violence. The play, she argues, addresses epistemological problems such as our engagement with fictional narratives of abuse. Ultimately, both essays make clear that the structural interlacing of epistemological layers in *The Author* prompts a critical reflection on questions of political representation and agency.

Bettina Auerswald's and José Ramón Prado's essays are both concerned with explicitly political forms of theatre. In her essay on Robin Soans's *Talking to Terrorists*, Auerswald identifies two strands of verbatim theatre, which she names 'political' and 'communal verbatim'. While the former counters communitarian tendencies by facilitating mediated encounters with others, the latter triggers critical thinking and emancipation via self-reflexive structures. In both strands, Auerswald argues, verbatim theatre addresses the sensitivity of audiences towards the Other by turning the act of witnessing into an event. Prado argues that the Theatre Uncut project challenges non-participatory theatrical practices by the stimulation of active spectatorship, by opening up the theatrical event in post-show talks and, above all perhaps, by releasing plays for performance rights free. Theatre Uncut thus creates something similar to what Jacques Rancière calls an "aesthetic community" (2009: 82). Through this call for participatory acts on the part of the audience, the exposure to the precariousness of the Other and the ethical obligation towards them are foregrounded.

Adina Sorian looks at the fragility and vulnerability of a globalised, post-ideological world as it is portrayed in Forced Entertainment's performance piece *Tomorrow's Parties*. Drawing, amongst others, on the theoretical work of Catherine Malabou, Sorian suggests that the show underlines the 'plasticity' of the future, a fluidity that is more creative than destructive and stands in contrast, therefore, with Bauman's more pessimistic 'liquid modernity'. In its aleatory structure, *Tomorrow's Parties* addresses the aesthetic as much as the ethical and the political. Precariousness is, thus, encountered in self-transforming aesthetic gestures of plasticity. With a similar focus on aesthetics and theatricality, Verónica Rodríguez's essay on David Greig and Suspect Culture suggests that both precariousness and precarity can be theatrically addressed through techniques of figuration of subjectivity. Viewed from this perspective, she finds two major formal strategies at work in Greig's theatre: 'ecstatic characterisation' and 'bleeding across'. Both strategies, she argues, turn the theatre into an utopian space that might, eventually, lead to the address and, consequently, to the transcending of both precarity and precariousness.

The essays by Elżbieta Baraniecka, Clara Escoda, Martin Riedelsheimer and Martin Middeke are devoted to the ethical interrelations of precariousness, responsibility and conceptions of community. Drawing on Nancy's reflections on love, Baraniecka's analysis of Dennis Kelly's *Love and Money* interrogates whether the myth of love can go some way towards protecting our lives from precariousness and meaninglessness. While love, as the analysis of Kelly's play brings to the fore, can be looked upon as an ecstatic experience of sharing which can eventually transcend individual isolation, it can offer neither permanent happiness nor security. Rather than that, love implies a constant exposure to a void, an opening to the Other which, paradoxically, is both the basis for all loving and also the precarious marker of love's limits. On her part, Clara Escoda investigates the unequal distribution of economic resources that underlies neoliberal precarity and examines how the (re-)structuring of social bonds in this context is dramatised in debbie tucker green's *dirty butterfly*, Laura Wade's *Posh* and Crimp's *In the Republic of Happiness*. Via their experimental formal structures, all three plays invite spectators to share an alternative conception of communal ethics. At the same time, by emphasising precariousness, they challenge consumerist values based on the acquisition and pursuit of objects and on the myth of self-sufficient individuality.

In a reading of Greig's *The Events* that draws on Butler and Levinas, Martin Riedelsheimer views the fragmentary structure of the play and the interaction of the female protagonist with multiple perspectives as a precarious way to overcome trauma. In a Levinasian way, the instance of the Choir becomes the epitome of a community of the precarious which can counteract traumatic experience and vulnerability. Both the theatrical space and the performance, thus, reconfigure Butler's existential claim of precariousness and become instances of ethical responsibility. Finally, Martin Middeke examines both Greig's *The Events* and Caryl Churchill's minimalist *Here We Go* in the light of Nancy and Roberto Esposito and their ontological approaches to community. The subject matter – death as ultimate precariousness – and the formal structure of both plays reveal how literature and theatre/performance become examples of unworkable and inoperative communities in Nancy's sense. Both plays emphasise the singularity of their characters rather than their individuality; both also highlight and, after all, hold on to the fluidity and creativity inherent in the precarious human condition.

* * *

The contributions in this volume prove how twenty-first-century British drama and theatre involve (implied) authors, texts, (implied) readers, directors, actors and spectators and their respective singularities in a creative, fluid, ever-changing community. In terms of both content and form, this community is permeated by the precarious, and the plays dealt with in this volume are characterised by their concern with ethical agency and the ways in which they address human vulnerability as well as human responsibility. In this, the plays often lay bare postmodern dilemmas in ethics in that they involve complex ethical reflection and, at the same time, implicate us in ethical difficulty and hesitancy. The unequal distribution of wealth and the uneven share in the achievements of globalisation are central thematic issues in all the plays discussed here. The ethical quandaries inherent to questions such as hospitality, vulnerability, responsibility, forgiveness, or indeed community are also major thematic hubs in the plays under discussion, and the precariousness they entail is reflected (upon) through complex aesthetic structures and such ambiguous leitmotivs as 'hinges' and 'thresholds'.[6]

Even though the plays examined in the chapters that follow are recognisably grounded in discernible real-life situations, they subvert conventional modes of representation via rich aesthetic structures and textures. As far as their rhetorics are concerned, repetition, iterability, irony and often the satirical heightening of language become important stylistic features. Many of them are characterised by a complex epistemological structure which merges or juxtaposes different layers of fiction and even virtuality and thus engenders a formal interaction of the real with the fictive and the imaginary. Such literary complexity is often enhanced by a high degree of intertextuality and intermediality that highlights the tensions between originality and simulation, fictionality and reality, or the unstable equilibrium between the past, the present and the future. The character configuration in many of the plays discussed in this volume turns away from traditionally realist character concepts and reaches towards intricate figurations of subjectivity. Much in the vein of postdramatic theatre, some of the plays entirely dissolve the

---

[6] For further engagements with ethics and spectatorship, see *Ethical Speculations in Contemporary British Theatre* (Aragay and Monforte 2014) and the *Theatre and Spectatorship* special issue of *Journal of Contemporary Drama in English* (Aragay and Monforte 2016).

idea of individuation in favour of an altogether ontological emphasis on singularity that resonates with the concept of precarious Being or Being-with (the Other). Interactions, dialogue, plotlines, character configuration, language structures, deixis, (inter-)textual structure, imagery and the rhetorics and poetics of the plays at issue formally address and reconfigure the topic of precariousness in that they lay emphasis on ambiguity, indeterminacy, liminality, elusiveness, uncertainty and even contingency.[7]

This is decisively enhanced by the performative means and the concept of theatre underlying the plays under examination. The theatre becomes a forum for the discussion of precariousness; it raises questions of vulnerability, responsibility and indeed community; and it deliberately turns audience members into active participants in the process of negotiating ethical agency. Many of the plays confront their audiences by laying bare and emphasising the contingencies visible in performative practice. Vulnerability is, hence, extended across the limits of the stage to the lives of audience members, who become active observers, witnesses, hosts/guests, or virtually accomplices of/in what they find themselves exposed to on stage. The aleatory aspects of performance and, especially, its unpredictability via improvisation (see, for instance, Forced Entertainment) give rise to the rich transformative experience that watching a play can entail.

No doubt, twenty-first-century British drama and theatre is characterised by a productive, complex and diverse aesthetics that ranges from more realistic forms through satire to more experimental, self-reflexive or autopoietic plays that entirely subvert traditional dramatic and performative elements and theatrical spaces. What emerges from the plays discussed in this volume across their very diversity, though, is the observation that contemporary (British) drama and theatre often realises its thematic and formal/structural potential to the full precisely by integrating, reflecting upon and finding representations for the category and the episteme of precariousness.

Works Cited

Agamben, Giorgio. 1993. *The Coming Community*. Trans. Michael Hardt. Minneapolis and London: U of Minnesota P.

Aragay, Mireia and Enric Monforte (eds.). 2014. *Ethical Speculations in Contemporary British Theatre*. Basingstoke and London: Palgrave Macmillan.

---

[7] For the interrelation of community and contingency, see Claviez's "A *Metonymic* Community? Toward a Poetic of Contingency" (2016: 39–56).

Aragay, Mireia and Enric Monforte (eds.). 2016. *Theatre and Spectatorship*. Special issue of *Journal of Contemporary Drama in English* 4.1.
Bauman, Zygmunt. 2000. *Liquid Modernity*. Cambridge: Polity.
Bauman, Zygmunt. 2006. *Liquid Fear*. Cambridge: Polity
BBC. 2016. "Migrant Crisis: Migration to Europe Explained in Seven Charts". bbc.com, 4 March. <http://www.bbc.com/news/world-europe-34131911> [accessed 11 May 2017].
Butler, Judith. 2004. *Precarious Life: The Powers of Mourning and Violence*. London and New York: Verso.
Butler, Judith. 2009. *Frames of War: When Is Life Grievable?* London and New York: Verso.
Butler, Judith. 2011. "Precarious Life, Vulnerability, and the Ethics of Cohabitation". Centre de Cultura Contemporània (CCCB), Barcelona. 11 July. Lecture manuscript.
Butler, Judith. 2012. "Precarious Life, Vulnerability, and the Ethics of Cohabitation". *Journal of Speculative Philosophy* 26.2: 134–151.
Butler, Judith and Athena Athanasiou. 2013. *Dispossession: The Performance of the Political*. Cambridge: Polity.
Claviez, Thomas (ed.). 2013. *The Conditions of Hospitality: Ethics, Politcs and Aesthetics on the Threshold of the Possible*. New York: Fordham UP.
Claviez, Thomas (ed.). 2016. *The Common Growl: Toward a Poetics of Precarious Community*. New York: Fordham UP.
Derrida, Jacques. 1995 [1992]. *The Gift of Death*. Trans. David Wills. Chicago: U of Chicago P.
Derrida, Jacques. 2000 [1999]. "Hostipitality". Trans. Barry Stocker with Forbes Morlock. *Angelaki: Journal of the Theoretical Humanities* 5.3: 3–18.
Derrida, Jacques and Anne Dufourmantelle. 2000. *Of Hospitality: Anne Dufourmantelle Invites Jacques Derrida to Respond*. Trans. Rachel Bowlby. Stanford: Stanford UP.
Johnson, Samuel. 1968 [1755]. *A Dictionary of the English Language*. London: W. Strahan. Repr. Heidelberg: Olms.
Korte, Barbara and Frédéric Regard (eds.). 2014. *Narrating 'Precariousness': Modes, Media, Ethics*. Heidelberg: Winter.
Levinas, Emmanuel. 1989 [1984]. "Ethics as First Philosophy". Trans. Seán Hand and Michael Temple. In: Seán Hand (ed.). *The Levinas Reader*. Oxford: Blackwell. 75–87.
Middeke, Martin. 2016. "The Art of Compearance: Ethics, (Reading) Literature, and the Coming Community". In: Martin Middeke and Christoph Reinfandt (eds.). *Theory Matters: The Place of Theory in Literary and Cultural Theory Today*. London: Palgrave Macmillan. 247–263.
Miller, J. Hillis. 2011. *The Conflagration of Community: Fiction Before and After Auschwitz*. Chicago and London: U of Chicago P.
Nancy, Jean-Luc. 1991 [1986]. *The Inoperative Community*. Ed. Peter Connor. Trans. Peter Connor et al. Theory and History of Literature 76. Minneapolis and London: U of Minnesota P.
Nancy, Jean-Luc. 2000. *Being Singular Plural*. Stanford: Stanford UP.
Pewny, Katharina. 2011. *Das Drama des Prekären: Über die Wiederkehr der Ethik in Theater und Performance*. Bielefeld: transcript.
Puar, Jasbir (ed.). 2012. "Precarity Talk: A Virtual Roundtable with Lauren Berlant, Judith Butler, Bojana Cvejić, Isabell Lorey, Jasbir Puar, and Ana Vujanović". *TDR: The Drama Review* 56.4: 163–177.
Rancière, Jacques. 2009. *The Emancipated Spectator*. London: Verso.

Ridout, Nicholas and Rebecca Schneider. 2012. "Precarity and Performance: An Introduction". *TDR: The Drama Review* 56.4: 5–9.

Mireia Aragay
On the Threshold: Precarious Hospitalities as Utopian Imaginings in *Pornography, Fewer Emergencies* and *The American Pilot*

Simon Stephens's *Pornography* (2007), set in London in the week that saw the Live 8 concert, the city winning the 2012 Olympic Games bid, the G8 summit in Scotland and the 7/7 bombings, is composed of seven scenes numbered in descending order from Seven to One, preceded by a brief prologue that reproduces the beginning of one of the 7/7 bombers' suicide speech, aired by Al Jazeera television on 1 September 2005. In scenes Seven to Two, a series of nameless characters tell six stories, all of which lead to the 7/7 bombings and to "*Images of hell*" being enacted on stage. Scene One functions as a kind of epilogue which lists and counts the 52 victims of 7/7; they remain unnamed, but tantalisingly incomplete biographical snapshots are provided.[1]

The lives depicted in scenes Seven to Two – including a working mum who avenges herself on her boss by leaking a top-secret report to a rival company (Seven); a bullied, viciously racist schoolboy with a crush on his teacher who fantasises about performing all kinds of violence on her (Six); a brother and sister who have an incestuous reunion (Five); and a student, eager for a job, who makes contact with her former university professor, who then attempts to seduce her (Three) – compose a fragmented mosaic of "a city whose citizens are disconnected from themselves and each other" (Gardner 2008: 1519). In such a context, scene Four, where a suicide bomber gets up in his house in Manchester, kisses his wife and children goodbye, and describes his train journey to King's Cross Saint Pancras and then on to Aldgate on the Circle Line, stands in the middle of the play as terrifyingly "normalized" (Mountford 2008: 1518).[2] And in the same context, there takes place in scene Two, near the end of the published script, what Stephens has described as "the play's touchstone moment" (qtd. in Logan 2007) – an 83-year-old solitary widow who has had to walk home

---
[1] The obituaries are trimmed down, anonymous versions of those provided on the BBC News website (see Rodgers, Offer and Mpini 2015).
[2] Stephens has insisted on numerous occasions that "there was something fundamentally British" about 7/7 (2008). Three of the 7/7 suicide bombers were British-born of Pakistani descent (Hasib Hussain, Mohammad Sidique Khan and Shehzad Tanweer); the fourth, Germaine Lindsay, was born in Jamaica and brought up in Britain. The lines that open the play come from Khan's suicide speech.

DOI 10.1515/9783110548716-002

from central London on 7/7 is drawn to a neighbour's door by the smell of barbecued chicken wafting from the house; she knocks on the door and asks her neighbour for some chicken.³ After laughing at and insulting her – "You're completely fucking retarded, sweetheart, aren't you?" (Stephens, *Pornography*: 274) – the neighbour eventually instructs the old woman to remain on the threshold while he fetches some chicken; on his return, he makes it clear that no napkins or beer are forthcoming. The scene closes on the woman walking home, munching the chicken and wondering about the tears running down her face – "I can't understand why there are tears pouring down the sides of my face. This makes absolutely no sense to me at all" (274–275).

The scene might easily be dismissed as overly sentimental or banal. Instead, this chapter reads it in the light of the ongoing debate on the figure of the neighbour and Jacques Derrida's interrogation of hospitality, in an attempt to unveil perhaps unexpected depths and resonances that point to concerns that have become increasingly pressing in the context of intensified global hostility in the wake of 9/11 and, of course, 7/7 itself. The scene is examined here alongside Martin Crimp's *Fewer Emergencies* (written 2001; first published 2002) and David Greig's *The American Pilot* (2005), which also address the figure of the neighbour in situations of global conflict, and interestingly do so in terms of expanding concentric circles vis-à-vis Stephens's play. Thus, the proverbial next-door neighbour in *Pornography* is replaced by an undefined mass of neighbouring strangers in *Fewer Emergencies*, while the focus on the eponymous American pilot and a group of people living in some far-away country in Greig's play "captures excellently [...] the idea of the world as a shrinking global village" (Billington 2005) where we are all everyone else's neighbours.

In their joint introduction to *The Neighbor: Three Inquiries in Political Theory*, Slavoj Žižek, Eric L. Santner and Kenneth Reinhard describe the Judaeo-Christian precept to 'love thy neighbour as thyself' as "an enigma that calls us to rethink the very nature of subjectivity, responsibility and community" (2006: 5).⁴ The neighbour itself is defined by Reinhard as an intriguing, liminal figure that com-

---

3 Stephens has indicated that "[the play] can be performed in any order" (2009: 214). Sean Holmes's premiere British production (Traverse Theatre, Edinburgh, 3–24 August 2008; revived at the Tricycle Theatre, London, 6–29 August 2009) fragmented the play even further: "Instead of playing the six stories in full one after another, he cut them all up into bite-sized fragments and interlaced them" (Sierz 2009: 879).
4 I wish to thank my colleague Rodrigo Andrés for generously pointing me in the direction of Žižek, Santner and Reinhard's book as well as other illuminating discussions on the neighbour, including his own publications (see 2014a and 2014b).

plicates any clear-cut distinctions between self/family/friend/proximity and other/stranger/enemy/distance (see 2006: 18). For Zygmunt Bauman, accepting the injunction to 'love thy neighbour as thyself' requires a "leap of faith" that amounts to no less than "the birth act of humanity", that is, "the fateful passage from the instinct of survival to morality [...] and the survival of *humanity* in the human" (2003: 78). "To live [in a city today]", Bauman adds elsewhere, "means to 'live with', to live with strangers" (2006: 61) whom "we have not invited" (2006: 28); and yet, "as mutual neighbours, we are bound to enrich each other" through the recurrent and inevitable rubbing together of our differences (2006: 72).[5] Emmanuel Levinas, whose perspective underlies Bauman's, insists in *Time and the Other* that the commandment to 'love thy neighbour as thyself' is predicated on the ineradicable difference of the Other: "The *for-the-other* responsive to the neighbor, in the proximity of the neighbor, is a responsibility that signifies – or commands – precisely the face in its alterity" (1987: 106).

Other contemporary thinkers are far less sanguine than Bauman and Levinas. Žižek, Santner and Reinhard wonder whether 'love thy neighbour as thyself' truly implies a movement from/of the self towards the neighbour's radical alterity and difference – a "dis-location" (1991: 25) or "ecstasy" (1991: 6) of the self in Jean-Luc Nancy's terms – or, rather, a (violent) gesture of appropriation and erasure of the neighbour's inassimilable specificity, materiality, corporeality and agency (see Žižek, Santner and Reinhard 2006: 7). In a chapter significantly entitled "Fear Thy Neighbour as Thyself!" in his book *Violence*, Žižek proceeds via Sigmund Freud's and Jacques Lacan's critique of the Judeo-Christian precept to answer the question in no uncertain terms – "The Neighbour", he claims, is radically incompatible "with the very dimension of universality. What resists universality is the properly *inhuman* dimension of the Neighbour" (2009: 48), that is, the Other as "imponderable [...] enemy", as "someone whose very reasoning is foreign to us, so that no authentic encounter with him in battle is possible" (2009: 47).

Žižek's argument is part of his profound questioning of the ethical turn in contemporary thought in general, and of Levinas's take on the neighbour/Other in particular. He claims that Levinas's gesture of "abandoning the claim to sameness that underlies universality, and replacing it by a respect for otherness" inevitably comes up against "the traumatic character of the Neighbour"

---

5 All three quotes from Bauman's *Confianza y temor en la ciudad: vivir con extranjeros* are my translation from the Spanish version of the original Italian *Fiducia e paura nella città* (2005). As far as I have been able to ascertain, this book has not been published in English.

(Žižek 2009: 47), his "inhuman [...] terrifying excess which, although it negates what we understand as humanity, is inherent to being human" (Žižek, Santner and Reinhard 2006: 9), a dimension which Levinasian ethics is ill-equipped to address.[6] This important difficulty is, in turn, inseparable from Levinas's tendency, despite his insistence on the radical alterity of the neighbour/Other, to turn him/her into an abstract notion and an occasion/object for the self's gesture (of love, compassion, responsibility), a gesture that paradoxically ends up reinscribing the self as privileged site (of love, compassion, responsibility). Žižek perceptively links this with Levinas's problematic singling out of the Jewish community as ethical touchstone:

> [I]s there not something radically *false* in [the link Levinas establishes] between the responsibility for/to the other and questioning one's own right to exist? Although Levinas asserts this asymmetry as universal (*every one* of us is in the position of primordial responsibility towards others), does this asymmetry not effectively end up privileging *one* particular group that assumes responsibility for all others [...] – in this case, of course, Jews [...]. In other words, do we not get here [...] a necessary passage from simple and developed form (I am responsible for you, for all of you) to the general equivalent and then its reversal (I am the privileged site of responsibility for all of you, which is why you are all effectively responsible to me.)? (2006: 155)

Judith Butler notes a related, deeply troubling contradiction at the heart of Levinas's ethical thought when she homes in on his difficulties in extending his vision of ethical obligation to Palestinians, proximate, embodied neighbours who nevertheless fall outside "his version of Judaeo-Christian and classical Greek origins" (Butler 2012: 140).[7]

Levinas's predicament may be seen as an expression of what I have described elsewhere as a "'political impasse' at the basis of [his] overhaul of the foundation of ethics" (2014: 13), deriving from the fact that "[a]s soon as there are three, the ethical relationship with the other becomes political" (Levinas 1986: 21). Clearly, there *always* are (at least) three, so the subject is never responsible only to one Other but to a plurality of others, which makes it necessary to negotiate, make decisions, choose alternatives.[8] Ultimately, this circles back to

---

[6] To the extent, Žižek polemically contends, that "[h]orrible as it may sound, the Levinasian Other as the abyss of otherness from which the ethical injunction emanates and the Nazi figure of the Jew as the less-than-human Other-enemy originate from the same source" (2009: 47).
[7] See also, in this connection, Levinas's reply when asked point blank about the Palestinians in a 1982 interview in the wake of the Sabra and Chatila massacre (see 1989: 294).
[8] See also Bauman's discussion of how Levinas navigates the hazardous crossing from an ethics based on the face-to-face encounter with the proximate neighbour/Other to the realm of politics (see 1993: 112–115).

Žižek's main objection to Levinasian and post-Levinasian ethics – its inability to envisage the neighbour/Other socially and politically as "traumatic intruder, someone whose different way of life [...] disturbs us, throws the balance of our way of life off the rails, when it comes too close", so that it can "give rise to an aggressive reaction aimed at getting rid of this disturbing intruder" (2009: 50). That is why, for Žižek, "the attitude of 'understanding-each-other' has to be supplemented by the attitude of 'getting-out-of-each-other's-way'" (2009: 50), given the ineradicable difference, as Žižek sees it, between me and my neighbour, and therefore the ultimate impossibility of an encounter between us.

The matter-of-fact realism of Žižek's argument runs the risk of "transform[ing] contingent social relations into immutable facts of history" (Szeman 2010: 72) and so, perhaps inadvertently, of buttressing what Imre Szeman calls the "master narrative" (2010: 77) of globalisation. As ideological discourse, globalisation insists on "the unchanging reality [...] of both what is and what will be" (Szeman 2010: 73) – that is, a present dominated by a world-wide neoliberal system that inevitably brings with it social and political relations characterised by (often traumatic) conflicts between neighbours on both a local and a global scale, which will be resolved in "a coming global community [through] the fluid shuttling of freely traded goods across the world" (Szeman 2010: 78), a harmonious future that somehow always fails to materialise.[9] It is precisely "the ideological attempt to seal off the future through the assertion of a present that cannot be gainsaid" (Szeman 2010: 76) that demands responses that interrupt the rhetoric of globalisation, particularly by producing "mutinous metaphors" (Szeman 2010: 67) that might enable "politically efficacious re-narrativizations of the present with the aim of creating new visions of the future" (Szeman 2010: 78), thus foregrounding, and perhaps even disputing, the "diminishment of utopian possibilities" associated with globalisation (O'Brien and Szeman 2001: 620). It is here, Szeman claims, that literary and cultural production and criticism have the potential "not only to shock us into recognition of reality through ideological critique, but also to spark the imagination so that we can see possibility in a world with apparently few escape hatches" (2010: 79). If, as Žižek

---

9 As Szeman notes (see 2010: 73), Francis Fukuyama's *The End of History and the Last Man* (1992) is a well-known, highly influential example of the master narrative of globalisation at work. While Samuel Huntington's response to Fukuyama in terms of his concept of the 'clash of civilisations' (see 1996) does highlight the instability of the rhetoric of globalisation by puncturing the fantasy of "endless accumulation without strife" (Szeman 2010: 74), it simultaneously partakes of the fundamental reifying strategy that characterises the dominant discourse of globalisation, that is, its claim on "the persistence of the present into the future" (Szeman 2010: 72) given the purported lack of alternatives to global capitalism.

reminds us in *The Year of Dreaming Dangerously* in a passage that goes some way towards belying his scepticism in *Violence*, the two French words for 'future', *futur* and *avenir*, underline the difference between, respectively, "'future' as the continuation of the present, as the full actualization of tendencies already in existence" and "a radical break, a discontinuity with the present [...] what is to come (*a venir* [sic]), not just what will be" (2012: 134), then the utopian imaginings Szeman refers to seek to interrupt *le futur* while opening up space for *l'a-ve-nir*.[10]

Derrida's deconstructive critique of hospitality, tantalisingly poised between Bauman's post-Levinasian vision of an enriching coexistence with our neighbours as uninvited strangers and Žižek's radically sceptical view in *Violence*, arguably spawns one such imaginative mutinous metaphor – that of the threshold. From Derrida's discussion in "Hostipitality" and *Of Hospitality*, unconditional hospitality – "graciously offered beyond debt and economy" and "invented for the singularity of the new arrival, of the unexpected visitor", unlike conditional hospitality, practised "*out of* duty" or obligation (Derrida and Dufourmantelle 2000: 83) – emerges as a quintessentially precarious experience, never securely held in position, dangerously likely to collapse, uncertain (re. Latin *precarius*). It is, in other words, an experience of vulnerability and mutual dependency that can "only be possible on the condition of its impossibility" (Derrida 2000: 5). That is, it is only through repeatedly enduring the "apparently aporetic paralysis on the threshold" that "beyond hospitality, hospitality may come to pass" (Derrida 2000: 14). Thus unconditional hospitality holds itself out towards the future understood as *avenir* – "a future without horizon", "always to come", which bestows "on [hospitality] its chance" (Derrida 2000: 14–15). "Such are the laws", Derrida concludes, "of [unconditional] hospitality" (Derrida and Dufourmantelle 2000: 125), a levelling, emancipatory experience that nevertheless can only be transient, "not a present being" but an "intentional act" (Derrida 2000: 8) that "come[s] from the future" (Derrida 2000: 11). In other words, a view of hospitality as desire (or desire as hospitality) at the heart of which there always remains "something to be desired" (Derrida and Dufourmantelle 2000: 127).[11]

---

10 In connection with Žižek's discussion of *futur/avenir*, see also Adina Sorian's chapter in this volume.
11 Derrida's argument here resonates with Nancy's notion of the 'inoperative community' of singular beings constituted by their capacity to 'compear', to be-in-common in the same limit or border – the same threshold – that also separates them by exposing and sharing their finitude through acts of dis-location or ecstasy – that is, by surrendering their ipseity, in Derrida's terms (see Nancy 1991: 24–33).

The threshold thus becomes, in Derrida's argument, a figure or site for the bestowing on hospitality of its utopian potential. When the old woman in *Pornography* knocks on her neighbour's door uninvited and is kept waiting on the threshold, to be eventually given the chicken she has asked for but no napkin or beer, the hospitality exercised by the neighbour is clearly conditional in Derrida's terms, eventually practised – grudgingly and illiberally – out of duty or obligation. The neighbour's attitude is characterised by hostility and an insistence on his role as patron and master of his household, rather than by an unreserved welcome that might dissolve the host/guest binary and produce a liberatory, if ephemeral, moment of unconditional hospitality. However, I would suggest that both the play's highlighting of the old woman's endurance of paralysis on her neighbour's threshold and her inexplicable tears as she walks away hold within themselves a utopian dimension that may be illuminated via Jill Dolan's discussion of utopian performatives, which resonates fascinatingly with both Derrida's vision of hospitality as desire and with the notion of the future as an *avenir* pregnant with possibility.[12]

As "small but profound moments in which performance [...] make[s] palpable an affective vision of how the world might be better" (Dolan 2005: 5–6), utopian performatives "allow a fleeting contact with utopia", understood not as "finished perfection", but as "always in process, always only partially grasped" (Dolan 2005: 6). Radically evanescent, utopian performatives are felt above all "as *desire*" (Dolan 2005: 7; emphasis added), as "moments of a future [*avenir*] that might feel like utopia in the present of performance" (Dolan 2005: 33), moments of "'not yet' [...] and 'not here'" replete with the potential of "'what if'" and of "elsewhere", whose fragile politics lie in "the complexity of hope in the presence of absence" (Dolan 2005: 20–21). Given that performance itself is an ephemeral experience, simultaneously and contradictorily predicated on presentness/presence and absence, and given also the difficulties attendant upon documenting spectators' affective responses, utopian performatives remain unpredictable, existing "as wishes, as desire, crystallizing from our labor", our belief "in a better future [*avenir*]" and in "human commonality despite the vagaries of difference" (Dolan 2005: 170–171). For me, the old woman's tears in *Pornography* and her stated inability to understand what they might mean crystallise as utopian performatives "tinged with sadness but akin to joy" (Dolan 2005:

---

12 Erika Fischer-Lichte argues that "the aesthetics of the performative emphasizes moments of transgression and transition", where "[t]he border turns into a frontier and a threshold, which does not separate but connects" in "an attempt to reenchant the world" (2008: 204). Unfortunately, there is no space here to explore the resonances between Derrida, Dolan and Fischer-Lichte any further.

8), transiently pointing to a utopian *avenir* even as "it disappears before us around the corners of narrative and social experience" (Dolan 2005: 6) – specifically, in the case of *Pornography*, as it is blown away by the harsh reality of the 52 victims of 7/7 evoked in the play's closing scene (One). In short, they are tokens of overwhelming desire for a utopian elsewhere where the precarious threshold dividing host from neighbour might dissolve and unconditional hospitality might come to pass.

Uncannily, Crimp wrote his short play *Fewer Emergencies* on 10 September 2001 (see Sierz 2006: 68).[13] The play addresses questions of vicinity and hospitality in a global context marked by an increasingly "unequal distribution of precarity" (Butler 2012: 148), questions that acquired a renewed urgency in the wake of 9/11. Through its radically experimental form – featuring three anonymous speakers and three absent protagonists rather than naturalistic *dramatis personae*, unspecified settings, and narration rather than on-stage enactment of events – the play explores the possibilities of imaginative re-narrativisation of a conflict-ridden present by focusing on a family house threatened by a crowd of dispossessed migrants.[14] Although Speaker 1 claims that "[t]he whole neighbourhood is improving. The trees are more established, they've kicked out the Mexicans, they've kicked out the Serbs, people are finally cleaning up their own dog-mess, nice families are moving in" and "there are fewer emergencies than there used to be", the family's child, Bobby, has to be "locked in for his own protection" (Crimp, *Fewer Emergencies*: 44–46).

When exploring the distinction between conditional and unconditional hospitality, Derrida writes of houses, doors and keys in a manner that resonates compellingly with Crimp's play:

> There is no hospitable house. There is no house without doors and windows. But as soon as there are a door and windows, it means that someone has the key to them and consequently controls the conditions of hospitality. [...] This is the difference, the gap, between the hospitality of invitation [conditional] and the hospitality of visitation [unconditional]. In visitation there is no door. Anyone can come at any time and can come in without needing a key for the door. (2000: 14)

In *Fewer Emergencies*, Crimp creates a mutinous metaphor for the hostility caused by global unevenly distributed precarity through imagining Bobby's

---

[13] See also Crimp's note on the last page of the 2002 Faber edition of *Face to the Wall* and *Fewer Emergencies*.
[14] The play text's experimental texture was enhanced in James Macdonald's Royal Court production (8–30 September 2005) by the absence of eye contact between the Speakers and a heightened use of light, among other devices.

room as the place where the accumulated riches of those who benefit from neoliberal economic policies are kept, from "a shelf full of oak trees, and another where pine forests border a mountain lake" to pornography (Crimp, *Fewer Emergencies*: 45). He keeps the island of Manhattan in a secret drawer, "the city of Paris" and "a Japanese golf course" in another cupboard, a "wardrobe full of uranium and another full of cobalt [...] and a row of universities – good ones" on a little shelf (45). And "hanging from the shelf, like the Beethoven quartets and fertility clinics, is the *key* to use in emergencies" (45; emphasis added), such as the one that is taking place right now in the streets outside the house – "Rocks are being thrown – shots fired [...] Cars are being [...] overturned and burnt" (46).

So far Bobby, the child master/host, has kept the contents of the house to himself and the door firmly locked against uninvited guests – his ipseity intact, a hostage to itself. But as the rioting crowd of unwelcome neighbours threaten to bring down the house and a shot hits him, the Speakers' complacent insistence that "[t]hings are definitely looking up [...]. Brighter light – more frequent boating – more confident smile – fewer / emergencies" (48) is troubled by their disturbing account of how a bleeding Bobby drags himself up the stairs in an attempt to reach the key (see 49). Speaker 2 exclaims that Bobby "wants to reach the key" and 1 adds he is going to use it to "open the door" (47). Although the Speakers concur he "must be / completely mad" (47), under the pressure of violence they are forced to make an attempt at re-narrativisation, that is, at envisaging the possibility that Bobby might perform an act of unconditional hospitality by addressing himself to his (migrant) neighbours "as stranger[s] in order to say 'Welcome' to them" (Derrida 2000: 8), thus interrupting the *futur* by opening up a space for an alternative *avenir*.

Admittedly, such a possibility is counterbalanced by the Speakers' suggesting that "what's going on in Bobby's mind" is that "if he opens the door, if he lets people in", if he invites them into his house as guests, "Then they'll always love him" (47). Such a scenario recalls both Žižek's critique of Levinas's tendency to erase the neighbour's/Other's alterity by envisioning it as merely an abstract occasion for the self's gesture of love and responsibility (see Žižek 2006: 155), as well as Derrida's warning that it is only when the master/host surrenders his place and his ipseity completely and becomes his guest's hostage that unconditional hospitality may take place (see Derrida and Dufourmantelle 2000: 123–125). In other words, the scenario conjured up by the Speakers "limit[s] the gift proffered [...] [to] *being-oneself in one's own home*" (Derrida 2000: 4), allowing at most for the conditional hospitality of invitation to maybe come about.

And yet, for me the play's closing moments, heightened through a potent combination of text and light work, function as a utopian performative that places both Bobby and, crucially, the audience on a threshold of desire for a less conditional, more encompassing kind of hospitality. As the key to Bobby's house is foregrounded in the Speakers' narrative, the stage gradually darkens until a complete blackout is reached and all spectators can hear is,

> 1 He's closer to the key [...] see how / it swings.
> 2 See how the key swings.
> 3 That's right, Bobby-boy. Watch the key. Watch the key swinging. (49)[15]

Thus, as the (inexistent) key becomes (doubly) invisible to Bobby, the Speakers and the audience alike, the fourth wall is discounted. And with that definite frontier replaced by a more fluid configuration – a kind of threshold – the performance space becomes an open space, and the hierarchical dyad stage/host vs. auditorium/spectator/guest gives way. As the play positions both Bobby *and* the audience to endure "an apparently aporetic paralysis on the threshold" (Derrida 2000: 14) – (possibly) jointly mesmerised, in the dark, by the Speakers' evocation of the key swinging above their heads – the choice between hostility and an unconditional hospitality without keys becomes palpable, almost (paradoxically) visible. It is the choice between a turbulently divisive "'as is'" and a "'what if'" (Dolan 2005: 21) ripe with desire for a more hospitable *avenir*.

Written in, and clearly inflected by, a post-9/11 atmosphere, Greig's *The American Pilot* opens on the badly injured Pilot, who has fallen from the sky onto "[a] small farm high up in a rural valley, in a country that has been mired in civil war and conflict for many years" (Greig, *The American Pilot*: 345).[16] The play, in other words, begins with a visitation, but one that complicates Derrida's vision of unconditional hospitality. In "Hostipitality", Derrida quotes from Kant's discussion of European colonialism, as follows:

> The *inhospitable* conduct of the civilized states of our continent, especially the commercial states, the injustice which they display in *visiting* foreign countries and peoples (which in their case is the same as *conquering* them) seems appallingly great. (2000)

---

15 As already noted, Macdonald's 2005 production at the Royal Court made a particularly effective use of light throughout, including the final moments in the play. For a detailed discussion, see Aragay and Escoda (2012).

16 Although *The American Pilot* was first performed in April 2005 (RSC, The Other Place, Stratford-upon-Avon), it was written in 2003 in the context of the war in Afghanistan. The play is geographically imprecise, but both the two-year gap before its first production and its very contents (including not least the uncannily prophetic scene where the Captain and the Translator attempt to videotape a message from the Pilot before executing him) meant that it was read as a response to the Iraq War (see Wallace 2013: 140–141 and Zaroulia 2011: 42).

However, he subsequently glosses over this acceptation of 'visitation', which would trouble his perhaps ultimately all-too-neat (Eurocentric) distinction between conditional and unconditional hospitality (invitation vs. visitation), where the host is always unambiguously the 'master of the house'. In *The American Pilot*, instead, as the Translator reminds the Captain, the host/visitor relationship is underpinned by a power structure where the former – the unnamed middle-Eastern country where the play is set – is "an ant", while the latter – the USA, embodied by the Pilot – is "an elephant" (337). In other words, *The American Pilot* addresses a question that haunts Derrida's "Hostipitality", namely, the limits and possibilities of hospitality when a visitation takes place under circumstances of global conflict and uneven distribution of precarity and power, where the (nominal) hosts are both the primary victims of such circumstances as well as the visitor's (nominal) enemies. How does the host/guest dynamic work in such a situation?[17] The play examines this question primarily from the perspective of the local characters – the nominal hosts – who, as Clare Wallace notes, are seen both "externally and internally while the pilot is never afforded the luxury of interiority, of directly speaking to the audience", and constitutes "the Other here" (2013: 142). The local characters, indeed, deliver eight monologues in the course of the play, where they articulate their personal reactions to the Pilot's presence in their midst.

To an extent, the play seems to endorse Žižek's argument, referred to earlier, that "the properly *inhuman* dimension of the Neighbour" means that "no authentic encounter with him in battle is possible" (2009: 47). Thus, the Captain wants to "keep [the Pilot] as a hostage. Make demands" (Greig, *The American Pilot*: 377); the Trader – who, rather than try to communicate with the Pilot, smashes his face with his rifle butt upon meeting him for the first time simply because "[h]e's American" (348) – dispels any utopian thoughts of a 'what if' and sees in the Pilot the possibility of doing business. As he says in his second monologue, "The margin exists in the deal and the deal exists in the world as it is – not in a dream of the world, not in the world as you would like it to be" (412). In contrast, there are fleeting moments in the play that point to an elsewhere where the uneven conflict dividing the (nominal) hosts from their visitor might give way before an assertion of the simple human duty of hospitality. A key one is Sarah's, the Farmer's wife's, first monologue – "I simply took it

---

[17] Marilena Zaroulia (2011) also reads *The American Pilot* – as well as *San Diego* (2003) and *Pyrenees* (2005) – with a focus on hospitality and in the light of Dolan's utopian performatives. However, both her key argument – that "cosmopolitanism constitutes Greig's utopia" (2011: 36) – and her reading of specific aspects of the play – particularly Evie's role and the play's final moments (see 2011: 43–44) – differ from my own.

that it was my duty to do what hospitality required of me, that's all. I cleaned his wounds and I bandaged his leg. I fed him. I brought him water" (355).

Most often, however, both kinds of moments are inextricably interlaced. Sarah's second monologue ends on a repudiation of any 'what if' – "It is painful and unnecessary to dream of a life in which it could have been otherwise" (408) – that stands in unresolved tension with her earlier avowal of the obligation of hospitality. The Farmer, who finds the wounded Pilot and hosts him in his shed, shares cigarettes, jokes and laughter with him, nevertheless ends his monologue on, "As far as I was concerned, the sooner he was gone from my shed, the better" (347). On his part, the Captain muses, "In another world we could have been friends. But he and I were not in another world. [...] He was my prisoner" (363). And, of course, there is the profound ambiguity of the play's final moments, when Evie, the Farmer's daughter, is raised up to the US rescue helicopter, together with the Pilot. While Peter Billingham finds here "a most disturbing reading of gender and power relations [...] ultimately providing a reactionary, sentimentalised fatalistic resolution" (2011: 178–179), it is possible to suggest a less stable, more open reading by placing the play's conclusion not only alongside Evie's earlier naïvely idealistic view of America – "America is on our side./ [The Pilot] told me this./ [...] We were lost but America sent him to tell us, we don't have to be alone any more./ [...] We can be American" (405–406) – and her liking for the Pilot, but also her proleptic objection to being lifted away by the helicopter – "I don't like just being lifted up to Heaven without so much as a 'please' or a 'thank you'" (357). Crucially, the play's anti-naturalistic linguistic strategy, whereby all the characters speak in English even though the locals and the Pilot are not supposed to understand each other, simultaneously and contradictorily points to the impossibility ('as is') and the possibility ('what if') of finding some common ground that might allow a sense of connectedness to emerge.

There is, in short, a profound indeterminacy in *The American Pilot* regarding the issue of hospitality and mutual recognition, with the characters caught on a precarious threshold composed of both the paralysing pull of a violently divisive present and the desire for a more hospitable *avenir*. It seems productive to view this in the light of Greig's account of Adornian dialectics, which, interestingly, might almost double as a description of the e/affect achieved by utopian performatives: "Adorno's concept of negative dialectic rests on the power of contradiction. [...] [T]he more profound the contradiction [...] the greater the chance that [...] the fabric of 'reality' will tear and we can experience transcendence" (2008: 220). In *The American Pilot*, through the recurrent clashes between 'as is' and 'what if' the spectator may catch a glimpse of an alternative *avenir*.

In relation to Susan Sontag's argument that war photography both overwhelms and paralyses us, Butler asks, "But is it possible that we might be overwhelmed and *un*paralyzed? [...] Must we, in fact, be overwhelmed to some degree in order to have motive for action?" (2012: 136). *Pornography, Fewer Emergencies* and *The American Pilot* seek to "articulate the possible" – the 'what if' leading to a more hospitable *avenir* – without losing sight of the "obstacles to human potential" (Dolan 2005: 2) – the 'as is' that will, if unchallenged, hijack the future – through utopian performatives that hinge on the mutinous metaphor of the threshold. If, as spectators, we experience such utopian imaginings as overwhelming – being as they are fleeting, evanescent, yet affectively intense and mesmerising – then they might unparalyse us and open a window for agency, moving us perhaps to change our mode of being in the world. Acutely aware that the precarious experience of hospitality always leaves "something to be desired" (Derrida and Dufourmantelle 2000: 127), the three plays nevertheless appeal to spectators to attempt the (im)possible.

Works Cited

Andrés, Rodrigo. 2014a. "Amor al vecino y cuestionamientos a la nación en la literatura del siglo diecinueve". *Lectora: Revista de dones i textualitat* 20: 15–46.

Andrés, Rodrigo. 2014b. "Opaque Encounters, Impossible Vicinities". In: Joana Sabadell-Nieto and Marta Segarra (eds.). *Differences in Common: Gender, Vulnerability and Community*. Amsterdam and New York: Rodopi. 161–173.

Aragay, Mireia and Clara Escoda. 2012. "Postdramatism, Ethics and the Role of Light in Martin Crimp's/James Macdonald's *Fewer Emergencies* (2005)". *New Theatre Quarterly* 28.2: 133–142.

Aragay, Mireia. 2014. "To Begin to Speculate: Theatre Studies, Ethics and Spectatorship". In: Mireia Aragay and Enric Monforte (eds.). *Ethical Speculations in Contemporary British Theatre*. Basingstoke and New York: Palgrave Macmillan. 1–22.

Bauman, Zygmunt. 1993. *Postmodern Ethics*. Oxford: Blackwell.

Bauman, Zygmunt. 2003. *Liquid Love: On the Frailty of Human Bonds*. Cambridge: Polity.

Bauman, Zygmunt. 2006 [2005]. *Confianza y temor en la ciudad: Vivir con extranjeros*. Trans. Josep Sampere and Enric Tudó. Barcelona: Arcadia.

Billingham, Peter. 2011. "'The bombing continues. The gunfire continues. The end': Themes of American Military-Cultural Globalisation in *The American Pilot*". In: Anja Müller and Clare Wallace (eds.). *Cosmotopia: Transnational Identities in David Greig's Theatre*. Prague: Litteraria Pragensia Books. 166–179.

Billington, Michael. 2005. Rev. of *The American Pilot* (The Other Place, Stratford-upon-Avon), by David Greig. *theguardian.co.uk*, 7 May. <http://www.theguardian.com/stage/2005/may/07/theatre> [accessed 14 November 2014].

Butler, Judith. 2012. "Precarious Life, Vulnerability, and the Ethics of Cohabitation". *Journal of Speculative Philosophy* 26.2: 134–151.

Crimp, Martin. 2002. *Face to the Wall and Fewer Emergencies*. London: Faber.

Crimp, Martin. 2005. *Fewer Emergencies (Whole Blue Sky, Face to the Wall, Fewer Emergencies)*. London: Faber.
Derrida, Jacques. 2000 [1999]. "Hostipitality". Trans. Barry Stocker with Forbes Morlock. *Angelaki: Journal of the Theoretical Humanities* 5.3: 3–18.
Derrida, Jacques and Anne Dufourmantelle. 2000 [1997]. *Of Hospitality: Anne Dufourmantelle Invites Jacques Derrida to Respond*. Trans. Rachel Bowlby. Stanford: Stanford UP.
Dolan, Jill. 2005. *Utopia in Performance: Finding Hope at the Theater*. Ann Arbor: U of Michigan P.
Fischer-Lichte, Erika. 2008 [2004]. *The Transformative Power of Performance: A New Aesthetics*. Trans. Saskya Iris Jain. London and New York: Routledge.
Fukuyama, Francis. 1992. *The End of History and the Last Man*. London: Penguin.
Gardner, Lyn. 2008. Rev. of *Pornography* (Traverse Theatre, Edinburgh), by Simon Stephens. *The Guardian*, 5 August. *Theatre Record Edinburgh International Festival and Fringe 2008 Supplement*: 1519.
Greig, David. 2008. "Rough Theatre". In: Rebecca D'Monté and Graham Saunders (eds.). *Cool Britannia? British Political Drama in the 1990s*. Basingstoke and New York: Palgrave Macmillan. 208–221.
Greig, David. 2010. *The American Pilot*. In: David Greig. *Selected Plays 1999–2009 (San Diego, Outlying Islands, The American Pilot, Being Norwegian, Kyoto, Brewers Fayre)*. London: Faber. 341–418.
Huntington, Samuel P. 1996. *The Clash of Civilizations and the Remaking of World Order*. New York and London: Simon & Schuster.
Levinas, Emmanuel. 1986. "Dialogue with Emmanuel Levinas". Interview with Richard Kearney. In: Richard A. Cohen (ed.). *Face to Face with Levinas*. Albany: SUNY Press. 13–33.
Levinas, Emmanuel. 1987 [1979]. *Time and the Other*. Trans. Richard A. Cohen. Pittsburgh: Duquesne UP.
Levinas, Emmanuel. 1989 [1982]. "Ethics and Politics". In: Seán Hand (ed.). *The Levinas Reader*. Oxford: Blackwell. 289–297.
Logan, Brian. 2007. "One Day in July". Rev. of *Pornography* (Schauspielhaus, Hannover), by Simon Stephens. *theguardian.co.uk*, 19 June.
<http://www.theguardian.com/stage/2007/jun/19/theatre> [accessed 7 July 2014].
Mountford, Fiona. 2008. Rev. of *Pornography* (Traverse Theatre, Edinburgh), by Simon Stephens. *Evening Standard*, 4 August. *Theatre Record: Edinburgh International Festival and Fringe 2008 Supplement*: 1518.
Nancy, Jean-Luc. 1991 [1986]. "The Inoperative Community". Trans. Peter Connor. In: Jean-Luc Nancy. *The Inoperative Community*. Ed. Peter Connor. Theory and History of Literature 76. Minneapolis: U of Minnesota P. 1–42.
O'Brien, Susie and Imre Szeman. 2001. "Introduction: The Globalization of Fiction/the Fiction of Globalization". *The South Atlantic Quarterly* 100.3: 603–626.
Reinhard, Kenneth. 2006. "Toward a Political Theology of the Neighbor". In: Slavoj Žižek, Eric L. Santner and Kenneth Reinhard (eds.). *The Neighbor: Three Inquiries in Political Theology*. Chicago: U of Chicago P. 1–10.
Rodgers, Lucy, James Offer and Ransome Mpini. 2015 [2005]. "7 July London Bombings: The Victims". *bbc.com*, 3 July. <http://www.bbc.com/news/uk-33259919> [accessed 12 April 2016].

Sierz, Aleks. 2006. *The Theatre of Martin Crimp*. London: Methuen.
Sierz, Aleks. 2009. Rev. of *Pornography* (Tricycle Theatre, London), by Simon Stephens. *Tribune*, 4 September. *Theatre Record* 29.16/17: 879.
Stephens, Simon. 2008. "*Pornography* – Simon Stephens Interview". Interview with Steve Cramer. *The List* 607, 17 July.
<http://www.list.co.uk/article/10159-pornography-simon-stephens-interview> [accessed 2 December 2010].
Stephens, Simon. 2009. *Pornography*. In: Simon Stephens. *Plays: 2 (One Minute, Country Music, Motortown, Pornography, Sea Wall)*. London: Methuen. 211–280.
Szeman, Imre. 2010. "Globalization, Postmodernism, and (Autonomous) Criticism". In: Petra Rethman, Imre Szeman and William D. Coleman (eds.). *Cultural Autonomy: Frictions and Connections*. Vancouver: UBC Press. 66–85.
Wallace, Clare. 2013. *The Theatre of David Greig*. London: Bloomsbury.
Zaroulia, Marilena. 2011. "'What's missing is my place in the world': The Utopian Dramaturgy of David Greig". In: Anja Müller and Clare Wallace (eds.). *Cosmotopia: Transnational Identities in David Greig's Theatre*. Prague: Litteraria Pragensia Books. 32–49.
Žižek, Slavoj, Eric L. Santner and Kenneth Reinhard. 2006. "Introduction". In: Slavoj Žižek, Eric L. Santner and Kenneth Reinhard (eds.). *The Neighbor: Three Inquiries in Political Theology*. Chicago: U of Chicago P. 1–10.
Žižek, Slavoj. 2006. "Neighbors and Other Monsters: A Plea for Ethical Violence". In: Slavoj Žižek, Eric L. Santner and Kenneth Reinhard (eds.). *The Neighbor: Three Inquiries in Political Theology*. Chicago: U of Chicago P. 134–190.
Žižek, Slavoj. 2009. *Violence*. London: Profile Books.
Žižek, Slavoj. 2012. *The Year of Dreaming Dangerously*. London and New York: Verso.

Enric Monforte
Staging Terror and Precariousness in Simon Stephens's *Pornography* and Mark Ravenhill's *Shoot/Get Treasure/Repeat*

The twenty-first century has so far been defined by the deadly effects of war, terrorism and neoliberal capitalism. The terrorist attacks on the Twin Towers of the World Trade Center that took place on 9/11, 2001 in New York City may be taken as signalling the actual beginning of the new century and triggered the subsequent War on Terror. Deadly mass attacks soon spread in the West, affecting Madrid (11 March 2004 [11-M]) and London (7/7, 2005). A number of plays written in Britain in the aftermath of the events of 9/11 and subsequent attacks and of the US reaction to them inevitably reflect on issues of war and terrorism. This chapter looks at Simon Stephens's *Pornography* (2007) and Mark Ravenhill's *Shoot/ Get Treasure/Repeat* (2008) in the light of the notions of precariousness, ethical obligation/solicitation, hospitality and cohabitation, and their recent theorisation. The plays selected share the background of a world increasingly atomised and fractured by the effects of terrorism, the War on Terror, neoliberalism and globalisation, and pose relevant, sombre questions about the way in which contemporary societies adjust to life in post-Holocaust, post-9/11, liquid, precarious times. The chapter offers a reflection on the particular ways in which the plays stage precariousness, bearing in mind their status as open texts that put formal experimentation on a par with conceptual experimentation.

Precariousness, Hospitality, Cohabitation

Precariousness can be understood in a double, interrelated sense, always having ethico-political connotations. On the one hand, precariousness is "an ontological condition" (Puar 2012: 163), "an existential problem" (Berlant in Puar 2012: 163) related to the "[v]ulnerability" (Butler 2004: xi) and "injurability" (Butler 2004: xii) intrinsic to human existence. On the other hand, precariousness – or, rather, precarity – taken in a socio-economic, political sense is "a byword for life in late and later capitalism" (Ridout and Schneider 2012: 7) and therefore inseparable from the effects of war and terrorism.

In *Precarious Times: The Powers of Mourning and Violence*, Judith Butler develops the notion of precariousness as vulnerability and links it to Emmanuel Levinas's ethical philosophy. She argues that acts of terror such as the 9/11 at-

DOI 10.1515/9783110548716-003

tacks expose "an unbearable vulnerability" (2004: xi) as well as the existence of a "fundamental dependency" (2004: xii) between ourselves and unknown Others – this being related to Lauren Berlant's definition of precarity as "a condition of dependency" (qtd. in Ridout and Schneider 2012: 6) in contemporary neoliberal times. Thus, according to Butler, being aware of our own vulnerability and injurability establishes a connection with other people and "offers a chance to start to imagine a world [...] in which an inevitable interdependency becomes acknowledged as the basis for global political community" (2004: xii–xiii). She identifies the call of the Other as a "structure of address" or "the demand that comes from elsewhere" (2004: 130). The response to the address will be an encounter with what Levinas calls the face – "the wordless vocalization of suffering" (Butler 2004: 134), something that "bespeaks an agony, an injurability" (Butler 2004: 135) that "summons me, calls for me, begs for me" (Levinas 1989: 83). Butler concludes, "To respond to the face, to understand its meaning, means to be awake to what is precarious in another life or, rather, the precariousness of life itself. [...] It has to be an understanding of the precariousness of the Other" (2004: 134) that will hopefully help us understand our own precariousness and trigger the emergence of selfless responsibility: "A responsibility for my neighbour, for the other man, for the stranger or sojourner, to which nothing in the rigorously ontological order binds me – nothing in the order of the thing, of the something, of number or causality" (Levinas 1989: 84).

As mentioned above, precarity, understood in a socio-economic, political sense refers primarily to living conditions in present-day, radical capitalist regimes and describes "the privatization of wealth and the slow and uneven bankrupting of so many localities (nations, states, regions) beginning in the 1970s" (Berlant in Puar 2012: 166). As such, it can be affiliated to other terms such as "*austerity*" (Puar 2012: 163), so that one of the inevitable outcomes of precarity is the appearance of a new class Guy Standing and other analysts have referred to as the "precariat" (qtd. in Ridout and Schneider 2012: 7).

The rise of an ethics that acknowledges the presence of the Other and the necessity of the encounter with the face can also be related to Jacques Derrida's formulation of the notion of hospitality and to Butler's articulation of the idea of cohabitation. In his seminal reflections on hospitality, Derrida discusses the difference between 'invitation' and 'visitation'. An 'invitation' implies "conditional hospitality" – "When I invite someone to come into my home, it is on condition that I receive him" (2000: 17) – and therefore it does not imply a real threat to the authority of the host, who dictates the rules of the household or nation that the guest must abide by. A 'visitation', quite on the contrary, implies "unconditional hospitality", which is what happens if I accept the coming of the other, the arriving [*arrivance*] of the other who could come at any moment without asking my opinion and who could come with the best or worst of intentions: a visitation could be an invasion by the worst. Unconditional hospitality must remain open without horizon of expectation, without anticipation, to any surprise visitation. (2000: 17)

According to Derrida, the total relinquishing of a position of authority in one's own home is an indispensable condition if the invitation is to fulfill its ultimate aim: the host becoming the visitor's 'hostage' (see 2000: 9). Therefore, only unconditional hospitality will yield positive results. This also resonates with Levinas: "It is the responsibility of a hostage which can be carried to the point of being substituted for the other person and demands an infinite subjection of subjectivity" (1989: 84).

Being hospitable in an unconditional way inevitably entails the sharing of the earth. Butler describes "[t]he unchosen character of earthly cohabitation" (2012: 143) as implying "the [ethical] obligation to live on the earth and in a polity that establishes equality for a population necessarily and irreversibly heterogeneous" (2012: 145) and to fight "against subjugation and exploitation" (2012: 150). According to her,

We live together because we have no choice, and [...] we remain obligated to struggle to affirm the ultimate value of that unchosen social world, an affirmation that is not quite a choice, a struggle that makes itself known and felt precisely when we exercise freedom in a way that is necessarily committed to the equal value of lives. (2012: 150)

The inevitable, powerful conclusion would be that "[w]e are all, in this sense, the unchosen, but we are nevertheless unchosen together" (2012: 146). No matter how unwilling we are, we must "struggle in, from, and against precarity" (2012: 150), thus underlining the necessity of non-hierarchical forms of cohabitation in contemporary, precarious times.

Staging Terror and Precariousness

Staging precariousness in the context of the War on Terror needs the commitment of playwrights who are not afraid to explore new avenues of representation. In this respect, Butler distinctly claims that "dominant forms of representation can and must be disrupted for something about the precariousness of life to be apprehended" (2004: xviii). At the same time, recent theorisations on the contemporary ethical turn have linked it with the use of experimental forms in order "to achieve an effective political response to the challenges of a consumer culture and a marketized world" (Rebellato 2007: 259). Nicholas Ridout, on his part, sees the theatre as a vital place to examine and debate the ethical, based on the striking similarity between the position of the spectator and that of the witness. In *Theatre & Ethics*, he effects what can be seen as a vindication of Levinas's work on alterity for the theatre, and proposes "a model of performance as an ethical encounter, in which we come face to face with the other, in a recognition of our mutual vulnerability which encourages relationships based on openness, dialogue and a respect for difference" (2009: 54). Such a model of performance, Ridout proceeds, will inevitably be characterised by a concentration on the process of artistic creation and by sheer formal experimentation, as traditional aesthetics have become obsolete and constraining.

In the light of this, staging precariousness would entail subverting conventional modes of representation in an environment that foregrounded the ethical and might therefore lead to political analysis, emphasising our exposure in the world, the necessity of re-assessing our relationship with the Other and establishing forms of earthly cohabitation. I will now discuss how *Pornography* and *Shoot/Get Treasure/Repeat* put forward their ethico-political reflections on the precariousness of contemporary existence through fragmented, episodic structures, a radical conception of character and, overall, through non-naturalistic aesthetics, thus enhancing both conceptual and formal experimentation. On their part, as will be shown, spectators are impelled by the plays to renegotiate their relationship with the theatrical experience, a process which proves to be empowering in that it fosters their emancipation (see Rancière 2009: 1–23) and their "response-ability" (Lehmann 2006: 185).

Pornography

Simon Stephens's *Pornography* (Schauspiel Hannover, 2007; Traverse Theatre, Edinburgh, 2008) elliptically depicts the events in the life of a number of individuals in the summer of 2005 in the days going from the G8 summit, the Live Aid concert in London's Hyde Park and the election of London as the site for the 2012 Olympic Games to the 7/7 London bombings, when four bombs were exploded on the London transport system, causing 52 deaths and more than 700 injured. The piece, a succession of four monologues and two duologues in decreasing order – "like a countdown" (Sierz 2009: 879; Innes 2011: 456) – is structured around the Shakespearean 'seven ages of man' – infancy, childhood, love, war, wisdom, old age, dementia – and depicts acts of "transgression" (Stephens 2009a: xviii) performed by its characters: the leaking of a business report, stalking, incest, mass terrorism, abuse, consumption of pornography and breaking of the norms of social courtesy. The play ends – Scene One – with brief descriptions of the 52 victims the attacks yielded, one of them intriguingly left blank.

Pornography can be read in the light of the notions of precariousness, ethical obligation/solicitation, hospitality and cohabitation. Precariousness is indeed a central characteristic in the characters' lives as different elements emphasise in each case a distinct vulnerability: the feeling of loss of the young mother caused by her boss's treatment of her and by her partner's potential lack of attention in Scene Seven is embedded in the late capitalist environment of the office where they are frantically working on the report that she will end up leaking, which was supposed to give them the upper hand in relation to other firms; the utter defencelessness of the working-class schoolboy in Scene Six in the face of his bullying at school and the domestic violence going on in his own home is sharply replicated by his racist and totalitarian feelings, not to mention his infatuation with his teacher and his final attack on her; the transgression of the brother and sister in Scene Five who commit incest places them in an impossible position from which there is no escape; the terrorist who, in Scene Four, meticulously describes his journey from the north of England to London and to the tube train where he explodes his bomb eerily introduces the looming presence of unexpected death; making a pass at a much younger ex-student who comes looking for help does nothing but exacerbate the feeling of loss of the university lecturer in Scene Three; finally, the utter solitude of the old lady in Scene Two who, on the day of the bombings, ends up asking an unknown neighbour for some food, is stressed by showing her to be addicted to internet porn. The feeling of alienation is what links the two voyeuristic aspects that seem to make up her life, the consumption of war – via the news – and pornography, both directly or indirectly related to the "objectification of humans" (Sierz 2009: 879).

Thus, all the characters in *Pornography* live in "the culture of dislocation and disaffection" that encourages a complete "*suppression of empathy*, [...] the inability, or refusal, to imagine what it is like to be 'the other'" (Bolton 2013: 119). At the same time, it is precisely the lack of empathy "which enables [them] to commit acts of sexual, physical, emotional or economic violence" (Bolton 2013: 119). Indeed, the characters embody different aspects of the newly created precariat, suffering from extreme vulnerability and injurability, which become physical on account of the actual threat to their lives posed by the terrorist attacks. In this sense, a connection between all of them is established as they all suffer directly or indirectly from the bombings – the former student in Scene Three perhaps eventually becoming one of the victims as she heads for a train going to the Edgware Road tube station at the end of the scene (see Stephens, *Pornography*: 267).

The fundamental dependency on the Other, as well as the ethical solicitation on his/her part and the act of hospitality are also manifest throughout the play, becoming especially relevant in the case of the old woman in Scene Two and the suicide bomber in Scene Four. Thus, when the woman finally reaches her neighbourhood after having crossed London twice on foot on the day of the bombings, she smells a barbecue being held in her street and feels an urge to call on an unknown neighbour and ask for some food:

> I just wanted you to know that I think your chicken smells delicious. [...] And I wondered what would happen if I just knocked on your door and said, your chicken smells delicious, please can I have some of it? [...] Don't laugh. [...] Don't laugh at me. [...] Don't laugh at me. (273–274)

Taken aback by her unsolicited visitation, the neighbour first mocks the old lady – "You're completely fucking retarded, sweetheart, aren't you?" (274) – but eventually brings her some of the food, for which she is very grateful: "This is fine. This is kind of you. This is lovely. Thank you" (274). As she leaves she starts crying, perhaps still unaware of her own precariousness: "I can't understand why there are tears pouring down the sides of my face" (274–275). This visitation emphasises the need for contact and communication (see Stephens 2009a: xxi) all characters seem to experience and, at the same time, through the "act of kindness" it triggers, "placed among a sea of destruction and terror" (Lane 2010: 35), it offers an indication of hope in an otherwise extremely bleak play (see Innes 2011: 458; Lane 2010: 35–36), thus making a call for empathy.

However, perhaps the most obvious encounter with the face of the Other in *Pornography* occurs in Scene Four, at the very centre of the play. The scene describes the terrorist's journey to London, as he kisses his wife and children goodbye, changes trains at different stations and eventually enters "the busiest carriage. At the heart of the train" (255) of a Circle Line tube heading towards Aldgate before his "body is transformed into a weapon, not in a metaphorical sense but in the truly ballistic sense" (Mbembe 2003: 36). His account of the journey is interspersed with graphic descriptions of the people he encounters, from a "young Bangladeshi boy" (249) he imagines shooting to a bus driver to whom he "send[s] psychic signals" to "[d]rive through the red lights. Turn right on the left turn only. Drive up and over the pavements" (250). Other descriptions are more detached: he aseptically watches the people going to work in the early morning as they sit on the train and imagines moments of their life, like a woman who has "been crying" (252) or a moment of intimacy in bed with another one (see 253). He suddenly bursts out: "fucking bewigged, myopic, prurient, sexless dead" (252) and verbalises his wish to "take a bomb to all of this" and thus "[w]ipe it all off the skin of the world. Scratch it away" (253). His description of contemporary England epitomises "the West's cultural decadence" (Lane 2010: 34):

> Here there are food-makers and the food they make is chemical. It fattens the teenage and soaks up the pre-teen. Nine-year-old children all dazzled up in boob tubes and mini-skirts and spangly eyeliner as fat as little pigs stare out of the windows of family estate cars. In the sunshine of mid-morning in the suburbs of the South Midlands heroin has never tasted so good. Internet sex contact pages have never seemed more alluring. Nine hundred television channels have never seemed more urgent. And everybody needs an iPod. (252–253)

At the same time, the highly critical view of the Western neoliberal lifestyle which contemporary England embodies, as put forward by the spectral, ghostly presence of the bomber, points to the race and class background of the terrorists in *Pornography*, who come from deprived areas in the United Kingdom and travel to the more affluent south – specifically to its capital city, which epitomises the splendour of radical capitalism in the West. Besides, in trying to offer clues to interpret the 7/7 terrorists' behaviour, Stephens introduces another element:

> Their actions seemed to be absolutely a product of the same Britain I'd grown up in. They were born and raised in a Britain built by one prime minister who denied altogether the existence of society and another who made a passionate plea for understanding to be valued less than unthinking condemnation of others. I wanted to write a play that put a terrorist action on equal footing with many of the other flaws and ruptures I saw around me. (2009a: xviii)

Thus, Stephens is explicit in his denunciation of the policies of the conservative governments of Margaret Thatcher and John Major, which sowed the seeds for the spectacular success of neoliberalism and the (northern) Eurocentric perspective, which, through a complete objectification, alienate people from each other and from themselves, making present times thoroughly "pornographic" (Stephens qtd. in Innes 2011: 457). In this respect, the fact that all the 7/7 terrorists had been born and raised in the United Kingdom – in Thatcher's and Major's Britain – together with the horror of the attacks undertaken on British soil, is what baffled people the most, what had the most "visceral *affect*" on them (Bharucha 2014: 163) – namely, their violation of "the basic codes of hospitality and equality" (Bharucha 2014: 161) by killing their fellow citizens in their own homeland and willingly dying in the process. In this connection, the play controversially prompts us "to consider the terrorist act as something located within, and produced by, Western culture" (Bolton 2014: xxxv).

In addition, according to Achille Mbembe, in suicide attacks,

> my death [the terrorist's] goes hand in hand with the death of the Other. Homicide and suicide are accomplished in the same act. [...] To deal out death is therefore to reduce the other and oneself to the status of pieces of inert flesh, scattered everywhere, and assembled with difficulty before the burial. (2003: 36–37)

The "unbearable intimacy" of a suicide attack (Jacqueline Rose qtd. in Bharucha 2014: 162), the paradoxical inseparability and indistinguishability of the Self and the Other after the explosion (see Gayatri Spivak in Bharucha 2014: 162), correspond, according to Adriana Cavarero, to the attacker's desire in contemporary 'suicidal horrorism' "to destroy the uniqueness of the body, tearing at its constitutive vulnerability", to do away with its "ontological dignity" (2009: 8–9), to deny their victims their own "irremediably singular being" (2009: 102; see also 89–115). Going back to Stephens's words, what might perhaps be inferred from them – echoing Levinas and Butler – is a plea for the necessity to respond to the call of the Other by trying to understand their plight. Perhaps the problem so far in contemporary Western democracies has been to treat the Other as a guest, as someone who has been invited, thanks to the immigration/mobility laws at work, instead of accepting him/her as a visitor in an unconditional way. This is what happened to the parents of the bombers, who perhaps, deep down, were never accepted as visitors in their new country, were never offered an unconditional type of hospitality. Or perhaps this is something their children experienced while growing up in their own homeland – which makes it even more problematic. In both cases, there seems to be a complete refusal on our part to acknowledge and meet the face, to respond to its ethical solicitations. The spectral, utterly disquieting presence of the terrorist in the play thus poses urgent questions about the (im)possibility of understanding and the urgency of earthly cohabitation.

As for the staging of precariousness in *Pornography*, Stephens has stated the intrinsic openness of the text: "[It is] a text that [is] as open as possible. [...] There are only a few stage directions and they are frankly impenetrable. There are no character names" (2009a: xix), and "[the] play can be performed by any number of actors. It can be performed in any order" (2009b: 214). He acknowledges the influence of German theatre on *Pornography* and on his work generally, valuing its "formal boldness" and its preference for "the metaphorical and the visual" (2009a: xix). As he has said, his use of duologues and monologues shows "an interest in dramatising a world that seems to be more atomised and fractured than it has been in the past and subsequently scorched by a need and an inability to connect" (2009a: xxi). In this respect, the British premiere production of the play, directed by Sean Holmes, chose to take fragmentation to its limits by breaking up the different scenes and interspersing them with one another. To this should be added the fact that actors repeatedly addressed the audience, that cast members remained on stage when not performing – which gave rise to a productive feeling of "Brechtian alienation" (Coveney 2009: 878) – and that no bombings were actually enacted in the course of the performance, thus hindering any feeling of catharsis from arising. All of this fostered "a position of interpretation" in spectators (Stephens 2009a: xii), who were "expected to fill in the blank" (Innes 2011: 456) and who, by becoming witnesses placed in the position of the Other, were therefore urged to pose uncomfortable ethico-political questions.

Shoot/Get Treasure/Repeat

Shoot/Get Treasure/Repeat (Traverse Theatre, Edinburgh, 2007; various venues, London, 2008), Mark Ravenhill's "most overtly ambitious work for the theatre" (Svich 2011: 417), is an "epic cycle of short plays" (Ravenhill 2008a: 5) that situates its characters at the centre of episodes of war and terrorism so as to "capture our urge to bring our model of freedom and democracy to the world, even as we withdraw into more and more fearfully isolated groups at home" (Ravenhill qtd. in Svich 2011: 416–417). Jenny Spencer describes the plays as a "political response to 9/11" (2012: 64), signals how they offer "both direct and oblique references to the war on terror" (2012: 68) and points out how "Ravenhill historicizes the affects that circulated between British and American governments and their citizens after 9/11 (and 7/7), making the war on terror more about 'us' than 'them'" (2012: 68).

The plays, which take their titles from major canonical works of literature, theatre, film, music and the media, are variously set in different war/occupied zones (*Crime and Punishment*, *Love (But I Won't Do That)*, *Twilight of the Gods*, *Odyssey*, *Birth of a Nation*) and in Western contexts (*Women of Troy*, *Intolerance*, *Women in Love*, *Fear and Misery*, *War and Peace*, *Yesterday an Incident Occurred*, *The Mikado*, *War of the Worlds*, *Armageddon*, *The Mother*, *Paradise Lost*), both in middle- and working-class environments, the middle-class ones characterised by the total isolation of their citizens, who live in walled communities completely insulated from their surroundings. At the same time, it is made clear that the elements of war gradually seep into the aseptic, insulated middle-class areas. The aim is to create "an epic narrative [...] to suggest a big picture through little fragments" (Ravenhill 2008a: 5). According to the playwright, the chosen structure of the play – his own or the one preferred by readers and spectators – "reflects the age we live in, an age in which we yearn for a grand narrative even as we suspect it is dead" (2008a: 5). This chapter discusses four of the plays taking place in Western, middle-class environments.

The different short plays, which can be performed in any order, allow themselves to be read from the perspective of an ethics of precariousness. They show the immense gap between the affluent West and deprived war zones and ponder on the unbridgeability of such a distance. At the same time, the urban, middle-class, late-capitalist environments that are depicted are haunted by the spectres of poverty, war and terrorism. Thus, references to the menace of looming terrorist attacks and the fear stirred by them are recurrent, contaminating the middle-class comfort and rendering it utterly unsettling. As an example, Helen, the main character in *Intolerance*, desperately tries to cling to her comfortable, "perfect" (Ravenhill, *Shoot/Get Treasure/Repeat*: 18) everyday life with her husband and child – a child who paints a "soldier with no head" (26) – and to her healthy eating habits while she avoids "read[ing] the newspapers or watch[ing] the news or anything" so as not to hear about "bombs and wars" (19) in a city where "immigrants [are] in offices cleaning" (23). However, recurrent abdominal pain ruins her desperate construction of such a happy, fulfilling narrative. Significantly, she feels "no personal responsibility" (Spencer 2012: 65) for the events surrounding her life, which is made even clearer as she crucially tries to silence the impact of the Holocaust on her own family, defining it as "the past. [...] history. [...] the last century" (24).

Fear and Misery further explores the issue of precariousness and lack of empathy by focusing on a similar couple, Harry and Olivia, in their desperate attempt to protect themselves from outside perils: "[T]he addicts. The madwomen. The bombers. The soldier with his head blown off" (44). Interestingly, unsettling elements filter into their conversation from the outset and demolish the apparent feeling of bourgeois domestic bliss and safety. Thus, prompted by domineering Harry, Olivia admits to having experienced a rape-like feeling the night their son was conceived (see 40), while Harry, on his turn, admits that he is scared "[t]hat [Olivia] won't wash [her] vagina. That [she]'ll fuck a black man. That [she]'ll have a breast removed" (44), encapsulating his revulsion at female physiology, other races and disease in one go. Olivia admits to washing her vagina "obsessively" and promises to "be washing extra hard tonight. Down there" (45–46). Both agree that "[s]ecurity is the most important thing in this life" (45) and protect their home compulsively, a "wise investment" (47) in an area undergoing gentrification, but still with a preoccupying presence of "[t]he poor, the ethnics, the, the..." (47). This is why Harry seems determined to move the family to a "new community. Gated community" (47), as he feels their area is not safe enough: "Walk down the street and your eyes are scanning, scanning, never meeting a gaze of course because that would be... but scanning" (48). The utter refusal to see, to acknowledge the Other and perhaps feel empathy, is here articulated in conjunction with Harry verbalising his vulnerability and injurability, his need for protection and security, his contempt for the poor and the racially different and his rejection of any idea of community: "SO DON'T YOU – COMMUNITY, THAT'S A LIE. THERE'S NO COMMUNITY, I HAVE NO COMMUNITY WITH THEM" (48–49). And all this takes place as a "[s]oldier covered in blood and mud enters and watches [them]", without them being able to see him (48).

The headless soldier's unsettling visits to Harry and Olivia's son Alex form the core of *War and Peace*. Recounted through an alienating use of language in which "the characters constantly quote themselves" (Spencer 2012: 69), the play shows the ambiguous necessity on the part of the young, working-class soldier, whose "brains are blown across the desert" (61), to touch – and ultimately take – Alex's head so he can go back to "[f]ight the big fight" (59). Alex considers himself "a perfect child" (51) who wants to work "in the City like my mummy and daddy" (55) and retire early. He eventually confronts the deprived soldier, an Other in terms of class who used to live in an estate that stood where Alex's home is and who declares he is "fighting for your freedom and democracy" (60). Alex is blunt – "We want to keep people like you out. Gated community. That's us" (58) – but cannot help pissing and shitting himself in the course of the soldier's frightening visitation. On his part, the soldier claims war is intrinsic to humanity – "But live without war? No human being's ever done that. Never will. It's what makes us human" (54) – and presents the child with a lucid account of his role in the war:

> [T]his world this country this... everything exists because of me, because I go out there and I fight the fucking towelheads. [...] And if we can't fight them fucking towelheads then this is over, right – yeah? Yeah? This place, gated community, hedge funds, that's over unless I'm fighting the fighting. You see? You see? You see? (58)

However, he ends up despairing of the unending war: "It's a war on terror and it goes on and on and on and on. There's no God, see? There's no end day. There's just this war on terror on and on and on and on and on and on and on and on and on and on..." (60–61). Alex shoots the soldier and makes him leave, not without keeping his gun and all the while assuming a clear position of authority in front of the Other, who gradually ends up "elicit[ing] our empathy" (Spencer 2012: 69).

Women of Troy, the first play in the cycle, presents us with a Brechtian "chorus of Women" (7) who powerfully begin by addressing the audience as possible suicide bombers from the perspective of their middle-class, Western identities: "We want to ask you this. [... W]hy do you bomb us? [... W]e want to understand" (7; 9). Speaking from their own belief that they are "the good people. The good guys. The righteous ones" (8) and that their "way of life is the right, the good, it's the right life" (9), their words, uttered from their comfortable positions, take it for granted that they are the ones on the side of "Freedom, Democracy, Truth" (9) – freedom and democracy being the recurrent trope that holds the plays together (see Hughes 2011: 120). Gradually, the lack of empathy for the Other becomes evident and the satirical thrust of the play increases:

> — We know your culture's very different.
> — And that's okay. We accept that.
> — We tolerate, we accept, we celebrate –
> — We celebrate – exactly – we celebrate difference.
> — It's all part of being a good people.
> — It's what makes us the good people that we are.
>
> [...]
>
> — I see nothing when I look at you.
> — I see... darkness. (10–11)

The women's position thus shifts from fake tolerance to fake celebration, to real rejection. When an announcement is made – in the form of a Brechtian interruption (see Spencer 2012: 71) – that a number of suicide bombers are attacking the hospital they find themselves in, their attitudes change, gradually revealing the hypocrisy of their apparently progressive positions and their actual hatred of the Other, whom they cannot "picture" (11):

> You bastards. [...] You cunts [...]. You are not a person. I don't see you as a person. I've never seen you as a person. You're a bomb. I look at you. And all I see is a bomb. I see you there now and I see you and I hear you ticking away and I feel frightened and angry and disgusted. That's what I feel. (12)

At the same time, the women verbalise the possibility of negotiating access to what sustains their wealth and comfort – "natural resources", "the multimedia environment", "shopping" – as well as the ultimate prerogative, bringing them "[d]emocracy and freedom. Freedom and democracy" (13), while simultaneously reinforcing their position of entitlement: "And the Lord made His earth for us, His earth with its resources and its... coffee, the bombs, the shops... they are for us. For us to use the good people" (15). Eventually, a suicide bomber detonates the bomb and all the women and the terrorist die, the former not before declaring war on the "evil, wicked, terrible [...] bad people" (15) and announcing the beginning of "the great war between good and evil" (16). A soldier, "half-man, half-angel" (16), appears and officially declares war. His words, as he "kisses the lips of each of the dead Women in turn", depict warfare as a never-ending process:

> Freedom and democracy and truth and light – the fight is never done. There are always enemies. We must fight. [...] I promise you that gun and tank and this flaming sword will roam the globe until everywhere is filled with the goodness of the good people. / There will be good everywhere. / And then, every day, peace will be war. Keeping the peace with the gun. It is my destiny. / I open battle. / I declare war. / Begin. [...] / Kill the bombers. Slaughter our enemies. In the name of the good people – begin. (17)

Ravenhill's experimental *Shoot/Get Treasure/Repeat* plays with form, with non-naturalistic characters, with dialogue – here showing his indebtedness to Martin Crimp in not assigning lines to specific characters – and with the way it was staged and presented at different venues (see Svich 2011: 418) in order to enquire about the *cul-de-sac* neoliberal capitalism and the foreign policies of the strongest potencies of the West have led the world to. He shows his familiarity with Brechtian practices, but also transcends them. As Spencer puts it, "the goal of the cycle is not simply to promote detachment in the service of analysis, but also to amplify audience affect in ways more likely to produce political change" through the use of alienation strategies "with the goal of producing social gests" (2012: 67–68). As the cycle's general title suggests, "the choices available to the free and democratic citizens of this new global order create the conditions for a state of emergency, which in turn produces the very terror it claims to be fighting" (Spencer 2012: 66). The plays underline the intrinsic precariousness of Western citizens of all classes and bleakly show their total lack of empathy with the plight of the dispossessed, their absolute lack of concern about the (racial, class) Other, and the impossibility of unconditional hospitality and cohabitation.

Conclusion

This chapter has shown how *Pornography* and *Shoot/Get Treasure/Repeat* can be read in the light of the notions of precariousness, ethical obligation/solicitation (the Levinasian address of the Other and its subsequent reformulations), hospitality and the urgent need to foster it, and cohabitation and the creation of feasible forms of sharing the earth. The characters in the plays embody the recently formed precariat, suffering as they do from extreme (social, political, economic, but also ontological) vulnerability and injurability, which become physical following the actual threat to their lives posed by terrorist attacks, on account of their living in war situations or simply because their lives are moulded by contemporary neoliberalism. In this sense, a connection between all of them is established as they all suffer directly or indirectly from the effects of war and neoliberal capitalism. The plays manifest both the fundamental dependency on the Other as well as the ethical solicitation – the visitation that requires unconditional hospitality – on the part of the Other, underlining in this way the necessity for connectedness and relationality in a world fractured by the effects of war and globalisation. As for the staging of precariousness, both plays are open texts, their fragmented, highly experimental forms reflecting their content and therefore allowing active, emancipated spectators to articulate their own responses to the deeply uncomfortable ethico-political questions they formulate.[1]

Works Cited

Bharucha, Rustom. 2014. *Terror and Performance*. London and New York: Routledge.
Bolton, Jacqueline. 2013. "Simon Stephens". In: Dan Rebellato (ed.). *Modern British Playwriting: 2000–2009*. London: Bloomsbury. 101–124.
Bolton, Jacqueline. 2014. "Commentary". In: Simon Stephens. *Pornography*. London: Bloomsbury Methuen Drama. xxi–lxxiv.
Butler, Judith. 2004. *Precarious Life: The Powers of Mourning and Violence*. London and New York: Verso.
Butler, Judith. 2012. "Precarious Life, Vulnerability, and the Ethics of Cohabitation". *Journal of Speculative Philosophy* 26.2: 134–151.
Cavarero, Adriana. 2009 [2007]. *Horrorism: Naming Contemporary Violence*. Trans. William McCuaig. New York: Columbia UP.
Coveney, Michael. 2009. Rev. of *Pornography* (Tricycle, London), by Simon Stephens. *The Independent*, 10 August. Theatre Record 29.16–17: 878.
Derrida, Jacques. 2000 [1999]. "Hostipitality". Trans. Barry Stocker with Forbes Morlock. *Angelaki: Journal of the Theoretical Humanities* 5.3: 3–18.
Hughes, Jenny. 2011. *Performance in a Time of Terror: Critical Mimesis and the Age of Uncertainty*. Manchester: Manchester UP.
Innes, Christopher. 2011. "Simon Stephens". In: Martin Middeke, Peter Paul Schnierer and Aleks Sierz (eds.). *The Methuen Drama Guide to Contemporary British Playwrights*. London: Methuen. 445–465.
Lane, David. 2010. *Contemporary British Drama*. Edinburgh: Edinburgh UP.
Lehmann, Hans-Thies. 2006 [1999]. *Postdramatic Theatre*. Trans. Karen Jürs-Munby. London and New York: Routledge.
Levinas, Emmanuel. 1989 [1984]. "Ethics as First Philosophy". Trans. Seán Hand and Michael Temple. In: Seán Hand (ed.). *The Levinas Reader*. Oxford: Blackwell. 75–87.

---

[1] I am grateful to Elisabeth Massana for bringing the work of Rustom Bharucha and Achille Mbembe to my attention.

Mbembe, Achille. 2003. "Necropolitics". Trans. Libby Meintjes. *Public Culture* 15.1: 11–40.
Puar, Jasbir (ed.). 2012. "Precarity Talk: A Virtual Roundtable with Lauren Berlant, Judith Butler, Bojana Cvejić, Isabell Lorey, Jasbir Puar, and Ana Vujanović". *TDR: The Drama Review* 56.4: 163–177.
Rancière, Jacques. 2009 [2008]. *The Emancipated Spectator*. Trans. Gregory Elliott. London and New York: Verso.
Ravenhill, Mark. 2008a. "Introduction". In: Mark Ravenhill. *Shoot/Get Treasure/Repeat*. London: Methuen. 5.
Ravenhill, Mark. 2008b. *Shoot/Get Treasure/Repeat*. London: Methuen.
Rebellato, Dan. 2007. "From the State of the Nation to Globalization: Shifting Political Agendas in Contemporary British Playwrighting". In: Nadine Holdsworth and Mary Luckhurst (eds.). *A Concise Companion to Contemporary British and Irish Drama*. Oxford: Blackwell. 245–263.
Ridout, Nicholas. 2009. *Theatre & Ethics*. Basingstoke and New York: Palgrave Macmillan.
Ridout, Nicholas and Rebecca Schneider. 2012. "Precarity and Performance: An Introduction". *TDR: The Drama Review* 56.4: 5–9.
Sierz, Aleks. 2009. Rev. of *Pornography* (Tricycle, London), by Simon Stephens. *Tribune*, 4 September. *Theatre Record* 29.16–17: 879.
Spencer, Jenny. 2012. "Terrorized by the War on Terror: Mark Ravenhill's *Shoot/Get Treasure/Repeat*". In: Jenny Spencer (ed.). *Political and Protest Theatre after 9/11: Patriotic Dissent*. London and New York: Routledge. 63–78.
Stephens, Simon. 2009a. "Introduction". In: Simon Stephens. *Plays 2: One Minute, Country Music, Motortown, Pornography, Sea Wall*. London: Methuen. ix–xxii.
Stephens, Simon. 2009b. *Pornography*. In: Simon Stephens. *Plays 2: One Minute, Country Music, Motortown, Pornography, Sea Wall*. London: Methuen. 211–280.
Svich, Caridad. 2011. "Mark Ravenhill". In: Martin Middeke, Peter Paul Schnierer and Aleks Sierz (eds.). *The Methuen Drama Guide to Contemporary British Playwrights*. London: Methuen. 403–424.

Christian Attinger
Staging Hobbes, or: Theseus Goes to the Theatre. Precariousness, Cultural Memory and Dystopia in Philip Ridley's *Mercury Fur*

> The most tragic form of loss isn't the loss of security; it's the loss of the capacity to imagine that things could be different. (Ernst Bloch)

London's East End: Hell's Kitchen

Although Philip Ridley's *Mercury Fur* has been subject to constant debate and scandal ever since it premiered at the Drum Theatre (Plymouth) in 2005, it is a play that has always been very popular among young adults (see Redman 2014). So far, most critics have condemned the play for its explicit language, drastic graphical images, violence and – over large parts of the play – absence of any moral (see, among others, Fisher 2005; Croggon 2007; Brantley 2012). These critical voices notwithstanding, I suggest a reading which focuses on three distinct, yet predominant, aspects of the play whose subtle interrelatedness has hitherto been neglected by scholarly research. My argument will be that Ridley's play needs (perhaps even demands) a culturally apt, well-read reader who, unlike the characters in the play, does not suffer from loss of memory or an eroding language. *Mercury Fur* adapts the literary utopia to the contemporary (British) stage by displacing the ancient myth of Theseus into a near-future dystopian version of London. Consequently, the key to *Mercury Fur* lies mostly within one of the largest archives of Western cultural memory and identity, classical Greek mythology. I contend that the play may be read as a dramatic, dystopian adaptation of the myth of Theseus, the legendary king of Athens who killed the Minotaur in Crete and became the archetype of good governance in Athens.[1] Additionally, and in contrast to this, Ridley's dystopianism draws heavily upon a

---

[1] For a clear, unmistakeable reference see Ridley, *Mercury Fur*: 81–85. Ridley himself mentions Theseus as a central aspect of the play in an interview with Aleks Sierz (see Ridley 2009: 114). Where the myth of Theseus is concerned, I mainly follow the standard account given by Gustav Schwab's *Gods and Heroes of Ancient Greece* (2001). Schwab's account is largely similar to other versions (see, for example, Hahnemann (2010); *The Oxford Classical Dictionary* (Hammond and Scullard 1970); Ranke-Graves (1974)). Where I refer to deviations from the standard account, I have consulted, above all, Ranke-Graves, Hammond and Scullard, and Henry J. Walker (1995), one of the most extensive comments on the myth of Theseus.

Hobbesian outlook in which the *bellum omnium contra omnes* dominates everyday life, creating a world of mutual mistrust, sheer fear, violence and destruction. His near-future version of London is, ostensibly, the epitome of a dysfunctional social and political order and, therefore, concepts such as vulnerability and the Hobbesian state of nature become relevant for a thorough analysis of the intricate interrelatedness of literary utopia, (cultural) memory and precariousness. The latter is constantly foregrounded in the play as it seeks to cross and/or re-negotiate (ethical) thresholds, asks painful questions about our willingness to admit outsiders into our community, and shows audiences a nightmarish world devoid of any sense of history or stable identities at all. Ultimately, as the play pushes its genre to the utmost limit, it contests commonly shared assumptions about the spectator and his or her "response-ability" (Lehmann 2006: 185), highlighting once more the importance of the political for any reading of *Mercury Fur*.

Staging Precariousness: Vulnerability and Insecurity

With Samuel Johnson's complaint in mind, that "no word is more unskilfully used than this [i.e. precarious] with its derivatives" (1968: 1549), this section is meant to pinpoint three distinct aspects of precariousness, before their connection to the play and its mythical pre-/intertext (i.e. the adventures of Theseus) is explained in subsequent sections.[2] Precariousness has recently received widespread attention in many research areas and disciplines, ranging from jurisprudence to philosophy. However, it is still possible to extract a core set of characteristics which are commonly used across disciplines to describe the condition of precarious life as, for instance, outlined by Butler (2012).

Firstly, precariousness is about a being's vulnerability, which can be understood as a certain aptness to be hurt or killed and the fear thereof. Secondly, another important aspect is the feeling or the fact of being (completely) dependent on or challenged and threatened by another person or, to use a more abstract concept, an Other (i.e. in the sense of 'not me' or 'not myself'). Emmanuel Levinas discusses this delicate, complicated relationship with the Other in his influential essay "Ethics as First Philosophy". The precariousness of human existence may best be circumscribed by his asking:

---

[2] My special thanks to Martin Riedelsheimer, who brought up Johnson's definition of the word in one of our discussions.

My being-in-the-world or my 'place in the sun', my being at home, have these not also been the usurpation of spaces belonging to the other man whom I have already oppressed or starved, or driven out into a third world; are they not acts of repulsing, excluding, exiling, stripping, killing? (Levinas 1989: 82)

Secondly, the fundamental, a priori quality of human existence, then, is a profound interdependency between two or more vulnerable beings. What deeply stirs any person and makes them aware of their "extreme exposure, defencelessness, [and] vulnerability" (Levinas 1989: 83) is the unmitigated, unprepared and uncalled for encounter with the "face of the Other" (Levinas 1989: 82), as it painfully reminds oneself of one's own vulnerability, finitude and, ultimately, mortality.[3] It is again Johnson's *Dictionary of the English Language* that guides the way along this idea of existential (inter-)dependency, which has also been prominent in jurisprudence and sociology of late (see, among others, Kaser and Knütel 2008; Standing 2014):

> PRECA'RIOUS. adj. [precarius, Lat. precaire, Fr.] Dependent; uncertain, because depending on the will of another; held by courtesy; changeable or alienable at the pleasure of another. [...] It is used for uncertain in all its senses; but it only means uncertain, as dependent on others. (Johnson 1968: 1549)

The socio-economic dimension of this uncertainty or insecurity led Guy Standing to describe and analyse the living conditions of 'the new dangerous class' of people, the so-called 'precariat' of his seminal study (see Standing 2014).

Thirdly, the precarious is often associated with the process of transgressing thresholds or borders, highlighting the indeterminacy of what comes of or after this transgression. This liminal state of vulnerability and indeterminacy has, for heuristic purposes, often been compared to a person boarding an airplane, when he or she is neither here nor there but in between two states. At this point, recent events that have to do with the (re-)current problematics of hospitality or asylum come to one's mind. Writing in late 2015 as a German citizen, it seems almost inevitable to establish this connection, given the multitudes crossing borders globally in search of asylum and safety, while they are forced into the liminal state of vulnerable beings by anonymous state powers and compatriots. As the subsequent sections pick up on these preliminary working definitions, they show

---

[3] Levinas emphasises this throughout the fourth and fifth sections of his essay (see Levinas 1989: 82–85), most ostensibly in the following lines: "But, in its expression, in its mortality, the face before me summons me, calls for me, begs for me, as if the invisible death that must be faced by the Other, pure otherness, separated, in some way, from any whole, were my business" (Levinas 1989: 83).

that *Mercury Fur* is a play about the world's disenfranchised and the dire consequences further inaction against rapidly growing inequality and spreading violence around the globe will bring to the core of well-developed Western societies. In this respect, theatre transforms the dark side of literary utopia from the read-only form of the novel or short story to the experiential (and experimental) world of the stage.

The Hobbesian Stage, or: A Normal Day in London

Right from the beginning, *Mercury Fur* uses stark imagery and bleak symbolism to underline its dystopian mode:

> DARREN (*calling, offstage*): Elliot? Ell? Where the hell *are* ya?
> ELLIOT *goes to front door.*
> ELLIOT: Where the hell are you?
> DARREN: Dunno
> ELLIOT: Can ya see the dead dog?
> DARREN: ... Yeah.
> ELLIOT: Step over the dead dog. Turn left. (3)

The dead dog symbolizes the prevalent and ensuing chaos of this near-future London. Traditionally a bad omen, a harbinger of imminent death(s) and, as Cerberus, also the mythical guide to the border or threshold between the realm of the living and the underworld, the slain dog hints at the play's inevitable catastrophe at the end (see Lurker 1991). Moreover, it is not by chance that the short form for 'Elliot' ('Ell') and 'hell' are homophones in the Cockney accent so widely spoken by locals in London's East End. With no one guarding the passage to and from the underworld, the world has entered a liminal state without clear borders, thresholds or any higher, discernible social and political order. It has become a place of instability, insecurity and *mésalliance* which, according to Mikhail Bakhtin (see 1984: 113–134), involves the combination and juxtaposition of the high and the low, the sacred and the profane and, in the context of the play, also of the living and the dead, as they now all share the same space, namely London's East End.[4]

---

[4] As will be seen below, this observation is of the utmost importance in connection with the general aesthetics of the play, their relationship to the mythical pretext of Theseus and the notion of cultural memory.

With its run-down, bombed-out houses and the rubble-strewn streets lined with looted museums and destroyed cars, the Hobbesian stage of *Mercury Fur* is a clear echo of the dysfunctional, poverty-stricken, failing city-states of the age of Theseus (see Ranke-Graves 1974: 297–299; Walker 1995: 3–9).[5] These images evoke memories of well-known depictions of war zones, either taken from history (WWI, WWII, Vietnam, etc.) or recent conflicts (Somalia, Palestine, Syria, Ukraine). With riots, looting, rape, murder and other unsanctioned war crimes, the audience bear witness to what is supposed to be quite a normal day in failed states all around the world. Furthermore, this underlines the fact that civilization, culture and social order are not much more than a very thin layer which can easily be stripped and give way to havoc and turmoil in the absence of a sovereign exercising the final and supreme power over a given polity. The resulting situation is a self-help system in which the claim of the survival of the fittest actually means the survival of the strongest. A general hostility to any foreign human being and an atmosphere of sheer fear dominates everyday life and social interactions, eventually leading to an age in which "the life of man [is again] solitary, poore, nasty, brutish, and short" (Hobbes 1968: 186).

As already stated, one of the play's predominant themes is the utter insecurity and vagueness of circumstances. On the level of characters, this is epitomized by the Duchess. Deep inside the Duchess there slumbers a desire for safety and company, as it does naturally in almost every human being. The simple reason why Spinx has to bring her along to the snuff video party is that she would just start defecating uncontrollably if she were left alone. This marks her as an extremely fragile, vulnerable being. Moreover, she only starts to really feel safe and comfortable when she is introduced to Darren, Elliot and Naz, who pretend to be generals (Darren, Elliot) and their *aide-de-camp* (Naz). Shortly afterwards, they assure her that nuclear weapons are present on the premises and can be put to use anytime, if necessary (73). By referring to weapons of mass destruction, normally used for tactical or strategic purposes in an all-out intercontinental nuclear war, Ridley goes beyond the limits of his dystopian version of the East End so as to imply that the whole world may now only exist in a state of emergency and self-help. That is to say, the macrocosm of *Mercury Fur*

---

5 Some sources speak of the Dark Ages of Greek Republics (roughly 1000 BC to 780 BC) after the fall of the Mycenaen kingdoms, which brought about relative poverty and obscurity (see, for example, Walker 1995: 3–4.) According to the myth, the streets and woods were full of scoundrels, robbers and other evildoers, as well as wild, dangerous animals. Like his idol Heracles, Theseus made vanquishing these foes and restoring order his task and overcame, among others, such adversaries as Periphetes, Sinnis, Sciron, Cercyon and Procrustes.

is structured and governed by the same principles as the microcosm shown on stage.

Theseus Visits the Theatre: Vulnerability and Hospitality

Nevertheless, vulnerability is not the only concept closely related to the myth of Theseus which can be observed in *Mercury Fur*. The characters also either experience, grant or revoke hospitality. Apart from Elliot, who experienced hospitality from a disobedient Lola after he fled the hospital chased by a rampant mob roaming the streets, Naz, a squatter who happens to have occupied a flat on the same floor, plays the most important role in this respect (see 54–55). In the first few minutes of the play, Naz forces the brothers Darren and Elliot to decide whether they will grant him, as a foreigner or stranger, access to their flat and enterprise. Unconditional hospitality would demand openly welcoming the foreigner and offering him everything they can without any questions asked (see Derrida and Dufourmantelle 2000: 9–13; 15–17 and 23–25). However, as the following excerpt shows, this does not happen in the play:

> NAZ *appears in doorway. He is a young-looking fifteen-year-old.*
> NAZ: Wotchya
> DARREN *pulls a knife from his pocket.*
> DARREN: Where'd you fucking come from?
> NAZ: End of corridor.
> DARREN: Thought the whole block was empty.
> NAZ: It is. Just me. Broke into a flat last night.
> DARREN: Well, fucking break back out and... and fuck off back out again. Go on!
> [...]
> ELLIOT: What's ya name?
> NAZ: Naz.
> ELLIOT: And what d'ya want in return for helping, Naz? (20–25)

In this scene, hospitality is something Darren and Elliot may choose to offer or simply deny.[6] With Naz finally being allowed to come into the flat and help with the preparations for the party, he enters a precarious state. He is completely dependent on his hosts and his status as a 'guest' or 'temporary helper' (see 49) can be withdrawn at any moment. This notion is backed up by Elliot's subsequent

---

6 Moreover, hospitality here is also based on reciprocity and granted only upon the revelation of the foreigner's name. Such demeanor stands in clear opposition to absolute or unconditional hospitality (see Derrida and Dufourmantelle 2000: 25–27).

allusion to the fate of those people who knew about an Egyptian pharao's secret tomb – once the pyramid containing the tomb was completed, they were killed and disposed of (see 26–27). Ironically, this comment foreshadows Naz's own sad reality towards the end of the play. He comes back to the party location to fetch champagne for the Duchess and is then used as *ersatz* for the party piece, the ten-year old boy who was originally meant to be tortured, raped and killed by the Party Guest. His status as *aide-de-camp*, friend or even human being is revoked on the spot and he is faced with Spinx's and the group's violence, rage and sheer desperation (see 110–112).

The scene illustrates various aspects of hospitality and precariousness. On the one hand, it shows the extreme vulnerability of the characters in a Hobbesian state of nature where, in the absence of any rules, even the strongest fears the weakest as he is constantly threatened and can easily be killed in a moment of debility or carelessness. So everyone's basic attitude is mutual mistrust (see Hobbes 1968: 183–188, in particular 183). This, again, leads to even more extreme vulnerability, resulting in a situation where every encounter with a stranger or foreigner is potentially dangerous and hostility is the first reaction towards other human beings. Yet, as Derrida suggests, unconditional hospitality and radical openness towards the foreigner or the Other may be much more difficult to embrace and offer than the "conditional and juridico-political" variety (Derrida and Dufourmantelle 2000: 135). However, as Pheng Cheah argues at length (of course by also referring to Derrida), it may be an impossibility altogether to actively grant or offer such hospitality, as this "absolute [i.e. unconditional] hospitality is fundamentally inhuman" and is more to be seen as "the structural exposure of any finite being or thing" than "a power that issues from and cobelongs with humanity" (2013: 72). Interestingly, hospitality is also a prominent aspect of the chronicles of Theseus. The Greek hero, too, experiences the precariousness of being a guest. First in the hands of the grateful Phytalides and later in Athens in those of a jealous and cunning Medea, the wife of his father Aegeus. Whereas his reception by the Phytalides is reminiscent of what Derrida calls "absolute hospitality" (Derrida and Dufourmantelle 2000: 25–26) because they offer him a place to rest and replenish his resources and also "purif[y] him of the blood he had shed" (Schwab 2001: 210; see also Ranke-Graves 1974: 301–303), the hospitality offered by Medea, fearful for her influence and position in Athens, is of a treacherous and hostile nature – she wants to poison him and she also displays a general hostility towards all strangers entering the city.

A Play on Precarious Memories, or: The World at Stake

Elaborating on Andrew Wyllie's reading of *Mercury Fur* in his short comparative study of Ridley's theatrical oeuvre (see 2013), I would contend that cultural and personal memory is the play's other major theme which is subtly interrelated with precariousness and the myth of Theseus. As a theoretical concept, cultural memory has often been described as linking the present to the past, making our present experiences meaningful by providing a framework for intersubjective orientation and interpretation. Moreover, it is not only useful and necessary for a group's or nation's identity, but it is also equally important to individuals, who update and even establish their own personal and social identity by relating to such a stable framework. Unlike communicative memory, which links the three most recent generations mostly through oral history and everyday communication, cultural memory, if it is meant to provide a mechanism for stabilizing a group or national identity, always needs a place where it can be preserved, as well as institutions by which it can be reviewed. These places are commonly known as museums, archives or myths, and they very much privilege written accounts or scripture over classical lore (see A. Assmann 2010; J. Assmann 2010; Basseler 2010; Harth 2010). In his article on (cultural) memory and trauma, Michael Basseler in particular hints at literary texts as key locations for concepts of collective and individual identity. He also highlights the fact that all forms of individual or collective memory deal with narrated identities, i.e. the act of narrating fosters or constructs identity (see 2010: 226–227). In *Mercury Fur*, a lot of characterization and identity construction happens by means of narrative flashbacks on stage. This is highlighted in the scene where Elliot remembers how he met Lola for the first time (see 52–55), or when Naz tells Darren about how his mother and sister were brutally killed by a street gang (see 32–35).

As regards individual memory, *Mercury Fur* confronts its audience with its problematic nature right from the start. In the opening minutes, for example, Darren and Elliot break and enter a flat whose windows and doors have been barred with plywood. As they remove more and more plywood from the windows, more and more light floods the room. The whole stage goes from pitch black to a warm late afternoon sun shining through its windows. This 'enlightenment' triggers a memory in Darren, who, just moments before, was described as "acting like a kitten after a twirl in the microwave" (5) – first he was dawdling behind and lost his orientation and then he did not know who they are and what they are supposed to do or where they actually come from:[7]

> DARREN: *hovers uneasily*
> ELLIOT: You bloody helping or what?
> DARREN: Yeah, but... who are we?
> ELLIOT: I told you who we fucking were.
> DARREN: When?
> ELLIOT: When we parked the fucking car.
> *Slight pause.*
> Do ya remember parking the fucking car?
> DARREN: What d'ya think I am? (4–5)

Shortly after this incident, the audience learn that the loss of memory and identity may be related to some sort of butterflies that have a similar effect to psychoactive drugs when eaten, especially repeatedly and excessively – they are responsible for altering or erasing memory in the customers' minds.[8] If they do not instantly erase an addict's memory, they at least lead to non-homogeneous, distorted memorized versions of reality. In the end, it becomes clear that something is indeed at stake in *Mercury Fur* – nothing less than the world as we know it. In this nightmarish version of (East) London created by drugs, orientation, be it chronological or spatial, becomes increasingly difficult as the characters not only struggle for survival but also for language, which, unfortunately, from time to time completely fails to mean anything.[9] This of course directly affects the characters' capacity to adequately describe, name and identify their immediate surroundings. Furthermore, their ability to recognize important landmarks of their own cultural heritage is called into question, too, because they are unable to even name places, buildings and things of utmost cultural significance, such as the British Museum or mummies (see 23–25). In this dystopian world, no common framework or cultural memory seems available anymore. Even if one were to explain Naz's difficulty in mapping his world and, for instance, Darren's

---

[7] This can also be seen to refer to the problematic nature of the myth of Theseus, in which origin and identity is a major theme.
[8] According to what can be discerned either from an actual performance of the play or from reading it, the butterflies are highly addictive.
[9] This may be best illustrated by the various times Elliot or Spinx swear at other people (mostly Darren) and end up spewing pleonasms of ethnic determinants used as swear words – for example, "you Paki, Yid, nigger, Catholic, Chink, spic cunt" (7 et *passim*; in some cases with very slight variations of the original quotation such as a different word order or the adjective 'Catholic' replaced by 'Christian').

language problems by their being confused and drugged up, one still does not know whether this is a permanent problem for people in this near-future dystopian London or not.¹⁰ As Elliot rightly states, "[e]*veryone* round here's a fucking customer" (23; emphasis added), meaning nothing less than everyone around the city is a drug addict. To conclude, not understanding or not knowing words as well as the lack of basic historical knowledge or the inability to access cultural memory is a recurrent problem throughout the play. Interestingly enough, most of the time Darren or Naz are the ones with deficient language skills and Elliot is the one who is able to explain words to them because he is the only character who is left with an intact sense and account of history, which automatically makes him the only (reliable?) source of cultural memory and identity.¹¹

After Memory, or: Pulp History

Shifting the focus away from individual memory and orientation, it seems intriguing that history and the recollection of it play such an important role contentwise as well as aesthetically. The following excerpt from the play can be seen as the pinnacle of the impact the drug-like butterflies have on memory, language and the play's aesthetics. It shows how history, mythology, fairytales and pornography build the kind of pulp history that informs the process of identity formation and construction, be it personal, cultural or national, in *Mercury Fur*'s fictional world. In the scene under scrutiny here, Darren tells Naz about a new sort of butterfly – red and with silver stripes – which allows you to experience or witness assassinations of political leaders. He recounts a strangely distorted story about the Kennedy assassination he witnessed in his mind some hours earlier:

> DARREN: Listen, mate, don't knock it. I saw the Dallas splat-head Kennedy get wasted this morning.
> NAZ: Dallas splat-head Kennedy?
> DARREN: He used to be President. He was married to this blonde tart called Marilyn Monroe. They went to Germany for a visit and they met this guy called Hitler.

---

10 At the beginning of the play, Darren has difficulties pronouncing the phrase "bloody biology" and instead says, "All right, all right, I don't wanna *bloddy bolligie* lesson" (7; emphasis added).
11 Sometimes, however, his explanations would not be adequate for publication in a dictionary, one prime example being his definition of the word 'alacrity', which, according to him, "means bright as a polished bullet up a nigger's arsehole" (9).

> [...]
> I'm the Camelot girl. I'm in the car with Kennedy.
> [...]
> I lean towards him to help and his head goes – Kapow! My cunt is getting juicy and creaming up. I fiddle with the bone and brains on me dress. I'm gonna come. I feel it. The sun. The heat. Bone. Brain. Blood. And then – gushhh! Me cunt sprays cunt juice all over the car. (38–39)

Thus, the play not only makes readers and spectators ask questions about what has happened to Darren's or other characters' personal short-time memories, but also about the general availability of any shared cultural or collective memory or what may be left of it after all. And just as this scene convincingly shows, aesthetics become more and more important as the play unfolds towards its moment of catastrophe. By using explicit language and therefore juxtaposing a serious subject like history with the profane and ridiculous, the former suddenly becomes pulp history. The account of Kennedy's assassination is not only completely worthless with regard to its historical accuracy, but it also combines the assassination with a very popular male sexual fantasy, namely female ejaculation, and furthermore adds elements of fairytales, folklore ("Camelot") and cheap comic books, so called pulp fiction, to it ("Kapow", "gushhh!").

In relation to this, one cannot help but be reminded of Bakhtin's concept of the *mésalliance*, which "brings together, unifies, weds, and combines the sacred with the profane, the lofty with the low, the great with the insignificant, the wise with the stupid" (1984: 122). Implicitly this of course also challenges society, based and constructed upon a hierarchical symbolic order, by erasing or diluting the borders between genres and registers.[12] What has hitherto only been identified on the level of content is thus mirrored more deeply on the structural level of the play by virtue of its mythical intertext again. The story of Theseus has always been a story about origin and *mésalliance* because Theseus is not only king and founder of a united Attica, but he is also the illegitimate son of Aegeus, the childless king of Athens. Theseus was secretly wed to Aethra, daughter of Pittheus, son of Pelops, once the mightiest king on the Peloponnesus. Theseus did not know about his real father until his mid-teenage years, because his grandfather Pittheus spread the rumour that he was the son of Poseidon, the protector of Pittheus's city Troezen. Consequently, Walker constantly refers to the problem of origin and fatherhood in his extensive study of Theseus and his relationship to Athens. It is not completely clear whether Theseus's father was really Aegeus

---

12 Naturally, this is what the carnivalesque *mésalliance* and the mode of satire may suggest. However, as this is not the key topic of this essay it cannot be elaborated further at this point.

or Poseidon, which qualifies him as the *mésalliance*-become-flesh, as ostensibly he brings together "the sacred with the profane, the lofty with the low, [and] the great with the insignificant" (Bakhtin 1984: 122).[13] In alternative versions of the myth's standard account, Theseus is also said to have been a wild bandit and a menace to those around him. Among his crimes, Walker counts, for example, the kidnapping of Helen, who was originally a Goddess worshipped at Thorikos, and his helping Peirithous to abduct Persephone, for which he was punished by detainment in the underworld (see 1995: 15–20).

Dystopia, or: From Lost Hope to Last Hope

The present chapter has shown that precariousness, (cultural) memory and the myth of Theseus provide a viable framework for the analysis of Ridley's *Mercury Fur*. The concluding section focuses on the remaining question of genre and how this can be related to the audience of the play. Like Anna Harpin (2011), I draw here upon Jacques Rancière's concept of the emancipated spectator (see 2011). Furthermore, I also provide a brief discussion of the ways in which the play comments and reflects on current political events and developments.

Mercury Fur transgresses and painfully re-negotiates certain thresholds and boundaries, the most obvious ones perhaps being moral boundaries. Keeping in mind what reviewers and scholars alike have said about the actual live experience of the play, I contend that entering the theatre for a performance of *Mercury Fur* means entering a liminal (or precarious) space. In his concise history of liminality as a concept, Bjørn Thomassen concludes that "in liminality there is no certainty concerning the outcome" (2009: 5). With regard to liminality, which originally described the transitional aspect of rites of passage (see Turner 1969; van Gennep 2005; Thomassen 2009), one may argue that watching the play involves a constant process of crossing thresholds which literally starts and ends with (ritually) entering or leaving the theatre. The outcome of a night out at the theatre thus becomes something unforeseeable that will, nevertheless, ultimately have an effect on individual members of the audience. The artificially created liminal space of the theatre confronts the spectator with a situation in or by which s/he is induced to act accordingly to his/her perception and

---

[13] However, with reference to Bacchylides 17, Walker mentions the fact that Theseus may be seen as neither coming from the earth nor from the sea, ultimately preventing both Aegeus and Poseidon from claiming fatherhood. The most likely place from which Theseus really originated is the *pontos*, the unknown sea, which is very close to the primordial chaos that only came to an end because earth was created (see Ranke-Graves 1974: 294–296; Walker 1995: 83–86).

experience of said situation. This is exactly where responsibility meets "response-ability" (Lehmann 2006: 185). Rancière's notion of an emancipated spectator, too, challenges the traditional assessment of theatre audiences as typically passive and immobile (see 2011: 2–5). His core argument is to restore theatre to its original virtue and purpose of letting spectators learn and critically asses what they see on stage in comparison to their own past or future actions. For Rancière, spectators have never been passive onlookers but rather actors in that they actively compare, listen, compose, interpret and observe (see 2011: 13).

In *Mercury Fur*, the emancipated spectator's full potential is unlocked by the play's dystopian quality. Generally, dystopias (a) begin *in medias res* and neglect or completely discard the longer expository parts of traditional utopias (see Baccolini and Moylan 2003: 5); (b) show or imagine a world in which the point of no return has been reached and the characters are faced with the consequences of man-made catastrophe (see Baccolini and Moylan 2003: 5; Sargent 1994: 5–10; Vieira 2010: 16–18); and (c) "[t]raditionally a bleak, depressing genre with little space for hope within the story, [they] maintain utopian hope outside their pages, if at all; for it is only if we consider dystopia as a warning that we as readers can hope to escape its pessimistic future" (Baccolini and Moylan 2003: 7). That being said, one may see that Rancière's argument may best be applied to *Mercury Fur* from a genre perspective. Thus, by virtue of its dystopian mode, the play tries to send out a warning and be as clear as possible about what is at stake. As it projects disturbing current socio-political developments into a near-future, *Mercury Fur* can of course be read as a comment on or criticism of Western politics, complacency and hypocrisy. It also gained unforeseeable relevance and immediacy in 2011, when several London boroughs provided the setting for violent riots after a police officer shot a 29-year-old black British Tottenham denizen (see, for example, Standing 2014: vi–xi, and among many news reports on the topic, "Technology and Disorder" 2011 and "Riots in Tottenham" 2011). In the end, *Mercury Fur* presents readers and audiences with a world in which the so-called periphery and the disenfranchised have struck back against the metropolis. Ironically, the near-future version of London, the European epitome of neoliberal capitalism, democracy, political and military power, suffers all the ills normally experienced by struggling least-developed and developing countries or failed states. The irony becomes biting sarcasm when it is contrasted with the original myth of Theseus, so prominently echoed in the play's content, structure and aesthetics. The chronicle of the virtuous hero and founding father of Athens's era of political unity, prosperity, and economic and military prowess has been transformed into the story of an anti-Theseus, Spinx, a powerless man of dubious motives and morals living in a derelict country, finally tasting the bitter fruits of what he did not care to prevent or actively had others spread in his name elsewhere. Such interpretation may sound overly didactic at first but, at a second glimpse, it seems a valid one with regard to the conventions of the genre of dystopia (see, among others, Baccolini and Moylan 2003: 10–11; Vieira 2010: 15–16) and the resulting de-mystification of Theseus.

Works Cited

Assmann, Aleida. 2010. *Erinnerungsräume: Formen und Wandlungen des kulturellen Gedächtnisses*. Munich: Beck.

Assmann, Jan. 2010. "Communicative and Cultural Memory". In: Astrid Erll and Ansgar Nünning (eds.). *A Companion to Cultural Memory Studies*. Berlin and New York: De Gruyter. 97–108.

Baccolini, Raffaella and Moylan Tom. 2003. "Introduction: Dystopia and Histories." In: Raffaella Baccolini and Tom Moylan (eds.). *Dark Horizons: Science Fiction and Dystopian Imagination*. London and New York: Routledge. 1–12.

Bakhtin, Mikhail. 1984 [1963]. *Problems of Dostoevsky's Poetics*. Transl. Caryl Emerson. Manchester: Manchester University Press.

Basseler, Michael. 2010. "Kulturelle Erinnerung und Trauma im afroamerikanischen Roman". In: Sonja Altnöder, Wolfgang Hallet and Ansgar Nünning (eds.). *Schlüsselthemen der Anglistik und Amerikanistik*. Trier: WVT. 223–248.

Brantley, Ben. 2012. Rev. of *Mercury Fur* (Trafalgar Studios 2012), by Philip Ridley. *NYTimes.com*, 29 June. <http://www.nytimes.com/2012/06/30/theater/in-london-minsk-2011-and-mercury-fur.html> [accessed 7 February 2015].

Butler, Judith. 2012. "Precarious Life, Vulnerability, and the Ethics of Cohabitation". *Journal of Speculative Philosophy* 26.2: 134–151.

Cheah, Pheng. 2013. "To Open: Hospitality and Alienation". In: Thomas Claviez (ed.). *The Conditions of Hospitality: Ethics, Politics, and Aesthetics on the Threshold of the Possible*. New York: Fordham UP. 57–80.

Croggon, Alison. 2007. Rev. of *Mercury Fur* (Theatreworks Melbourne 2007), by Philip Ridley. *theatrenotes.blogspot.de*, <http://theatrenotes.blogspot.de/2007/09/review-mercury-fur.html> [accessed 4 January 2015].

Derrida, Jacques and Anne Dufourmantelle. 2000 [1997]. *Of Hospitality: Anne Dufourmantelle Invites Jacques Derrida to Respond*. Trans. Rachel Bowlby. Stanford: Stanford UP.

Fisher, Philip. 2005. Rev. of *Mercury Fur* (Menier Chocolate Factory 2005), by Philip Ridley. *britishtheatreguide.info*, n.d. <http://www.britishtheatreguide.info/reviews/mercuryfur-rev> [accessed 7 February 2015].

Johnson, Samuel. 1968 [1755]. *A Dictionary of the English Language*. London: W. Strahan. Repr. Heidelberg: Olms.

Hahnemann, Carolin. 2010. "Theseus". In: Michael Gagarin (ed.). *The Oxford Encyclopedia of Ancient Greece and Rome*. Vol. 7. Oxford: Oxford UP. 43–45.

Hammond, Nicholas G.L. and Howard H. Scullard. 1970. *The Oxford Classical Dictionary*. 2nd ed. Oxford: Clarendon.

Harpin, Anna. 2011. "Intolerable Acts". *Performance Research* 16.1: 102–111.

Harth, Dietrich. 2010. "The Invention of Cultural Memory". In: Astrid Erll and Ansgar Nünning (eds.). *A Companion to Cultural Memory Studies*. Berlin and New York: De Gruyter. 85–96.
Hobbes, Thomas. 1968 [1651]. *Leviathan*. Edited with an introduction by Crawford B. Macpherson. London: Penguin.
Kaser, Max and Rolf Knütel (eds.). 2008. *Römisches Privatrecht. Ein Studienbuch*. München: Beck.
Lehmann, Hans-Thies. 2006 [1999]. *Postdramatic Theatre*. Trans. Karen Jürs-Munby. London and New York: Routledge.
Levinas, Emmanuel. 1989 [1984]. "Ethics as First Philosophy". Trans. Seán Hand and Michael Temple. In: Seán Hand (ed.). *The Levinas Reader*. Oxford: Blackwell. 75–87.
Lurker, Manfred (ed.). 1991. *Wörterbuch der Symbolik*. Stuttgart: Kröner.
Rancière, Jacques. 2011 [2008]. *The Emancipated Spectator*. Trans. Gregory Elliott. London: Verso.
Ranke-Graves, Robert. 1974 [1960]. *Griechische Mythologie. Quellen und Deutung*. Vol. 1. Reinbek: Rowohlt.
Redman, Bridgette M. 2014. Rev. of *Mercury Fur* (The Ringwald 2014), by Philip Ridley. *encoremichigan.com*, 19–25 August. <http://www.encoremichigan.com/article.html?article=4466> [accessed 3 December 2014].
Ridley, Philip. 2005. *Mercury Fur*. London: Methuen.
Ridley, Philip. 2009. "'Putting a New Lens on the World': The Art of Theatrical Alchemy". Interview with Aleks Sierz. *New Theatre Quarterly* 25.2: 109–117.
"Riots in Tottenham after Mark Duggan shooting protest". 2011. *bbc.co.uk*, 7 August. <http://www.bbc.co.uk/news/uk-england-london-14434318> [accessed 7 February 2015].
Sargent, Lyman Tower. 1994. "The Three Faces of Utopianism Revisited". *Utopian Studies* 5.1: 1–37.
Schwab, Gustav. 2001 [1946]. *Gods and Heroes of Ancient Greece*. New York: Pantheon.
Standing, Guy. 2014. *The Precariat: The New Dangerous Class*. 2nd ed. London: Bloomsbury.
"Technology and Disorder: The BlackBerry Riots". 2011. *economist.com*, 13 August. <http://www.economist.com/node/21525976> [accessed 7 February 2015].
Thomassen, Bjørn. 2009. "The Uses and Meaning of Liminality". *International Political Anthropology* 2.1: 5–27.
Turner, Victor. 1969. *The Ritual Process: Structure and Anti-Structure*. London: Routledge & Kegan Paul.
van Gennep, Arnold. 2005. *Übergangsriten*. Frankfurt: Campus.
Vieira, Fátima. 2010. "The Concept of Utopia". In: Gregory Claeys (ed.). *The Cambridge Companion to Utopian Literature*. Cambridge: Cambridge UP. 3–27.
Walker, Henry J. 1995. *Theseus and Athens*. Oxford: Oxford UP.
Wyllie, Andrew. 2013. "Philip Ridley and Memory". *Studies in Theatre and Performance* 33.1: 65–75.

David Kerler
Jez Butterworth's *Jerusalem* and Postmodern Precariousness

When Jez Butterworth's three-act play *Jerusalem* (2009) opened at the Royal Court Theatre it was showered with rave reviews – an appraisal that would last until the play's last performance at London's West End in January 2012. Aside from Mark Rylance's outstanding performance of the main character Johnny 'Rooster' Byron, the play was particularly praised for its "defiant celebration of freedom" (Spencer 2011) and anarchic sense of vitality (see Spencer 2011, Brantley 2011 and Barton 2011), most notably embodied by Johnny Byron with his "fast, vital Falstaffian appetite for pleasure, for independence, for life itself" (Brantley 2011). With its liveliness and evocation of the mythic, *Jerusalem* seems to strike a chord in its audiences and critics, as Ben Brantley (2011) puts it outright in his review for the *New York Times*: "We theatergoers too are starved for a sense of the mythic". In fact, William Blake's eponymous poem sets the stage for a play that likewise questions England's current state, thereby evoking its cultural, mythic legacy. This time, however, it is not the industrial revolution with its "dark Satanic Mills" that is threatening "England's green & pleasant Land" (Blake 1988: 95–96, ll. 8 and 15), but the insecurity and fragmentation of a postindustrial, postmodern world that has deconstructed all stable certainties and notions of (collective) identity. It appears that the postmodern(ist) credo of a liberating, free-playing 'anything goes' based on radical ontological uncertainty does not turn out to be that satisfying after all: despite (or precisely because of) its carnivalesque inversion of established hierarchies and orders, Butterworth's *Jerusalem* is marked by a strong sense of the precarious, suggesting that there indeed is something at stake beyond all postmodern playfulness.

The play opens with a prologue citing the first two stanzas of Blake's poem "And did those feet in ancient time", in which he identifies England('s ancient past) with the holy land in a series of rhetorical questions, implicitly asking what has now remained of that divine heritage. The last two stanzas – in which Blake prophetically calls for revolution, to rebuild Jerusalem in England – are, however, left out for the action of the play to set in. The intertextual context thus suggests that Butterworth's *Jerusalem* takes the place of the missing part of Blake's poem, providing a counter-discourse to the aforementioned question of England's place in a fragmented, postmodern world. These issues are scrutinized by foregrounding the notion of boundaries, i.e. by focusing on the precarious character of Johnny Byron, who epitomizes both the fears and (unconscious) desires of society. A drug dealer, anarchistic hedonist and heavy drinker, Johnny lives in a mobile home amidst the woods of the fictitious town Flintock in Wiltshire. Both despised and celebrated by his fellow townspeople, he attracts the local youth to his place with his notorious parties and bewitching tales. On St. George's Day, his reclusive existence is suddenly threatened as the county officials Linda Fawcett and Luke Parsons bring him a letter from the Kennet and Avon Council, stating that he has to leave the woods within 24 hours. Byron, however, chooses to ignore this resolution and goes on with his life as usual: we witness his parties and hangovers, meet his friends (such as the unemployed would-be deejay Ginger, Lee, who wants to emigrate to Australia, or a babbling professor who has been drugged) and eventually hear stories about his reckless jumps over several busses, injuries and even about his supernatural encounter with giants. Meanwhile, the annual fair and parade are taking place in the background or, to be more precise, taking place in the center, the city. As it will be shown later, however, these alternative categories of center and margin, in and out, are called into question. As the play progresses we learn that Johnny has a six-year-old child, Marky, whose mother Dawn strongly disapproves of her ex-boyfriend's lifestyle. Yet Byron seems to be a caring person, for he hides Troy Whitworth's stepdaughter Phaedra, last year's May Queen, who appears to have been abused by her stepfather, in his trailer. The play eventually reaches its climax when Troy beats Byron up shortly before the eviction and a mob of two dozen townspeople who want to expel the outcast is approaching. Thereupon, Byron sets his trailer on fire, delivers a curse and invokes his mythic line of ancestors – and the giants.

In the following it will be argued that *Jerusalem* is a reflection on as well as an antithesis to a postmodern *zeitgeist* that is fundamentally characterized by its precariousness. The play's central character, Johnny Byron, epitomizes both this postmodern spirit of the age and the ensuing desires/attempts to overcome its precariousness. By combining these opposing tendencies, i.e. being both a symptom of and a reaction to the postmodern crisis, his ambivalence is further stressed and additionally exposes the very precariousness of such endeavours. But what does the notion of (postmodern) precariousness refer to exactly? In order to approximate and understand it, we need to have, in the first place, a closer look at its most basic definitions. Whereas the *Oxford English Dictionary* describes the meaning of 'precarious' as "not securely held or in position; dangerously likely to fall or collapse" and as "dependent on chance; uncertain" (2010: 1397), the *Collins Cobuild Advanced Dictionary* rather stresses the loss of control: "If your situation is precarious, you are not in complete control of events and might fail in what you are doing at any moment" (2009: 1217). Hence, we can already see that the word describes a state of uncertainty that is on the threshold of collapsing. This uncertainty may not only be subjected to chance or arbitrariness but is also dependent on a third party, society, as the word's Latin etymon *precarius* – "obtained by entreaty" (*Oxford English Dictionary* 2010: 1397) – further reveals.[1] In any case, however, the concept of precariousness implies a strong notion that there is something at stake. With that said, striking resemblances can be discerned between the precarious uncertainty just outlined and Zygmunt Bauman's diagnosis of the postmodern (moral) crisis. According to Bauman, the latter emerges from the "pluralism of rules" (1996: 20), the fragmentation of the self into the numerous roles it performs and the death of the author with regard to (social) responsibility. That is, globalization and the division of labour have abolished any individual responsibility inasmuch as certain actions or effects can no longer be traced to any individual 'authorship'; responsibility is rather "floating, nowhere finding its natural haven" (Bauman 1996: 18). The price for postmodern plurality, its boundless freedom of choice, however, is that it "cast[s] us into a state of uncertainty never before so agonizing" (Bauman 1996: 21). Put differently, precariousness is generated by incertitude, indeterminacy, liminality and incommensurability.

All these attributes are condensed in the play's social outcast Johnny Byron. By constituting the radical Other, and thus foregrounding the precariousness of society itself, he can be identified with the Levinasian concept of the face, i.e. "the extreme precariousness of the other" (Levinas qtd. in Butler 2004: 134), "the wordless vocalization of suffering" (Butler 2004: 134). Through his precarious character and existential situation, Byron transcends the mere phenomenal and points at a fundamental ontological condition of society, of our existence. That is, on behalf of the play's central character the irreconcilable yet inextricable poles of nature and civilization, individual and society, host and guest, Other and self, pleasure principle and reality principle, in and out, are scrutinized, thereby exposing their/our unstable, precarious nature. It is precisely this uncertainty that reveals a vulnerability that addresses us and opens up a discourse of ethics, responsibility: the encounter with the radical Other, the precariousness of the face, constitutes our own identity at the same time as it defines the insecure,

---

[1] Also see in this regard Butler (2012: 148): "We can make this [the vulnerability to destruction by others that follows from a condition of precarity in all modes of social interdependency] into a broad existential claim, namely, that everyone is precarious, and this follows from our social existence as bodily beings who depend upon one another for shelter and sustenance and who, therefore, are at risk of statelessness, homelessness, and destitution under unjust and unequal political conditions".

vulnerable boundaries of our very existence.[2] The precariousness of society and (collective) identity as well as the ensuing desires for and attempts at stability/definiteness shall be analyzed in four consecutive steps: (1) semantics of space, (2) laughter and precariousness, (3) identity and performativity. Finally, I will readdress the play's aesthetics and ask how the notion of precariousness is represented formally and which aesthetical consequences arise from it (4).

Precarious Spaces

In his essay "Ethics as First Philosophy", Emmanuel Levinas poses the question whether the "*Da* of my *Dasein* is not already the usurpation of somebody else's place" (1989: 85). In this way, he regards the "crisis of being" (1989: 85) from a spatial perspective as he focuses on the local, spatial aspect of being, i.e. "the being of a being (*de l'être de l'étant*) in the human domain" (1989: 85). Accordingly, the subject's very existence, its being-in-the-world, is inevitably a violation of the Other's space, thereby exposing a fundamental vulnerability that makes claims for responsibility (see Levinas 1989: 82–85). This crisis of (spatial) being, its uncertainty, is scrutinized in *Jerusalem*'s depiction of spaces, their various (re)appropriations and in the disclosure of their underlying power structures.

A closer look at the depiction of the scenery in the first act shall further elucidate this:

> England at midnight. A clearing in a moonlit wood. At the back of the clearing stands an old forty-foot mobile home [...] Now we can see that the mobile home stands in a fairly permanent state. The old Wessex flag (a golden Wyvern dragon against a red background) flies from one end. An old rusted metal railway sign screwed to the mobile home reads 'Waterloo'.
>
> A porch stands out front – an old mouldy couch stands on the porch deck. Lots of junk. An old hand-cranked air-raid siren. Stuck to the porch post is an old submarine klaxon. An old record player, with a stand-alone speaker. An old American-style fridge. Stacks of old LPs.
>
> Underneath, a chicken coop. Chopped wood under a lean-to. Rubbish. Empty bottles. A car seat, a swing. An old windchime. A garden table, and four red Coca-Cola plastic chairs. A rusty Swingball set.
>
> In the middle of the copse, a smashed television. (Butterworth, *Jerusalem*: 6)

---

[2] See Butler (2004: 128–135 and 2012: 140–142; 148) for the notions of precariousness, (her reading of) Levinas's concept of the face and the ensuing imperative it casts upon us.

Already the point of time, midnight, describes a liminal phase where neither has the current day ended nor has a new day begun. This temporal uncertainty is furthermore matched by the play's decentered spatial center, Johnny's mobile home: not only does the concept of a mobile home already imply an impermanent, transitory quality, but this particular one is characterized by further indeterminacy as it features elements of a submarine (the klaxon) and seems to transform into a tank when Byron, wearing a Second World War helmet, looks out of the hatch (see 8). This protean arbitrariness is eventually underlined by the attached railway sign reading "Waterloo", which is completely out of place in this particular context: a signifier without a signified that exposes, especially with regard to the mobile home's polymorphism, the arbitrariness of signification. Finally, the opposition between inside and outside is undermined as the couch, the fridge, a record player and a smashed TV – altogether an image of a waste land of civilization – are standing in front of the mobile home, i.e. outside amidst untamed nature. In short, in is out and out is in. We can see, then, that from the start the setting figuratively situates the play in a postmodern condition of uncertainty and liminality, suggesting a sense of the precarious that mainly arises from spatio-temporal indeterminacy.

This inversion of the dichotomy of inside and outside and the disclosure of its precarious nature hints, in a wider sense, at the equally precarious relationship between nature and civilization, individual and society.[3] In fact, Byron and his woods mirror society's fears and desires. In this sense, the woods are not on the town's outskirts but in its very center as they can be regarded as the unconscious of society/the town.[4] On the one hand, the woods are an image for society's estrangement, as suggested by the aforementioned semantics of space, which depict a postmodern, precarious wasteland of civilization. It is moreover striking that the May Day festivities are planned meticulously and are taking place off-stage, i.e. in the town and hence outside nature.[5] This further adds

---

[3] In fact, Johnny Byron's woods are attributed a universal quality: Lee, for instance, considers it a holy, mythical place – "this wood is holy. This is holy land" (72) – and Johnny affirms that Flintock could indeed be any other place – "Flintock's no worse than anywhere else" (101).
[4] See, for example, Johnny Byron's depiction of the woods, which, in the darkness (an image for the irrational, unconscious), reveal the mysteries and (repressed) secrets of the townspeople: "I seen lots of ghosts. (*Beat.*) I seen women burn love letters. Men dig holes in the dead of night. I seen a young girl walk down here in the cold dawn, take all her clothes off, wrap her arms round a broad beech tree and give birth to a baby boy. I seen first kisses. Last kisses. I seen all the world pass by and go. Laughing. Crying. Talking to themselves. Kicking the bracken. (*Beat.*) Elves and fairies, you say. (*Beat.*) Elves and fairies" (102).
[5] Ginger announces the detailed programme: "Ladies and gentleman, I give you... The annual St. George's Day Pageant and Wessex Country Fair in the village of Flintock sponsored by John

to society's estrangement inasmuch these festivities seem to be, figuratively speaking with regard to the semantics of space, artificially alienated from their folkloric, natural origin.[6] Consequently, Byron – who was the attraction of previous fairs precisely because of his anarchistic actions (see 30–32) that challenged the festivities' civilizational artificiality – does not participate in the festivities this time, but chooses to celebrate his own in his mobile home instead. This, on the other hand, shows that Byron and his bucolic woods seem to fulfill society's – almost Romantic – desires for the natural/primitive, irrational and anarchic suspension of artificial norms. Nevertheless, he turns out to be a deeply ambivalent character as he is welcomed as a liberating amusement attraction and host of notorious parties, but also despised by many and partly excluded from the festivities due to his numerous transgressions of limits (which, in turn, constitute his attraction in the first place). In short, Johnny Byron and, by extension, his woods represent both the in and out of society, thereby inhabiting a precarious, liminal space between normative boundaries and boundlessness.

Against this backdrop it can be furthermore said that Byron figures both the instance of a host as well as that of a guest, thereby deconstructing the notion of hospitality. As Jacques Derrida shows in "Hostipitality", hospitality is an impossible concept which "deconstruct[s] itself – precisely – in being put into practice" (2000: 5). This impossibility primarily arises from the fact that "the host, he who offers hospitality, must be the master in his house, he [...] must be assured of his sovereignty over the spaces and goods he offers or opens to the other as stranger" (2000: 14). Hospitality, however, presupposes an unconditional quality that inevitably becomes conditional as soon as it is realized. As a consequence, the power relations between host and guest are reversed, thus undermining their very opposition and rather hinting at their irreconcilable interdependence (see Derrida 2000: 3–18). To take the example of *Jerusalem*, on one side, Johnny Byron clearly plays the role of a host as his fellow townspeople come to his

---

Deere Tractors and Arkell Ales. (*Flicks through.*) Introduction from the Mayor... Blah blah blah. Picture of him and his fat missus. Here we go. 10 a.m., The Flintock Men – outside the Cooper's Arms. 11 a.m., Floats. 11.30, Ploughing competition. 11.45, Bell-ringing. 12 o'clock, Donkey drop. 12.15, Yoga demonstration. 12.30, Wheelbeero race. 12.45, Dancing dog display. 1 p.m., Knobbly knees. 1.15, Clown-town. Welly wanging, 1.30–" (46).

6 See also Boll (2012: 7): "It [rural England in *Jerusalem*] is home to an overlooked part of the population, the disillusioned middle class, [...] void of a distinctive identity. The local public houses are under the control of large breweries, the annual fair mirrors stereotypical fame and talent shows, and the common culture of the English countryside is largely being destroyed, replaced by commercialised Englishness".

place and experience through him a sense of mythical unity and primitiveness that they seem to lack and long for. That is, Byron receives the townspeople at his woods (i.e. a space that he usurped in the first place)[7] and offers them a space for identification (or, at least, a space for acting out their unconscious desires/drives), therefore acting as a powerful host. On the other side, Byron needs this particular society and its norms in order to construct his own identity via his various transgressive performances, thus becoming a guest (or even hostage) of society and its norms – albeit his transgressive behavior has to be likewise regarded as an usurpation of the host, therefore inverting the opposition again. Most significantly, however, he still is part of a larger context, i.e. the space of society with its laws and norms. And it is the latter that wants to expel him precisely because he has taken its hospitality to the extreme by his transgressive behavior. In other words, hospitality's prerequisite of unconditionality suddenly turns here into conditionality, for as soon as the host becomes a hostage of the guest, the former feels impelled to impose a certain conditionality that inverts the relationship between host and guest anew: the *Da* of the *Dasein* (be it the host or the guest) is unavoidably a usurpation of the Other's space (see Levinas 1989: 85), which underlines the precarious line between host and guest, between conditionality and unconditionality, strongly putting the concept of hospitality into question.[8]

Taken as a whole, it can be concluded that the spatial inversion of inside and outside is paralleled by the highly ambivalent character of Johnny Byron, who further points to the equally ambivalent oppositions of nature/civilization and individual/society. He unites the mentioned oppositions and also deconstructs them by unveiling their unstable relationship. In so doing, Byron turns out to be the epitome of precariousness, as he embodies the very threshold that separates these seeming opposites. These are, in turn, mirrored by the respective (uncertain) spaces they occupy, for Byron is both inside and outside of his mobile home, nature, civilization and ultimately society. Precariousness, therefore, is exposed not only abstractly in the permeability of these categories/spaces, but also concretely in Byron's vulnerability, i.e. by the fact that he is beaten up and expelled by the end of the play (which, once again, inverts the host/guest relationship). In that sense, Byron's vulnerability as well as the

---

[7] Byron tells Wesley about the wood, "You tell Sue's brother Jim to tell all his South Wiltshire bandits and all them fuckers on the New Estate that this is called Rooster's Wood. I've been here since before all you bent busybody bastards were born" (45).
[8] See Derrida (2000: 9) for the notion of the host as a hostage of the guest.

various uncertainties/instabilities he represents ultimately constitute an encounter with the radical Other, the Levinasian notion of the face: his precariousness and the ontological condition he embodies open up a discourse of ethics in which we have to recognize the boundaries of our being-in-the-world, and negotiate the conflicting yet indivisible poles of conditional and unconditional hospitality (see Derrida 2001: 3–24), individual and society, and notions of host and guest.[9]

Carnivalism and Laughter

As has been argued, the spaces depicted in *Jerusalem* are characterized by an inversion, or rather ontological uncertainty, of inside and outside. Nevertheless, there is no denying the fact that the play centers on Byron's mobile home exclusively, while the May Day festivities are taking place outside (i.e. in the town and off-stage). We only get to know about these festivities through the reports of other characters and various offstage sounds (see, for example, 19–20; 71 and 92), altogether suggesting a paradoxical presence/absence. Given the aforementioned artificiality of the festivities and Byron's transgressive behavior, however, we need to ask whether the fair is really taking place in the town or rather in the woods. For, as Ginger affirms with regard to Byron's stunts at the fair, "[t]wenty year back, Johnny Byron *was* the Flintock Fair" (30) and, as will be shown in the following, he still *is*: both constituting a scapegoat and a liberating Pied Piper, the threshold between normative boundaries and boundlessness, Johnny Byron stages a carnivalesque suspension of hierarchies and norms that provides society with a (temporary and hence precarious) sense of liberty and satisfaction of its (repressed) desires.[10] Laughter and notions of precariousness are thereby closely intertwined.

The carnivalesque suspension of hierarchies/norms is, to begin with, achieved by the use of grotesque aesthetics (and laughter). According to Mikhail Bakhtin, the grotesque is primarily characterized by the dissolution of the boundaries between different bodies (e.g. human and animals) as well as between body and world. The body's inside and outside are oftentimes merged to one shape, thereby connoting a continuous process of becoming that is never completed (see Bakhtin 1968: 52 and 315–318). Seen from another perspec-

---

[9] In this regard, see also Butler (2011: 2): "[V]ulnerability is the name for a certain way of opening onto the world. In this sense, it not only designates a relation to the world, but it asserts our very existence as a relational one".
[10] See Bakhtin (1968: 10–11 and 87–91) for the concepts of carnival and laughter.

tive, the grotesque (body) and precariousness are closely related insofar as they both describe an ephemeral, indeterminable state that is on the verge of changing into something different, on the threshold of collapsing. In this respect, it is quite striking that Johnny Byron features many grotesque qualities. Not only is he described as an ambiguous figure that combines human and animal traits ("*he moves with the balance of a dancer, or an animal*" (9); or as indicated by his middle name, 'Rooster'), but he also embodies a protean quality that is in the process of becoming. Already by the play's very beginning, Johnny assumes the role/body of the historical Lord Byron (his "*slight limp*" (9) alludes to Lord Byron's clubfoot), a soldier ("*A head appears, wearing a Second World War helmet and goggles*" (8)) and a dog ("This is Rooster Byron's dog, Shep, informing Kennet and Avon Council to go fuck itself. Woof woof!" (9)), until he eventually lifts his goggles and takes his helmet off in order to transform into an 'ordinary' civilian. The polymorphic, grotesque quality of Byron's character and appearance is furthermore completed by the numerous intertexts he can be related to – an issue that shall be scrutinized at a later point. But prior to this we need to reconsider the Bakhtinian notion of the grotesque from a wider perspective: does not the play itself, its aesthetics, constitute a grotesque body inasmuch as the abovementioned precarious spaces – i.e. the inversion of inside and outside, the merging of these seeming opposites – suspend the boundaries of/between body and world? Is not this grotesque inversion and uncertainty, its transient and interminable quality, precisely at the root of the notion of precariousness? Put differently, the (grotesque) dissolution of these oppositions is a source of precarious laughter that follows the logic of carnivalesque eccentricity (see Bakhtin, 1984: 122–124) as it exposes and gives voice to the subliminal dimension of human nature, thereby hinting at its unstable condition.

Such carnivalesque eccentricity is most notably staged in Johnny Byron's woods. With his loudhailer (in a sense, modern panpipes), his lewdness, and due to the simple fact that he lives in the woods, Byron resembles the mythological character of Pan. Beyond that, he also acts as the carnival prince (i.e. as host) who invites his guests – in tune with his mythical counterpart – to music and dance. To be more precise: he invites them to *his* fair, a place of excessive reveling, of drug- and alcohol-induced Dionysian frenzy that exposes irrational and suppressed desires, liberating the pleasure principle from the clutches of the reality principle. This liberating reign of the pleasure principle, the suspension of norms and hierarchies, however, is just temporary and in danger of changing abruptly: not only is Byron's fair seriously threatened by the approaching eviction, but also the guests usurp the host as they urinate on a heavily drunken Byron and film this humiliating episode with their mobile phones. In Bakhtin's terms, this corresponds to the "decrowning" (1984: 124) of the carnival prince and constitutes – together with his preceding exaltation or "[c]rowning" (1984: 124) – the essence of carnival: an ambivalent interplay of renewal and change, of death and rebirth, indicating the relativity and uncertainty of every order or hierarchy (see 1984: 124–127). In other words, carnivalesque laughter is fundamentally based on ambivalence, indeterminacy and instability – a state of ontological uncertainty that unveils the precarious nature of human existence, its vulnerability.

But how are laughter, vulnerability and precariousness intertwined in particular? As Charles Baudelaire shows, laughter is a paradoxical phenomenon as it combines two contrasting emotions. On the one hand, laughter is based on the degradation of the Other, evoking emotions of power and superiority, while on the other, its demeaning power brings about at the same time a moment of absolute weakness in ethical terms, exposing the abyss of human nature (see Baudelaire 1977: 289–294). In *Jerusalem*, we both laugh with and at Johnny Byron. In the former case, we are his accomplices, taking part in his antisocial behavior and laughing at society and its norms; in the latter, we laugh at his vulnerability, his helpless subjection to a third party (i.e. at his aforementioned degradation). In each case, however, it is an instance of precarious laughter, i.e. we will soon be laughing on the other side of our face. For this kind of laughter not only involves the extreme precariousness of the Other but also our own as it mirrors our own abyss, our deep-rooted weaknesses.[11] In a sense, this type of laughter very much resembles the Levinasian notion of the confrontation with the face, since we are faced with the vulnerability or precariousness of the Other as well as that of our existence at the same time. Put another way: whereas Heinrich Anz (see 1989) rather favorably identifies the ceasing of (postmodern) laughter as a destruction of metaphysics which unveils a new metaphysical quality of unlimited possibilities, I would suggest that laughter's ceasing in *Jerusalem* is at its root precarious. The deconstruction of all stable orders and hierarchies, unlimited freedom and possibilities, are achieved by instances of precarious laughter that hint at the incommensurability, incertitude and eventually vulnerability of our very existence – a precarious, threatening existence where something is indeed at stake, namely (the desire for) definiteness, stability and identity faced with a condition of postmodern precariousness.

---

11 In this regard, it is quite striking that Byron actually seems to mirror the fears (the abyss?) of those who want to expel him: for example, the county officials – "I ain't scared of Kennet and Avon. [...] I'm in their dreams and their worst nightmares" (24) – or Troy – "When was it you were last up here, Troy. [...] We poured a glass of wine into a plate, a silver plate, like a blood-red mirror, and you took the candle and you gazed into the mirror. (*Beat.*) You shook like a leaf. You couldn't stop shaking. Couldn't speak. You were terrified, boy" (81).

(Collective) Identity and Performativity

How does the play negotiate the issue of (collective) identity in view of the aforementioned conflicting poles, i.e. the precarious threshold between radical ontological uncertainty and the desire for stability and definiteness? Again, it is through the highly ambivalent character of Johnny Byron that these issues are scrutinized. Hence we have to ask to whom the framing context of St. George's Day may refer: is Johnny Byron the dragon slayer or the dragon itself, i.e. is he the *embodiment of* or the *solution to* the precariousness of (collective) identity?

To begin with, it is striking that Johnny proves to be a highly intertextual character. Critics generally see him as a trickster figure, identifying him with Falstaff, Prospero, Robin Hood or, as has been shown before, Pan (see for example Boll 2012: 4; or Brantley 2011). In addition to this, his special "Byron blood" (107) may be related to the legendary dragon slayer Siegfried, and due to his surname, slight limp and excessive, rebellious manner he resembles the historical Lord Byron. Finally, he places himself within a vast mythic and folkloric lineage by the end of the play, including Norse mythology (Búri, Woden/Odin, Vili and Vé), giants from folkloric tales (Jack-in-Irons, Thunderdell, Blunderbore) and eventually Brutus of Albion (see 109). With that said and due to the fact that the whole play takes place amidst the festivities of a rich folklore tradition, it becomes clear why Johnny Byron has such a strong appeal: an intertextual conglomerate of numerous mythological, literary and folkloric figures, he embodies a (Romantic) sense of unity and mythic completion in face of postmodern estrangement. In other words, he fills in for "the lost gods of England" (Butterworth, *Jerusalem:* 18), the perceived loss of origin and society's desire for "a sense of the mythic" (Brantley 2011), i.e. for a sense of stable (collective) identity in a globalized, fragmented world. Against this backdrop, it comes as no surprise that Johnny additionally features many similarities to Jesus Christ, hence also connoting a messianic figure: from his resurrection after a failed jump over several buses, his virgin birth (see 31–32; 48) through to his banishment and death by the end of the play (which can be loosely related to the crucifixion). While it goes without saying that the notion of a stable identity has always been a chimera, the resort to myths and folkloric traditions, models that suggest and (pretend to) provide ahistorical significance and identity, seems to undergo a renaissance in *Jerusalem* regardless of postmodernism's proclaimed end of *grands récits*.

At the same time, however, Johnny Byron is the very embodiment of postmodern fragmentation, indeterminableness and estrangement. His aforementioned liminality and precarious identity are ultimately underpinned by the numerous intertexts he refers to: similar to his grotesque polymorphism, he is an intertextual patchwork that cannot be reduced to a coherent, stable identity. It is therefore hardly surprising that many of those intertexts are alluded to in an ironical way: his special "Byron blood" is, in fact, Romany blood, therefore breaking with Siegfried's noble descent (quite the contrary, Johnny is a degenerated, antisocial drunkard and drug dealer); his Christlike resurrection was very likely indebted to fortune which, as is known, favors fools and their foolish actions; and his *excessive* recital of his (mythical) ancestors can be equally regarded as an utterly absurd, arbitrary mix of folklore, Norse mythology, medieval British legends and ultimately made-up persons. In short, he may be everything or simply just nothing *ipso facto*, i.e. his identity lies disseminated along a chain of (intertextual) signifiers.

Turning back to the initial question, we can conclude that Byron is *both* the dragon *and* the dragon slayer, thereby exposing the precariousness that is inherent to the construction of (collective) identity. That is, identity is highly elusive and unstable, if anything temporarily and performatively established. Accordingly, story-telling features prominently in *Jerusalem* – be it Byron's numerous tales (such as his virgin birth, his encounter with giants or his rare blood), society's stories about Byron (e.g. his notorious activities at the fair or his 'rebirth') or the play itself which is clearly marked as enactment/fiction due to the framing prologues (see 5; 47). Whereas Byron needs society and its norms (the big Other) to construct his own identity via his transgressive performances and stories, society likewise needs the radical Other (Byron) as projected embodiment of its unconscious desires/drives as well as to define the boundaries of its existence and construct a stable (collective) identity. In any case, however, we can see that (collective) identity is an utterly unstable category, i.e. an ongoing process of (self-)reflections that unveils the negativity and precariousness of identity. Story-telling and myths may help to close, or rather soothe, this gap only temporarily within the act of performance, in the precarious encounter with the (big) Other.

Conclusion: Aesthetics of Precariousness – Precarious Aesthetics

On the basis of the foregoing analysis I can now, in conclusion, readdress the notion of precariousness in relation to the play's aesthetics. It has been shown that *Jerusalem* is fundamentally characterized by the dissolution of oppositions (nature/civilization, individual/society, host/guest, pleasure principle/reality principle) which are central to the constitution of (collective) identity, thereby exposing the precarious threshold that lies between the interdependence yet incommensurability of these categories. This instability, or rather ontological vulnerability, is represented by aesthetics which are equally precarious, stretching from the semantics of space which deconstruct the relation between in and out, grotesque ambiguity and instances of Janus-faced laughter right through to the play's intertextuality – the latter acting as host for cultural memory and thus providing a sense of (collective) identity, but at the same time being the epitome of postmodern fragmentation and estrangement. Regardless of its varied manifestations, the play's aesthetics can be therefore summarized as being ambiguous, indeterminate, liminal and elusive. This precarious aesthetics is eventually unified in the figure of Johnny Byron – a highly fragmented and inconsistent figure who represents the face *precisely because of* its liminality and representational failure:

> For Levinas, then, the human is not *represented by* the face. Rather, the human is indirectly affirmed in that very disjunction that makes representation impossible, and this disjunction is conveyed in the impossible representation. For representation to convey the human, then, representation must not only fail, but it must *show* this failure. [...] The face is not 'effaced' in this failure of representation, but is constituted in that very possibility. (Butler 2004: 144)

With this in mind, we can conclude that *Jerusalem* indeed testifies to the ontological instability that underpins postmodernism's loss of sense/certainties, yet provides a counter-discourse at the same time. That is, although the play is very much aware of the discrepancy between our lifeworld and notions of (mythical) wholeness, it nonetheless offers a space for identification, sense, identity and ethics – highly precarious categories that have to be (performatively) realized in the encounter with the (big) Other and continuously negotiated anew.

Works Cited

Anz, Heinrich. 1989. "Wenn einem das Lachen vergeht... Überlegungen zum metaphysischen Charakter des Lachens in der Postmoderne". *Jahrbuch für internationale Germanistik* 20.2: 44–56.
Bakhtin, Mikhail M. 1968 [1965]. *Rabelais and his World*. Trans. Hélène Iswolsky. Cambridge: MIT Press.
Bakhtin, Mikhail M. 1984 [1963]. *Problems of Dostoevsky's Poetics*. Ed. and trans. Caryl Emerson. Manchester: Manchester UP.
Barton, Laura. 2011. "Why I love Jez Butterworth's *Jerusalem*". *theguardian.com*, 25 October. <http://www.theguardian.com/stage/theatreblog/2011/oct/25/why-i-love-butterworths-jerusalem> [accessed 3 September 2014].

Baudelaire, Charles. 1977 [1855]. "Vom Wesen des Lachens". In: Friedhelm Kemp and Claude Pichois (eds.). *Charles Baudelaire: Sämtliche Werke/Briefe*. München: Kemp & Pichois. 284–305.
Bauman, Zygmunt. 1996. *Postmodern Ethics*. Oxford: Blackwell.
Blake, William. 1988 [1804]. "And did those feet in ancient time". In: David V. Erdmann and Harold Bloom (eds.). *The Complete Poetry and Prose of William Blake*. Berkeley: U of California P. 95–96.
Boll, Julia. 2012. "The Sacred Dragon in the Woods: On Jez Butterworth's *Jerusalem*". *Forum* 14. <http://www.forumjournal.org/article/view/633/918> [accessed 3 September 2014].
Brantley, Ben. 2011. "This Blessed Plot, This Trailer, This England". *nytimes.com*, 21 April. <http://www.nytimes.com/2011/04/22/theater/reviews/jerusalem-with-mark-rylance-review.html?pagewanted=all&_r=0> [accessed 3 September 2014].
Butler, Judith. 2004. *Precarious Life: The Powers of Mourning and Violence*. London and New York: Verso.
Butler, Judith. 2011. "Precarious Life, Vulnerability, and the Ethics of Cohabitation". Centre de Cultura Contemporània (CCCB), Barcelona. 11 July. Lecture manuscript.
Butler, Judith. 2012. "Precarious Life, Vulnerability, and the Ethics of Cohabitation". *Journal of Speculative Philosophy* 26.2: 134–151.
Butterworth, Jez. 2009. *Jerusalem*. London: Nick Hern.
Derrida, Jacques. 2000 [1999]. "Hostipitality". Trans. Barry Stocker with Forbes Morlock. *Angelaki: Journal of the Theoretical Humanities* 5.3: 3–18.
Derrida, Jacques. 2001. *On Cosmopolitanism and Forgiveness*. London and New York: Routledge.
Levinas, Emmanuel. 1989 [1984]. "Ethics as First Philosophy". In: Seán Hand (ed.). *The Levinas Reader*. Oxford: Blackwell. 75–87.
"Precarious". 2009. In: John Sinclair (ed.). *Collins Cobuild Advanced Dictionary*. 6th ed. Boston: Heinle Cengage Learning. 1217.
"Precarious". 2010. In: Angus Stevenson (ed.). *Oxford Dictionary of English*. 3rd ed. Oxford: Oxford UP. 1397.
Spencer, Charles. 2011. "*Jerusalem*, Apollo Theatre, review". *telegraph.co.uk*, 17 October. <http://www.telegraph.co.uk/culture/theatre/theatre-reviews/8833062/Jerusalem-Apollo-Theatre-review.html> [accessed 3 September 2014].

Christoph Henke
Precarious Virtuality in Participatory Theatre: Tim Crouch's *The Author*

> A couple of clicks before bed!
> I see a baby. This baby has a dummy in its mouth.
> I have the choice to continue.
> I have the choice to stop. (Crouch, *The Author*: 201–202)

In the closing scene of Tim Crouch's much debated 2009 play *The Author*, the character Tim tells the audience about facing a choice concerning the 'consumption' of child pornography from the Internet for his sexual arousal. The ethical repercussions of this choice are grave; it is a moral choice between good and evil, one that is also precarious because the audience's assessment of the character depends on it, a fact of which Tim, giving in to the temptation, is fully aware ("You won't forgive me anyway", he says; Crouch, *The Author*: 203). Structurally, this choice is reduced to a simple, binary either-or decision, much like a decision that players typically face in an adventure-type video game (should I take that path or not? should I pick up the item or not?). In other words, Tim is confronted with the problem of agency, but it is one that is narrowed down to a bifurcating choice. His state of reduced agency thus mirrors the situation of the audience in *The Author*, whose own range of agency in what seems to be a play inviting audience participation is, at this point, limited to a simple either-or decision as well (should I walk out or not?). In reality, my choice is in fact not limited to that – I may scream, I may attack the actor, I may do all sorts of things. But in the scenario of *The Author*, in a situation where every audience member is supposed to be not just a passive spectator, but also to *play* themselves in the play ("We're all going to have to *pretend ourselves!*" says the spectator-character Adrian; 167; emphasis original), the play establishes what I will call a range of *virtual agency* for the spectator, comparable to player agency in the virtual world of a video game.[1] It seems no coincidence that the problematic of virtual agency is addressed in the play by having recourse to the virtual space of the Internet, where Tim retrieves the paedophilic video clip, which is further refracted in the 'virtual' form of a story (i.e. not explicitly performed on stage).

---

[1] I refer to the planted spectator as 'Adrian' according to the published version of the play. In the 2009 Royal Court production, the character was played by Adrian Howells, while in the later tour of the play the part was taken over by Chris Goode.

What I thus seek to explore in this essay are such levels, and limits, of virtuality of action in Crouch's play.

The Author is counted among the prime examples of the ongoing trend in contemporary theatre to involve (and explicitly invite) audience participation. Partly as a reflection of this trend towards immersive, interactive or participatory performances, and partly due to the impact of Jacques Rancière's concept of the 'emancipated spectator' (2009), the ethical dimension of theatre spectatorship has become a major interest in theatre and performance studies of late (see Grehan 2009; Ridout 2009; Aragay and Monforte 2014). Nicholas Ridout, for example, highlights theatre's potential for encouraging ethical reflection in a play's audience, as "[w]e watch ourselves watching people engaging with an ethical problem while knowing that we are being watched in our watching (by other spectators and also by those we watch)" (2009: 15). Regarding *The Author*, Stephen Bottoms celebrates Crouch's play for lending "credence to Ridout's sense of theatre's too infrequently realised potential for ethical encounter", in that the audience is not only invited to respond to the actors' questions and addresses, but spectators are made aware of "being 'watched in our watching'" (2011: 446) due to the particular arrangement of opposite rows of seats without a stage. However, in this deconstruction of the theatre as spectacle, there is comparatively little interactivity between actors and audience. The characters, who bear their actors' real names (the author-figure Tim Crouch, the planted spectator Adrian Howells, the actor-figures Esther Smith and Vic Llewellyn)[2] mostly present monologic speeches that narrate their experiences with staging a play about war atrocities in Eastern Europe, which is apparently full of graphic representations of acts of violence of the most horrific sort imaginable. Occasionally, there are short-lined dialogues between characters (such as in Tim's interrogation of Esther playing the child-abuse victim 'Karen'; see Crouch, *The Author*: 185–188), but for the most part characters turn to the audience with the stories they have to tell concerning their production of a gruesome play-within-a-play, thus leaving little room for audience intervention. What seems at first to be a play stirring us into action in the face of violence, atrocities and abuse, ultimately thwarts any attempts at active intervention. James Frieze justifiably argues that "*The Author* depends upon a scripted failure to intervene" (2012: 13).

In what follows I want to pursue the question of ethical agency with which Crouch's play confronts us, and I will do so by referring to the concept of virtual-

---

[2] This is the cast of the original Royal Court production. Character names are always to bear the names of the actors playing them, "with the exception of the author, whose name should always be Tim Crouch" (Crouch, *The Author*: 164; performance note).

ity. *The Author* opens up a precarious virtual space for its spectators, seemingly to grant them 'virtual' agency, while actually manipulating and restricting it severely. This has a disconcerting effect on the audience: the initial ease of the characters' seductive invitations for audience participation makes way for an unsettling experience of visceral discomfort – the audience, a *host* for the actors seated in their midst, is turned into *hostage*, especially to the author-figure Tim. As a result, this troubling trajectory of audience manipulation, while prodding spectators into reflection about ethical responsibility, ultimately limits spectatorial agency and thus promotes ethical hesitancy at best. On the whole, *The Author* sends out a bleak satirical message not just about the answerability of art, but also about ethical limitations of the subject and postmodern dilemmas of agency. By discussing the particular case of *The Author*, I also hope to promote virtuality as a useful concept for describing the potential range of agency offered in participatory, interactive or immersive modes of the theatre. Hence, I shall begin by taking a slight detour through theory in order to define the concept that I would like to apply here.

Virtualization in Participatory Theatre

Virtual reality is usually associated with a computer-simulated space or world with which users can interact, up to the point of complete sensory immersion, via some technological interface connecting the human body to a world-generating machine. The Internet is the most widely known global framework for such virtual spaces. But there is another meaning of 'virtual' in which I am interested here. Marie-Laure Ryan (see 2001: 12–13) distinguishes between three distinct senses: (1) illusory or imaginary (the 'optical' sense of the word), (2) potential (Ryan calls this the 'scholastic' philosophical sense), and (3) computer-mediated (its information-technological sense). In the following, I shall mainly concentrate on the second aspect of virtuality as potentiality in order to adapt it to the reception of fictional worlds in general and the role of spectatorship in contemporary plays like *The Author* in particular.

Loaded with an entire conceptual tradition in Western philosophy since antiquity, the virtual comes to play a crucial role in the poststructuralist ontology of Gilles Deleuze, who conceives of the virtual not as something in opposition to the real, but as an integral part of it (see 2004: 260). Reality consists of *actual* things (existing in time and space, matter and form) as well as *virtual* aspects and structures (belonging to the 'Idea' of the real), which may or may not be *actualized* at some point. Deleuze further sets off virtuality from *possibility*, the latter of which, wherever *realized*, merely doubles existence. The simple statement "It is snowing today" (Ryan 2001: 35) is an example of how the possible can come to exist without adding any new quality to reality, because the realization of the possible is generally predictable (maybe not always precisely when and where, but in principle). By contrast, the virtual, whenever it actualizes itself, follows a generative principle that *makes* a difference and adds new quality to existence: "The actualisation of the virtual, on the contrary, always takes place by difference, divergence or differenciation. [...] In this sense, actualisation or differenciation is always a genuine creation" (Deleuze 2004: 264).³ A technological invention or a scientific paradigm shift are actualizations of the virtual that create a new quality or new order of reality.

Pierre Lévy takes over Deleuze's ontological concepts for the dynamic processes of being – "realization (the occurrence of a predetermined possible) and actualization (the invention of a solution required by a problematic complex)" (1998: 26) – and adds a third one, which he calls 'virtualization':

> Virtualization can be defined as the movement of actualization in reverse. It consists in the transition from the actual to the virtual, an *exponentiation* of the entity under consideration. Virtualization is not a derealization (the transformation of a reality into a collection of possibles) but a change of identity [...]. It transforms an initial actuality into a particular instance of a more general problematic, one on which the ontological accent is now placed. Having done so, virtualization fluidizes existing distinctions, augments the degrees of freedom involved, and hollows out a compelling vacuum. (Lévy 1998: 26–27)

Lévy speaks of virtualization as a process of "heterogenesis, a becoming other, an embrace of alterity" (1998: 34), which opens, widens and deterritorializes the field of the real, unlocks its virtual potential, by dissolving and deconstructing fixed actualities into heterogeneous, free-floating ones.⁴ Virtualization is to be found in contemporary media (where information/content has become deterritorialized), but also in modern decentred companies in which employees use mobile or private spaces as workspaces instead of stationary offices (see Lévy 1998: 26–27; 33–34).

In general, I want to propose virtuality and virtualization as fruitful concepts to grasp interactive, fluidizing aspects of fictionality. Virtuality in aesthetic fic-

---

3 Deleuze (2004: 258 *et passim*) uses the spelling of 'differenciation' (both in French and English) for the generative or creative processes of actualization, by which existence is qualitatively changed, and contrasts it with 'differentiation', which denotes the analytic process of determining the structure and potential of the virtual as an Idea (before it is actualized).

4 As becomes clear from this definition, Lévy's concept of virtualization, in Deleuzian terms, may still be subsumed under the ontological process of actualization, which is generally defined by changing and 'differenciating' pre-existing identities.

tion can be defined as *mediated*, *immersive*, and *interactive*. These adjectives correspond to three constitutive aspects: (1) the mediation of a fictional world (i.e. its material basis in cultural sign systems); (2) the recipient's (cognitive and/or bodily) immersion in the fictional world; (3) the recipient's (limited) agency of interaction with the fictional world.[5]

In the present context, I specifically want to employ the 'virtual' as an analytical term for interactive modes of experiencing fictionality in theatre spectatorship. The physical presence of the audience in a confined space shared with the actors offers a potential for agency and immersion that is qualitatively different from conventional fictional communication. In a standard fourth-wall theatrical setup, this potential remains largely untapped: the spectator, comfortably seated in a darkened auditorium, still resembles the reader of a fictional text, even though the spectator will use a wider array of sensory channels to become immersed in the fictional world of the play. However, theatre is generally constituted by what Erika Fischer-Lichte calls an "autopoietic feedback loop" (2008: 39) between performers and spectators, which principally turns live performance into an emergent system in which even the slightest 'input' by the audience (laughter, groans, applause etc.) influences the production and "renders the parameters developed for a distinct aesthetics of production, work and reception ineffectual" (2008: 18). Nevertheless, interaction is augmented considerably in performances that allow for some degree of direct exchange between actors and spectators within the fictional scenario of the play.

Participatory or interactive types of theatre, as long as they are still predicated on fictional representation, partake in the same ontological double mode of reality that characterizes all aesthetic fictions, but offer heightened degrees of interactivity and bodily immersion, which constitute a form of *virtual reality*.[6] Spectatorial awareness in the theatre is generally split into two modes of perception: on the one hand, we perceive real actors acting their roles in a present spa-

---

[5] I use 'agency' here with full awareness of its problematic philosophical underpinnings. As White discusses (see 2013: 62–65), personal agency is commonly associated with *intention* and the *power* to make a choice. By contrast, a forced response, an accidental act, or being manipulated into action would not derive from 'true' agency. However, as such true agency is an ideal hardly to be found in social reality – our actions always depend on others and on (partly unconscious) variables limiting our choices – 'agency' shall be understood here as a potential range of action whose choice will never be entirely free for the agent, but which presupposes at least a minimum degree of intention.

[6] There are certainly types of participatory performance art whose aesthetics involve 'role-play' or 'games' that are neither representational nor fictional (i.e. participants no longer *pretend* to be someone). In order not to over-complicate matters at this point, such types shall be omitted here, although virtual agency and virtualization are presumably important in them too.

tiotemporal setup; on the other hand, we perceive fictional characters acting in a fictional setting. What is added when the audience is physically/verbally involved in the performance is that the condition of ontological doubleness – the co-presence of reality and fiction – extends to the actions of audience members. They come to act both as persons in the actual spatiotemporal situation of the theatre and as agents immersed in the fiction. On the fictional level, the spectators' participatory actions *actualize* the virtual agency granted to them by the fictional framework of the performance: audiences enter a fictional world in which they can participate physically. The interactive agency in such an environment is evidently of a different order than in merely mental acts of interaction with a fixed text or pre-recorded fictional medium (film, TV programme etc.), since spectators-as-agents are part of a feedback loop and may have a genuine impact on the course of performance. Therefore I propose to adopt the term 'virtual reality' here – in analogy to the common usage of a digitally simulated world with which I can interact – to highlight this enhanced degree of interactivity in participatory theatre and to set it off from a merely fictional reality in which the recipient's agency is limited to mental acts.

In fact, the truly virtual dimension of spectatorial agency is the extent to which spectators can participate in unpredicted ways and thus change the script of the performance. Participatory theatre facilitates, to adopt Lévy's terminology, *virtualization* during performance: the ontological doubleness of reality and fiction is augmented by a virtual plane, on which the agency of the spectator actualizes itself in potentially unpredictable turns so that it has an impact on both real and fictional action of the actors/characters of the play. But it is not for spectators-as-agents alone to have virtual agency: actors themselves are granted an agency whose range goes beyond their scripted roles. In other words, play-acting in participatory theatre should be differentiated into *fictional* action, i.e. performing according to a pre-rehearsed script, and *virtual* action, which opens, i.e. virtualizes, the fiction by improvisation and potential digression from the play-script. Despite the fact that the interpretation of a role by an actor always has a virtual dimension, as not every little detail in performing a role can be scripted or controlled by an author/director, I would propose to speak of virtualization as a distinct aesthetic feature only in cases of theatrical performance that allow for a significant degree of virtual agency.

Finally, virtualization in participatory theatre has a profoundly ethical dimension. According to Deleuze (see 2004: 264), the virtual always 'differenciates' itself into an actuality that makes a *real* difference because it is radically unpredictable and not simply a realization of anticipated possibles. Such unpredictability bears many practical risks for the participants in a performance. For the audience who is invited to participate, action is always risky, as Gareth

White maintains: "Some activities clearly risk humiliation; some are evidently physically dangerous; some more likely to provoke an adverse reaction from people in the audience" (2013: 78). For the actors or performers, who exert what White calls "procedural authorship" (2013: 29) – a term adopted from game studies (see Murray 1999: 152) – in that they set up the framework and rules of play, the invitation of audience participation involves several risks too. Participants may considerably deviate from the expected or anticipated behaviour, up to the point of a complete loss of 'authorial' control over proceedings and the 'failure' of the performance as intended. These risks show that virtual agency in participatory theatre is precarious: it is aesthetically precarious due to the unpredictability of virtualization for the performance as a procedural work of art. It is ethically precarious due to the choices that participants make in a live performance. These choices entail ethical responsibility since participants affect each other in what Judith Butler calls a precarious ethical relation due to "our vulnerability to the claims of others" (2012: 141).

Furthermore, there is ethical potential in the virtual reality of audience participation insofar as it may be transferrable to the world outside the theatre as a model for intervention. In this way, the virtual agency of spectators-as-agents may contribute to fulfilling the optimistic vision of the emancipated spectator that Rancière has formulated for the theatre: "Emancipation begins when we challenge the opposition between viewing and acting [...]. The spectator also acts, like the pupil or scholar. She observes, selects, compares, interprets" (2009: 13). Even though Rancière is not thinking of participatory theatre here, the question remains whether virtual agency in participatory theatre is particularly conducive to ethical reflection and intervention.[7] One may have doubts here. Alan Read has countered Rancière's much vaunted 'emancipated spectator' with the claim that it is rather an 'emaciated spectator' we encounter in the theatre, one that is bereft of any real political power, despite all cultural protestations to the contrary, among which the concept of an emancipated spectator is just another "testament to the mobility of this 'emaciated' force, masquerading as democratic power" (Read 2013: 92). Within this discursive context, I shall go on to examine Tim Crouch's *The Author* in light of the overarching question of

---

7 See White, who observes: "Ranciere's 'emancipated spectator', however, knows no feedback loop. He or she meets a performance as a set of 'things', 'signs', that are autonomous, and in the face of which he or she remains autonomous" (2013: 23). In fact, Rancière seems to be rather suspicious of forms of theatrical performance in which the "separation of stage and auditorium is something to be transcended" (2009: 15). What is really at stake for Rancière is "that theatre assign itself the goal of assembling a community which ends the separation of the spectacle" (2009: 15).

whether the virtual agency offered to spectators has any ethical efficacy, or whether the play must be rather viewed as a case of furthering ethical hesitancy.

Precarious Virtuality in *The Author*

Participatory theatre can be awkward for audiences because "it presents special opportunities for embarrassment, for mis-performance and reputational damage" (White 2013: 73). Seemingly to prevent this, the audience in *The Author* is to be lulled into a comfort zone at the beginning of the play. This strategy of audience seduction is clarified in the play's performance note:

> This must not be a confrontational configuration. The request the play makes is for us to be okay about ourselves, to gently see ourselves and ourselves seeing. There should be plenty of warm, open space in the play. The audience should be beautifully lit and cared for. [...] Music is present in the play as a release valve. It brings us into the here and now and helps the audience to feel good about being together. It is a treat! (Crouch, *The Author*: 164)

Crouch's note hints at a structural contrast in the setup of the play, where lurking confrontation is to be concealed by creating a soothing atmosphere. The special seating arrangement, making the performance physically immersive for the audience, is potentially discomforting. By doing away with the stage and having audience members face each other in two opposing banks of seats, the conventional spatial boundaries of the theatre are dissolved and the spectators are confronted with each other, as well as with the actors, who are seated among them and, at first, are indistinguishable from the audience. This arrangement suggests an awkward, intrusive sense of community – a community that is seemingly safe and immune to the evils of the outside world (Adrian declares: "This is the safest place in the world!"; 192). Evidently, this emphasis on safety is a thinly veiled ploy to achieve the very opposite – a calculated provocation to make us feel uneasy. But the feeling of growing uneasiness is also connected to our own precarious situation as participating agents in a performance that is becoming increasingly claustrophobic and surreptitiously menacing as the characters' stories of violence, atrocities and abuse unfold.

Hence, *The Author* creates a situation of ethical encounter that forces itself upon the audience in a way that allows no flinching or ducking, as Wendy Hubbard has stressed: "It refuses me the illusion of absenting myself into a detached, observational stance: I am palpably on-show and amidst – surrounded" (2013: 23). This scenario can be construed as a theatrical version of what Butler calls "unwilled proximity and unchosen cohabitation" (2012: 145), which mark the precariousness of human life: "our interdependency constitutes us [...] as social and embodied, vulnerable and passionate" (2012: 148). What is ethically at stake for humanity in its state of unchosen cohabitation are life conditions on egalitarian terms and the prevention of genocide. While such extreme points of human precariousness are in fact the topic of *The Author*'s gruesome play-within-the-play, the miniature version of an unchosen cohabitation – the physical proximity of audience and cast – only creates milder states of interdependency and vulnerability. But even there we get an idea of ethical precariousness as soon as the actors' "concerned solicitude for us" turns into solicitation, "setting up a creepy tonal dissonance when their words become troubling" (Hubbard 2013: 23). While at the beginning of the play the audience is politely invited to grant consent or voice an opinion – TIM: "Is it okay if I carry on? Do you want me to stop?" / VIC: "What do you think?" (170; 171) – such invitations become more infrequent later or deteriorate into offensive rudeness – ESTHER: "What do you fuckin' think?" / ADRIAN: "All of us, all us dirty mother-fucking cunts!!" (187; 193). The actors' provocations of the audience take a form that seems to parody Butler's phrase of an "ethical solicitation", where we are "affronted by something that is beyond our will, not of our making, that comes to us from the outside, as an imposition but also as an ethical demand" (2012: 135). Initially a host to the performers (who are seated in their middle), the spectators are progressively taken hostage by them. This atmospheric change from invitation to confrontation may also be attributable to the seductive ambivalence of the signifier 'host', as Jacques Derrida has alerted us to "the troubling analogy in their common origin between *hostis* as host and *hostis* as enemy, between hospitality and hostility" (2000: 17).

The Author's strategy of audience seduction has an implicit didactic function that ties in with the play's leaning towards satire in its self-conscious metatheatrical design. The play holds up a rather conventional mirror to the spectators, who are to understand the precarious nature of their seemingly sheltered place in the theatre, which cynically serves them atrocities and ethical provocations for their delectation.[8] Spectators are supposed to criticize the putative safety of the theatre, given its ethically questionable productions of sensationalist spectacles of reality, especially by the Royal Court brand of new British theatre from Bond to Kane and beyond, and they are to feel guilty about themselves being consum-

---

[8] 'Shelter' ("shelter for women"; 185) and 'theatre' are linked in the play as a reversible image, a *Kippfigur:* "TIM: Do you want to talk about what happened to you? About why you're here? / ESTHER: What? / TIM: In this place. / ESTHER: In the shel'er? / TIM: the shelter or in the theatre. It's up to you. Wherever you want to be" (186).

ers of such spectacles.⁹ But far from just attacking spectatorial voyeurism, the play advances a comprehensive cultural critique of violence and the ethics of its representation: "Tim talked about the play – about violence in a culture, about what happens to you when you live with that violence around you all the time. [...] We have to show it" (183). Such an apparent 'obligation' to represent violence visually is clearly rejected by the play. The argument is that violence cannot be contained by (fictional) representation, but will contaminate those who represent it 'for real', as shown in Vic's account of his violent kicking of the stunned spectator Adrian, whom he, being himself in a state of PTSD induced by representational violence, mistakes for an attacker after a performance of the play-within-the-play.¹⁰ *The Author*'s entire short-circuiting of reality and fiction amounts to this: conventional boundaries of fiction will not hold up in the play to contain the violence and shelter those who are exposed to it. For spectators to participate in a play in which they are to play themselves as spectators, in which the actors play themselves as actors, in which even the author plays himself as the author, the unspoken threat is that violence will break out all over the place and destroy the sheltered community of the theatre ("a private club for the depraved", in Adrian's words; 192).

At the same time, all this poignant and unsettling discourse of violence and its contagious effects is offset by the very metadramatic aesthetic that enables it in the first place. *The Author*'s approach to break the frames of fictional illusion for didactic purposes is Brechtian in kind in that it uses epic elements of narration (in the mode of telling rather than showing, to use Wayne Booth's terms), which have a distancing effect on the audience in order to instigate ethical reflection, instead of being gripped by visual immersion in various extreme brutalities. Thus, the attempted erasure of boundaries of reality and fiction in the play is accompanied by erecting new ones of aesthetic distancing. The ethical motive for this is clear: *The Author* withholds from its audience the visual presentation of spectacles of brutality in order not to become an accomplice to the very practices of theatrical representation that it criticizes. Still, the atrocities that the charac-

---

9 Adrian's rant could not make this any clearer: "It's all safe! I've seen everything imaginable here. I've seen bum sex and rimming and cock sucking and wankings and rapings and stabbings and shootings and bombings. Bombings and bummings!! I've seen someone shit on a table! I've seen a man have his eyes sucked out. I've seen so many blindings! And stonings. Um. I've seen a dead baby in a bag. A baby stoned to death. I've seen a dead baby get eaten! That was great!" (192)
10 Vic comments on the effects of his playing the war criminal/rapist/tormentor Pavol: "My girlfriend said that the theatre should pay for us both to have counselling – to deal with post traumatic stress!" (196).

ters describe in connection with their production of the play-within-a-play are graphic even in their narratively distanced form. "Paradoxically", in Clare Wallace's view, "the play-within-the-play attains this ambivalent proximity precisely because it is not performed" (2014: 130). It is indeed an ambivalent proximity between audience and characters that unfolds in the seemingly casual but increasingly claustrophobic setting of personal storytelling, while the details of horrific acts of violence and mutilated bodies alienate and distance the listeners.

But how does this leave room for the agency of the participating spectator? For a play that is considered one of the primary examples of contemporary experimental theatre involving audience participation, there is relatively small leeway for genuine interaction with the audience. White rightly observes that the "procedure of audience participation" in *The Author* "is unusual, generally moving from small contributions to none at all" (2013: 191). Moreover, audience responses and spontaneous interjections during performance are generally not encouraged or responded to by the cast, which greatly limits the range of interactive audience participation.[11] Thus, virtualization, the audience's entering into a virtual reality that offers agency in the interaction with the actors, is severely limited throughout. Since consequential audience interaction is neither encouraged nor procedurally appropriated by the performers in *The Author*, walking out is the only option of intervention left to audience members if they are to renounce the position of apathy into which the play has cornered them. A walkout, however, is a liminal act in the context of virtual agency as it abandons the fiction and shuts down virtuality by the real act of leaving the theatre. Yet it is part of the frame-breaking logic of *The Author* to provoke just such a frame-break. Walkouts are in fact suggested and pre-empted by the play itself; the first scripted walkout arrives early on in the play (see 168) and sets an example for the actual audience, as White asserts: "it gives permission for one of the few acts of spectatorial disapproval conventionally allowed, helping some to take this choice for themselves" (2013: 191). In other words, *The Author* dares the audience to sustain the growing pressure of solicitation and confrontation, while suggesting a way for spectators to bail out as well.

---

11 This critical aspect has been addressed by Bottoms as one of *The Author*'s controversial points, "since – in circumstances where unexpected interjections have suddenly been made – the four actors will make no effort to respond and incorporate them through spontaneous ad-libs. An accommodating pause will be left, and then the actors will resume delivery of the scripted text" (2011: 455). Bottoms has tried to justify this strategy of non-engagement as "ethically consistent with the play's commitment to eliciting individual rather than group responses" (2011: 455–456), although this argument seems rather moot (how does ignoring an individual spectator's interjection encourage anybody to respond and feel listened to?).

Ethical responsibility at this point lies with each individual member of the audience, who has to make his or her own decision on whether to quit the performance – a responsibility that arises from the *virtual* reality of the play (I act with a virtual agency that is both granted and withheld by the play) but weighs more strongly as it is felt to be *real* (I take responsibility for no longer wanting to be solicited or harassed by a discomforting performance). This 'reality effect' in the constitution of the play's virtual reality is systematically achieved by *The Author*'s blending of reality and fiction, most strikingly signalled by the use of the performers' real names for the play's characters. While the characters technically still belong to the realm of fiction, performers and participants become actualized versions of their virtual selves during performance. Rather than a self-referential postmodern game or a self-conscious instance of metatheatrical navel-gazing, the reality effect supposedly heightens the participants' feeling of ethical responsibility.[12] Not only does this effect concern our behaviour as complicit consumers of aestheticized violence in contemporary media culture, it also extends to a guilty self-critique of authorial responsibility. As Hubbard has it, with a view to the suicide of the author-character Tim in the final scene: "*The Author* stages an authorship that seems compelled to draw attention to its continued and still potentially violent power, in order to finally empty itself out" (2013: 28). However, such a deconstruction of authorial power reveals an ethical double-bind: *The Author* unmasks the seductive, manipulative power of authorship, but reinforces that very power by controlling and manipulating the audience into suggested responses (e.g. walkouts). What is more, walking out may be misconstrued as a symbolic act implying that I renounce my ethical responsibility, that I turn my eyes away from the violence, harm and injustice committed against the Other, from the precariousness of human life.

Virtuality and Ethical Hesitancy

> I have the choice to continue.
> I have the choice to stop. (Crouch, *The Author*: 202)

---

[12] The virtual reality of the play can become so deceiving as to make it difficult for participants to separate fiction from reality. Chris Goode, who played the spectator-character in the 2010 tour of the play (i.e. Adrian Howells's part in the Royal Court premiere), reported on his Internet blog about the incident of an audience member fainting during a performance in Bristol, which brought it to a temporary halt so the person could get medical aid. Despite the cast's best attempts to convince the audience that this was *not* part of the show, many still thought it had been scripted (see Goode 2010; Hubbard 2013: 26).

In principle, participatory theatre permits a virtualization of performed action by granting virtual agency to spectators-as-agents who, during performance, act within the virtual reality of the play (as an aesthetic blend of reality and fiction that offers interactivity). Participatory theatre may therefore unleash the unpredictability of virtualization to facilitate heterogenesis, "the transition to a problematic, the shift from being to question" (Lévy 1998: 34). By contrast, *The Author* largely denies its spectators such agency. Just as it is down to an either-or choice for the author-character Tim in his temptation to view child pornography, *The Author* reduces the virtual agency of its spectators to the bare minimum of an either-or choice about their continuation or termination of the performance. Such a denial of agency seems to be in line with the deep suspicions the play harbours toward the seductions of virtuality, especially via visual media, which is one of its underlying themes. The virtual space of the Internet is exclusively associated with violence and abuse, since it serves as a vast repository for their visual mediation and distribution (the author-character Tim and other cast members become obsessed with them; see 177–178; 183; 201–203). The use of such consumable media makes their consumers complicit in the suffering and exploitation behind them. At best, such images may operate on us, in Butler's sense, as an "ethical solicitation" (2012: 135) of human precariousness and thus overwhelm us with a sense of ethical responsibility. This is, of course, the *modus operandi* in which *The Author* confronts us with such atrocities and abuse, and it even ethically shelters us from the seductions of the visual by narrativizing them instead of representing them directly on stage.

The problem remains, though, that ethical responsibility is based on agency, and it is for this reason that *The Author* is profoundly ambivalent, if not contradictory in its aesthetic design. The seductive power of the virtual is to be contained by manipulatively playing with the virtuality of audience participation. As the spectators' virtual range of ethical action collapses towards the end of the play, impulses for real action outside of the theatre remain elusive. If *The Author* really wants us to consider, as Frieze contends, whether "we are perpetuating a chain of production and consumption [of violence and abuse] in which we surrender our agency and ethical responsibility" (2012: 11), how efficacious is it then that we are forced to surrender our virtual agency in the choking of audience interaction, which the play so seductively holds out for us initially? Inevitably, Crouch's play stages the practical dilemma of postmodern ethics: while it engages us in complex ethical reflection, it arrests us in ethical hesitancy. The only solution it structurally suggests is to turn away from it all and abort consumption. As a satire, it is certainly successful at putting the finger on the limitations of our agency as interpellated subjects in consumerist societies. Ultimately, the self-ironic, self-effacing message of *The Author* may be that the play itself is part of the cultural evils that it stages. So in order to stop the unethical commodification of violence in capitalist culture and art, one has to stop consuming plays such as *The Author*, which are still part of its consumptive cycle. Once you get the message, you should walk out as quickly as you can.

Works Cited

Aragay, Mireia and Enric Monforte (eds.). 2014. *Ethical Speculations in Contemporary British Theatre*. Basingstoke and New York: Palgrave Macmillan.
Bottoms, Stephen. 2011. "Materialising the Audience: Tim Crouch's Sight Specifics in ENGLAND and *The Author*". *Contemporary Theatre Review* 21.4: 445–463.
Butler, Judith. 2012. "Precarious Life, Vulnerability, and the Ethics of Cohabitation". *Journal of Speculative Philosophy* 26.2: 134–151.
Crouch, Tim. 2011. *The Author*. In: Tim Crouch. *Plays One*. London: Oberon. 161–206.
Deleuze, Gilles. 2004 [1968]. *Difference and Repetition*. Trans. Paul Patton. London: Athlone.
Derrida, Jacques. 2000 [1999]. "Hostipitality". Trans. Barry Stocker with Forbes Morlock. *Angelaki: Journal of the Theoretical Humanities* 5.3: 3–18.
Fischer-Lichte, Erika. 2008 [2004]. *The Transformative Power of Performance: A New Aesthetics*. Trans. Saskya Iris Jain. London and New York: Routledge.
Frieze, James. 2012. "Actualizing a Spectator like You: The Ethics of Intrusive-Hypothetical". *Performing Ethos* 3.1: 7–22.
Goode, Chris. 2010. "The Theatre Is on Fire; or, feu d'artifice". *Thompson's Bank of Communicable Desire*. <http://beescope.blogspot.com/2010/10/theatre-is-on-fire.html> [accessed 17 September 2014].
Grehan, Helena. 2009. *Performance, Ethics and Spectatorship in a Global Age*. Basingstoke and New York: Palgrave Macmillan.
Hubbard, Wendy. 2013. "Falling Faint: On Syncopated Spectatorship and *The Author*". *Performance Research: A Journal of the Performing Arts* 18.4: 22–29.
Lévy, Pierre. 1998 [1995]. *Becoming Virtual: Reality in the Digital Age*. Trans. Robert Bononno. New York: Plenum.
Murray, Janet. 1999. *Hamlet on the Holodeck: The Future of Narrative in Cyberspace*. Cambridge: MIT Press.
Rancière, Jacques. 2009 [2008]. *The Emancipated Spectator*. Trans. Gregory Elliott. London and New York: Verso.
Read, Alan. 2013. "The Emaciated Spectator and the Witness of the Powerless". In: Peter Lichtenfels and John Rouse (eds.). *Performance, Politics and Activism*. Basingstoke and New York: Palgrave Macmillan. 87–104.
Ridout, Nicholas. 2009. *Theatre & Ethics*. Basingstoke and New York: Palgrave Macmillan.
Ryan, Marie-Laure. 2001. *Narrative Virtual Reality: Immersion and Interactivity in Literature and Electronic Media*. Baltimore: Johns Hopkins Press.
Wallace, Clare. 2014. "Playing with Proximity: Precarious Ethics on Stage in the New Millennium". In: Mireia Aragay and Enric Monforte (eds.). *Ethical Speculations in Contemporary British Theatre*. Basingstoke and New York: Palgrave Macmillan. 117–134.
White, Gareth. 2013. *Audience Participation in Theatre: Aesthetics of the Invitation*. Basingstoke and New York: Palgrave Macmillan.

Cristina Delgado-García
"We're All in This Together": Reality, Vulnerability and Democratic Representation in Tim Crouch's *The Author*

In studies on Tim Crouch's theatre, much attention has been paid to spectators' intellectual and affective engagements.[1] However, the ethical resonances of his work have only begun to be interrogated (see Wallace 2012; 2014), and its political reverberations remain largely underexplored. As I have noted elsewhere (see Delgado-García 2014; 2015), this means that many of the timely questions raised by Crouch's work remain to be addressed: the pervasiveness of exploitation, the limits of responsibility in a globalised context, and the convivial façade of authority are among such questions. By rethinking Crouch's 2009 piece *The Author* in relation to our specific historical conjuncture, this chapter begins to resituate Crouch's work more firmly on politicised ground.

My argument is threefold. First, I contend that *The Author* articulates its ethical inquiry through a complex layering of fiction, autofiction, and recognisably real details. This spirals outwards from the performers to current Anglophone theatre practices, and also, crucially, to recent events in Anglo-American politics. Second, I show how the play lays bare the potential pitfalls of representation in both theatrical and cultural performances, and suggest that Crouch's piece articulates a universalist ethical stance through its language-driven aesthetic. Finally, I argue that *The Author* theatricalises the crises of political representation that have affected Europe in the past decade. This situates the play precisely at the moment when foreign and economic policy have augmented the material and affective precariousness of some, while indulging in a rhetoric of justice, solidarity and community. Bringing these three strands together, it is apparent that *The Author*'s ethical and political position is grounded on a distrust of representation as a means to bring about social change. Theatrical, cultural and political performances that claim to tactically portray reality or speak on behalf of vulnerable Others are pessimistically framed by *The Author* as ethically questionable and incapable of inducing nonviolence.

---

[1] For more on the interplay between Crouch's aesthetics and spectators' involvement, see Bottoms (2009; 2011a; 2011b), Freshwater (2011), Frieze (2013), Hubbard (2013), Radosavljević (2013: 151–161) and White (2013: 188–194), as well as Christoph Henke's chapter in this volume. Crouch has also consistently identified spectators' engagement as crucial for his dramaturgy in interviews and public conversations (see e.g. Crouch (2006; 2011a; 2011b)).

Fiction, Autofiction, Reality

Premiered at the Royal Court's Jerwood Theatre Upstairs, *The Author* follows the events surrounding the fictional run of a hyperviolent play at the Jerwood Theatre itself – a play that was never written or produced in reality, but that is nonetheless described in terms reminiscent of well-known Royal Court productions. Addressing their lines to the audience throughout, the four performers present themselves as the author, the two main actors, and one spectator of the alleged piece. In a fragmentary manner, the spectators learn that the show focused on the relationship between a man called Pavol, "[t]he abuser", played by Vic (Crouch, *The Author*: 25), and his daughter Eshna, "[t]he abused", played by Esther (28). Details of the fictional performance itself are scant, albeit evocative, but the playwright and actors self-assuredly recount how they embarked on a compulsive process of research in order to create the violent world of the play.

The author and cast of the fictional show acknowledge having tracked down and consumed images of real, extreme violence uploaded on the Internet – namely, videos of gang-rapes, torture, mutilations and beheadings taking place in the context of war. They describe their visit to the unnamed, war-scarred country where the play was set (see 37–38). They give an account of and even re-enact encounters with individuals who had undergone similar experiences to the characters in the play (see 38–42). According to the author, whom Tim Crouch names Tim Crouch,[2] these research activities were intimately linked to the aims and aesthetic of his piece, which attempted "to create a – an amateur war zone on the stage" in order to "represent what was happening in the real world" (32). Here and elsewhere, the author and cast suggest that the alleged play secured its political credentials through its direct relation to reality. As this chapter argues, unfolding events in the metatheatrical play challenge this assumption, yet *The Author*'s own political gestures ironically hinge on evocations of real events – from the War on Terror to austerity measures in Britain.

The resolute ambivalence of the image of pain enables *The Author* to problematise our artistic encounters with the real as unequivocally ethical. Tim, Vic and Esther's research on violence while working on the fictional piece is correlated with their own violent acts. Affected by his role as Pavol, Vic explains how he mistook a spectator (Adrian) for a physical threat on the last night of the run and "just lash[ed] out" (53), assaulting him. Instances of psychological abuse also abound. The most notoriously uncomfortable confession comes from the

---

[2] For clarity, henceforth I refer to the writer of *The Author* as Crouch, and to the character of the playwright within this piece as Tim.

playwright of the disturbing play. Tim describes to the audience how he watched a clip of child pornography while alone in his study with Esther's baby. His account crucially blurs the boundary between the actions captured by the image on the computer screen and the reality in Tim's house, and even insists on the innocuous effects of the action itself (see 56–58). Thus, while the characters in *The Author* frame the consumption of violent images as ethically legitimate and necessarily informative, their subsequent actions suggest that such images can also be desensitising and exploitative.

The form of *The Author* redoubles these philosophical speculations, inviting us to consider the power that the real has over our assessments of both artistic value and ethical judgement. Although the theatre show to which *The Author* refers is overtly marked as fictional, the four performers bear their own first names, appear without costume, and loosely embody characters with personal profiles similar to theirs, repeatedly addressing the audience *qua* audience.[3] The set design situates actors and spectators in the same space: occupying two banks of seats facing one another, with no stage in between. The performers' autofictional characterisation (see Angel-Pérez 2013), together with this spatial configuration, initially creates a sense of immediacy, intimacy and togetherness that is pivotal for the play's affective punch. As the characters reveal their own participation in various acts of violence, the carefully orchestrated atmosphere of conviviality is set to become increasingly questionable, perhaps resisted. The ethical questions that surround the image of suffering are therefore expanded to the narratives of violence, and to the imagined scenes these stories conjure up. Similarly, considerations about reality are extended beyond the source materials of art to include the reality of the theatrical experience, as the play invites a reflection on audiences' own engagement with fictional narratives of abuse. The listening that takes place in the theatre is absolutely real.

The Author therefore clearly grapples with a series of familiar notions in ethical philosophy. The image of violence (see Nancy 2005: 15–26) and the possibility of holding a "guiltless responsibility" for the lives of others (Levinas 1989: 83)

---

[3] During the first run, Tim Crouch played the role of the playwright called Tim Crouch, and actors Esther Smith and Vic Llewellyn played actors Esther and Vic. The character called Adrian in the script is the only exception to this overlapping of performers' professions with those of the characters: a passionate theatre-goer, the role was first played by theatre-maker Adrian Howells, renowned for his intimate theatre work. In the 2010–2011 tour, another theatre practitioner, Chris Goode, replaced Howells and the character was therefore renamed Chris. As specified by the text, the characters' names should always be the names of their actors, with the exception of the author, who should always be named Tim Crouch (see Crouch, *The Author*: 16). Following the published script, I refer here to the spectator character as Adrian rather than Chris.

are among these. My suspicion, however, is that to focus exclusively on how *The Author* dovetails with such theoretical frameworks is to risk missing much of its topicality and political nuance. Instead, *The Author*'s ethico-political engagement should be considered alongside its referred reality – even if this is consistently destabilised. I further suggest that the play's evoking, blurring and falsifying of the real has well-timed cultural resonances. In the next section I interrogate these ideas by placing *The Author* in the context of the War on Terror.

Against Artistic Representation: Rethinking Ethical Commitment and the Mediation of Reality

In *The New War Plays*, Julia Boll argues that changing methods of contemporary warfare have motivated a shift in the theatrical representation of conflict. These so-called New Wars are characterised by blurred beginnings and endings, elastic geographical delineations, and fighting sides that are more difficult to demarcate. While the Western world certainly participates in these New Wars, and may indeed become a target, it is not the geographical site of conflict (2013: 1–2). For Boll, plays such as Sarah Kane's *Blasted* (1995), Caryl Churchill's *Far Away* (2000), and Zinnie Harris's *The Wheel* (2011) "show how the disturbing experience of war may be represented on stage and mediated to an audience that, for the most part, does not have its own war experience" (2013: 2). The commitment to reflecting theatrically (on) an obfuscated reality is particularly apparent in verbatim theatre. Writing about the rise of this practice in Britain since 2003, Chris Megson notes that much verbatim work "responded to issues raised by the Iraqi conflict and the fall-out from the 'War on Terror'" (2005: 370), which Ariane de Waal summarises as "a desire for authenticity, facts, and truthful accounts" at a time when "politicians (mis)led the UK into war" (2015: 16). It is precisely this contemporary commitment to bringing a violent and elusive reality closer to theatre audiences that *The Author* problematises.

The protagonist of *The Author*, the playwright called Tim, offers a questionable embodiment of this salient interest in mediating war for contemporary audiences.[4] Tim consistently frames his work on his hyperviolent play as an ethical imperative and a much-needed cultural intervention in social consciousness. As

---

[4] I am not arguing here that *The Author* itself could be characterised as a New War play in Boll's terms, but rather that the play about Pavol as described fits those parameters. *The Author* is less interested in the mediation of war for a privileged audience than in the articulation of a philosophical enquiry into universal vulnerability and a political critique of current forms of democratic participation and representation.

he recounts to audiences, when his wife expresses astonishment at his ability to bear images of abuse in preparation for his play, Tim responds: "How can we not?" (31). He thus flags up what he sees as a collective responsibility to research, cast a light on and acknowledge otherwise obscured violence in the real world: "If *we* do not represent *them*", Tim continues, "then we are in danger of denying their existence" (31; emphasis added). It is worth noting how Tim's response diverts the focus from his individual consumption of violent images to the representative duties of a tacitly imagined collective. It is crucially unclear whether this 'we' refers to artists, the British, or the privileged international communities who only experience war atrocities second-hand – but a distinction between 'us' and 'them' is nonetheless drawn. Tim's binary expression reproduces the heavily criticised humanitarian divide between helper and victim (see Wickstrom 2012: 88–90), but also the "the division of the world into 'civilised' and 'barbaric'" that, according to Maryam Khalid, provided the American government with "[o]rientalist justifications for intervention in the War on Terror" (2011: 20).

Tim's self-appointed duty to mediate otherwise obfuscated events strongly resonates with the implicit ethos of the contemporary New War plays studied by Boll. Yet his interpretation of ethico-political commitment relies not only on questionable self/Other binaries but also on the false dichotomy between representation and inaction. Throughout *The Author*, Tim implies that artists have two options: to represent violence or to remain oblivious to it. Vic recounts how "Tim talked about the play – about violence in a culture [...]. About how we have to recognise it, confront it, absorb it. We have to show it" (37). As described by Tim, the author's wife epitomises a wilful refusal to endure or reproduce violent scenes: "She deals with all this by cooking fabulous meals and spoiling the children! That's her way of dealing with it" (31). Her indulgence is implicitly contraposed to Tim's self-appointed martyrdom, as he explains: "I took it upon myself to look at images of abuse, at beheadings, for example! [...] To bombard myself with all the gory details!" (31), "to reveal things, things for other people to solve" (44–45).

As events in *The Author* unfold, it becomes apparent that research, representation, knowledge and ethical behaviour are not necessarily correlative. Reproducing images of violence does not give the playwright or cast of the fictional play a solid understanding of conflict. The decontextualised way in which these images are consumed in the process of research and documentation is in fact enveloped in an astounding lack of precision. When Esther describes a video recording of an American contractor being beheaded, she is unable to tell whether this is perpetrated by a "terrorist or soldier" (50), with the two identities implicitly presented as interchangeable. Her account evokes the recorded beheading of Nick Berg in 2004, whose killing was presented as "revenge against abuse and humiliation carried out by US guards at Abu Ghraib prison, west of Baghdad" (Associated Press 2004). However, by presenting this as one among many instances of violence, Esther's description is at once misinformed and uninformative. Vic's encounter with the man who inspired his rendition of Pavol is equally confused, as he cannot ascertain who killed this man's son: "the militia or someone" (38). While the characters' difficulty in distinguishing between terrorism and military action is revealing of the features of the New Wars, the lack of clarity in these accounts suggests that aesthetic representation might be neither illuminating nor empowering. Similarly, the artistic mediation of images of suffering does not guarantee ethical awakening on the audience's part. Adrian's list of atrocities contained in the theatrical canon culminates in the gleeful exclamation: "It's such an education!" (47). What the results of such an education are remain to be specified. Hence, *The Author* offers no reassurances as to the ways in which mediating real violence through performance might inform or raise consciousness on either side of the stage.

The rehearsal process for Tim's play also suggests that ethical intentions can materialise in self-serving, exploitative and damaging practices. *The Author* recurrently presents the suffering of some as the conduit for others' exciting professional opportunities. The cast's research trip abroad is described in somewhat utilitarian terms: it was "amazing" for Vic, as he "really found Pavol there" and "[t]ook him into the rehearsal room" (37; 38). The suffering of the man Vic meets abroad is valued for its beneficial effects on his acting. In a more subtle way, the visit also gives Tim an opportunity to work on his public profile: writing a piece for *The Guardian* and publishing striking photographs on his blog (see 37). Esther's relationship with Karen, whom she met at a shelter for women who had experienced domestic violence, is coloured by the delight the actor feels at being able to mobilise some of the techniques she learnt in her training: "It was brilliant because we'd done loads of that kind of stuff at Drama Centre" (39); "[i]t was just incredibly helpful to have her as – as a reference point" (43). The creative team in Tim's play holds an egotistic and, crucially, ahistorical stance towards the world. Every experience and encounter is partially seen as a resource to further one's career, without fully registering the material and affective conditions of the world they represent.

Thus, while Tim discursively vindicates the ethico-political potential of researching, artistically reproducing and spectating otherwise obfuscated images of suffering, *The Author* makes apparent that these representational practices are not inherently enlightening. The methodologies and impact of contemporary politicised theatre works (such as those explored in Boll's and Megson's studies) are therefore called into question. Importantly, what is missing from the characters' compulsive retrieval of violent online videos and photographs – and their transposition of such violence onto the stage – is what, in Judith Butler's thought, is necessary for any ethically and politically grounded account of traumatic events: namely, "a thorough understanding of the history that brings us to this juncture" (2004a: 10). The characters of *The Author* compulsively research bodily violence without grasping how and why it originates, or situating the institutional and ideological structures that activate and sustain it. It is in this sense that *The Author* further taps into its historical conjuncture despite its vague spatio-temporal references. The characters' expressions share the same tense and structure as contemporary accounts of New Wars, and responses to institutional and terrorist violence – from the narratives about 9/11 that focused on the injury to the social fabric but were not accompanied by a "relevant prehistory of the events" (Butler 2004a: 6) to current reports presenting the violence of the so-called Islamic State *in medias res*.

Acting Politically

The Author's problematisation of representational practices in the arts is mirrored by an anxiety about existing forms of political representation. Tim's suggestion that artists have a duty towards real suffering in the world is echoed by his cast, inside and outside the theatre. Both Esther and Vic unconvincingly reproduce existing political strategies in their fulfilment of this obligation, prompting questions about their efficacy. Early in the play, Esther tells spectators about her participation in the anti-war protests that took place in London during "an anniversary of the war starting" (27). With an indeterminacy that is typical of Crouch's writing, the war mentioned lacks specificity, but the description of the events strongly evokes the anti-war march in London in February 2003 at the onset of the conflict, and its subsequent iterations.[5] As Esther explains, London

---

5 The military intervention in Iraq, initially part of the War on Terror, is evoked elsewhere in *The Author*. Early in the play, Tim mentions that "there are tanks at the airport" (26) on the day of his suicide attempt; this conjures up the unsettling images of military vehicles at Heathrow Airport, London, in February 2003, when over 400 soldiers were deployed following intelligence reports of a potential terrorist threat from Al-Qaeda (see Hopkins, Norton-Taylor and White 2003; BBC News 2003). The threat took place days before the onset of the invasion of Iraq in March 2003. Later on, Tim concedes that the extreme aesthetics of his play about Pavol were prompted by his own feelings regarding a specific military conflict: "I was angry because we were at war" (32). This 'we' is, of course, indeterminate; yet, in being delivered by Crouch, a British performer aiming for a presentation of his character with a strong effect of authenticity, the line resonates with the most recent and controversial conflict in which Britain has been involved: the Iraq War.

theatre professionals joined *en masse* following an initiative from their unions or professional circles: it was "a West End or an Equity thing" (27). Esther's gleeful narration somewhat undermines protesters' sensibilities and motivations for their participation in the rally. She describes joyful cohorts of actors singing modified West End musicals while marching, her newfound sense of freedom exacerbated by the act of "having fun" while "the serious" theatre companies "looked down their noses" (27). Esther's account of the day ends with the highly charged image of protesters leaving the event and stamping on abandoned placards illustrated with photographs of one particular war victim (see 28). Her self-absorbed, celebratory narrative jars with the brutality of the war, and destabilises the ideal image of the concerned and selfless ethical subject.[6]

For his part, Vic confesses that he "never really understood" the playwright's explanations "about violence in a culture, about what happens to you when you live with that violence around you all the time" – "But it's not my job to understand", he adds (37). Alongside this unabashed ignorance of the play's ethical rationale, he is unable to comprehend and empathise with the real suffering that Tim's play is allegedly representing. When describing a visit to a war-scarred country to undertake research for Tim's play, Vic jokingly compares the wounded bodies to "Cardiff on a Friday night" (37).

Esther and Vic thus act out two well-known politicised subject positions: the public demonstrator in a cultural performance of dissent, and the artist partaking in a politically-charged theatrical performance. Their behaviour nonetheless calls into question the nature of such familiar actions: Esther is drawn to the anti-war rally by peer groups and personal excitement, and Vic takes part in Tim's show for professional reasons. These culturally-scripted forms of behaviour appear as roles to be embodied, played out. Written and premiered in 2009, after years of failed public opposition to the Iraq War, *The Author* hints at the possibility that traditional politicised subject positions and actions, both in activist

---

More loosely, Tim's reference to "soldiers being flown home in coffins" (26) similarly conjures up images made familiar during the protracted military conflict in Iraq (see BBC News 2004). These references are evocative, yet ambivalent. Their openness certainly allows for readings in other contexts.

6 The dancing and singing of the West End actors while marching for peace can easily be the target of criticism for its aesthetic dissonance with the seriousness of suffering. Yet the joy produced by such acts can also be recast as politically productive and necessary. Working in the field of applied theatre, James Thomson persuasively argues for such a reconsideration of affect: "[P]articipation in the joyful is part of a dream of a 'beautiful future' [...]. Far from being a diversion, it acts to make visible a better world" (2009: 2).

and creative terrains, may have exhausted their potential.[7] I return to this in the final section of this chapter, after examining how the play's non-representational aesthetic articulates a strong ethical position.

Non-Representational Ethics

In one of the first academic responses to *The Author*, Stephen Bottoms comments on the ethical potential of the spatial design of the play. For Bottoms, Crouch's play "lend[s] credence to [Nicholas] Ridout's sense of theatre's too-infrequently realised potential for ethical encounter" (2011b: 446). The article does not focus on ethics, and therefore what this encounter may entail or whom it may involve is not pursued. Yet, his use of the term "ethical encounter" and the suggestion that this is foregrounded by spectators' being "watched in our watching" (Ridout qtd. in Bottoms 2011b: 446) is nonetheless reminiscent of the ethical philosophy of Emmanuel Levinas. For Levinas, it is the sheer presence of the Other in a face-to-face encounter that triggers an epiphany, an ethical interpellation: the Other disarms my freedom, autonomy and self-centred apprehension of the world (see 1989: 83–84), and renders me "inescapably responsible" for their life (1989: 84). The Levinasian ethical scene is therefore resolutely centred on the Other, and demands that I act "as if I were devoted to the other man before being devoted to myself" (1989: 83). Considering *The Author* in relation to Levinas's thought, however, highlights striking differences between the two. While spectators in Crouch's play may encounter other audience members and the cast in a reciprocal and self-aware form of spectatorship, the face-to-face encounter as envisioned by Levinas pivots on facing *the suffering Other*. Arguably, in the performance space of *The Author* the Other is absent – spectators' eyes never directly meet the gaze of the victims of decapitation, the distressed foreign man, or Karen. The Other is fictionalised, on occasion ventriloquised.

However, the absence of the Other need not compromise the play's ethical commitment – in fact, this is central to its articulation. First, the non-representational aesthetic of *The Author* resonates with a different aspect of Levinas's own ethical thought.[8] As Butler reminds us, "[f]or Levinas, the human cannot be cap-

---

[7] See David Cortright's *Peace: A History of Movements and Ideas* for a reflection on the political effects of the anti-war movement despite its inability to halt the military invasion of Iraq (2008: 174–175).
[8] The play's refusal to represent acts of violence mimetically has also been interpreted as an ethical strategy to avoid proliferating violent images that brutalise, desensitise and generate spectacle (see Wallace 2012: 59; 61). Writing on US reports about the Iraq War, Butler interesting-

tured through the representation" (2004a: 145). Indeed, *The Author* eschews the visual representation of Otherness, as the set design dictates that audiences are looking onto a mirror image of themselves. Whenever there is an attempt to represent the Other, the (ethical) limits of representational practices become apparent. These limits are particularly acute when Vic and Esther describe and impersonate for the audience the individuals who inspired their character work. The un-symbolisable and therefore un-representable experiences of trauma (see Felman and Laub 1992) that these individuals suffered, together with the complex socio-cultural and historical contexts in which their lives are situated, are reduced to body gestures that Vic and Esther imitate – essentially as tokens of their own craft as actors: "Her name was Karen. She was like this. Can you see that? Her tension here. Her eyes like this" (39). The characters' self-centred attempts to represent the Other mimetically demonstrate both the incommensurability of suffering and the possibility of appropriation, representational injustice or violence. Reductionist and even parasitic, these instances make apparent Levinas's suspicions as summarised by Butler: that "some loss of the human takes place when it is 'captured' by the image" (2004a: 145).

Second, structurally and formally, *The Author* reflects on how we are all exposed to violence, suffering and loss. The extent to which universal precariousness is central to the play's form is not immediately apparent. For example, Rebellato has recorded Crouch's perplexity about the fact that a lengthy description of a man's beheading in *The Author* did not receive any complaints, while the play's notorious account of child abuse generated walkouts, as well as vocal and written opposition (see Rebellato 2013: 141; see also Crouch 2011b). Crouch's surprise at the range of reactions to different evocations of violence could be read as somewhat disingenuous: babies epitomise extreme human vulnerability in their absolute dispossession and dependence on others for survival, and stories involving child abuse are therefore likely to elicit strong responses (see Freshwater 2013: 180). Yet Crouch's observation resonates with one of Butler's core theses in *Precarious Life: The Powers of Mourning and Violence* – namely, that physical vulnerability and interdependence are not contingent on a situation or a particular state of being, but are universal properties of human ontology, intricately linked to the fact that we are relational beings.

---

ly notes a different withdrawal of violent images: "[T]he graphic photos of US soldiers dead and decapitated in Iraq, and then the photos of children maimed and killed by the US bombs, were both refused by the mainstream media, supplanted with footage that always took the aerial view, an aerial view whose perspective is established and maintained by state power" (2004a: 149).

Although the baby constitutes the play's most memorable figure of injurability, precariousness is ubiquitous in *The Author*'s multi-layered structure. The physical and/or emotional safety of everyone represented by or involved in Tim's fictional show is openly fragile. In the fictional play within the play, there is Eshna, abused by her father, and Pavol, victim himself of the violence of a war. In the fictional-real world, there are Karen, also raped by her father; the countless victims of real violence appearing in the videos and photographs uploaded online; and perhaps Finn, Esther's son, who may have been abused by Tim. In circumstances that reveal our affective vulnerability, there are Karen, Esther and Vic, subjected to Tim's irresponsible professional practices; Esther, whose baby son is left with Tim; and Tim himself, suicidal with the certainty that he will not be forgiven. To a lesser extent, the unsuspecting spectators of *The Author* are in a position of emotional vulnerability too: rather like Adrian in the fiction, they open themselves to receiving an unexpected blow in the theatre, "the safest place in the world!" (46). This constellation of always-already vulnerable figures, traversing both the fiction and the performance event, highlights our ontological openness to being destabilised, injured and dispossessed in bodily, affective, social or material ways. *The Author* does not visually represent but linguistically evokes the experience that our safety and well-being depend on others: that relationality and vulnerability are universal conditions "from which we cannot slip away [...] but which can provide a way to understand that none of us is fully bounded, utterly separate, but, rather, we are in our skins, given over, in each other's hands, at each other's mercy" (Butler 2005: 101). Or, in the words of the *High School Musical* song fragment that Esther sings to the audience, the universality of precariousness implies that "we're all in this together".[9] The universality of precariousness complicates the powerful binaries at work in Tim's justification, in Levinasian ethical philosophy and in the political discourses mobilised during the War on Terror – 'us' and 'them', self and Other. It suggests the existence of a universal community that is neither represented nor representable but is nonetheless real.

Importantly, Butler notes that the essential dependency derived from our common vulnerability "require[s] not just one other person, but social systems of support that are complexly human and technical" (2012: 165). As she puts it elsewhere, "politics must consider what forms of social and political organization seek best to sustain precarious lives across the globe" (2004b: 23), and "[m]indfulness of this vulnerability can become the basis of claims for non-mili-

---

9 The script does not specify what West End song Esther will sing, but this is indeed the piece chosen (see Crouch 2014: 74).

tary political solutions" (2004a: 29). For Butler, precariousness is then inextricably linked with social and political practices, to which the final section of this chapter briefly turns.

Democratic Representation

In line with Crouch's austere, metatheatrical aesthetics, the political context in which *The Author* was produced is not overtly portrayed; rather, it is evoked, inscribed in the experience of spectatorship. To date, however, the mode of spectatorship in *The Author* has been examined in relation to the economy of the performance event and wider artistic debates, with only two exceptions. Dilating the terms 'performance' and 'spectatorship' to embrace activities and subject positions resonant with our cultural and economic situation, James Frieze argues that *The Author* makes us consider whether we, as spectators, "are perpetuating a chain of production and consumption in which we surrender our agency and ethical responsibility" (2013: 11). As Frieze notes, if *The Author* demonstrates a collective relinquishing of ethical agency and responsibility, this is because the show actually scripts our failure to intervene in the situation (see 2013: 13). Indeed, Crouch himself has made clear that if and when audience members express discomfort and a wish for the narration of violence to stop, the performers must continue (see Bottoms 2011a: 424). Writing from a political stance, Janelle Reinelt has recently argued that *The Author* "challenges the disaffiliation of liberal citizenship or flexible citizenship that trades on its passports but does not take up responsibility for the communities with which it is linked" (2015: 47). These arguments about consumption and citizenship are compelling, but perhaps it is possible to situate the design of spectatorship in Crouch's play in other, more concrete political contexts.

Rather than re-stating spectators' scripted failure to interrupt and intervene in *The Author*, or recasting this as a sign of unresponsiveness or irresponsibility, I want to foreground the resonances between spectators' powerlessness to change the course of events and the ongoing crisis of democratic legitimacy in the UK.[10] As Richard M. Buck notes, "the fundamental characteristic of any democracy is that [...] citizens are effectively the source of the political authority of the polity", and therefore "[d]emocratic legitimacy [...] requires that the structure and actions

---

[10] This is not exclusive to the UK. See Matthias Matthijs's "Mediterranean Blues: The Crisis in Southern Europe" (2014) for more on the relationship between the debt crisis and the erosion of democratic legitimacy in the European Union.

of a democratic polity reflect this collective aim" (2012: 223). A disjunction between polity and collective decision-making is precisely a characteristic of the political conjuncture in which *The Author* was written.

The play premiered after the British military intervention in Iraq – which occurred despite the most multitudinous peace demonstration to have ever taken place in the UK (see Jeffery 2003) – and just before the first wave of austerity measures, announced by the coalition government in 2010 amidst extraordinary public opposition (see Townsend et al. 2011). *The Author* therefore playfully absorbs a very contemporary dynamic between citizens and authorities. On the one hand, there is the *appearance* of political participation and consent; for example, through electoral participation and the delegation of responsibility inherent to democracy. On the other, however, there is the implementation of policy with or without public endorsement. Similarly, much of the beginning of Crouch's play is devoted to generating the experience of consensus, and the sense that spectators can indeed determine the future of the show. Adrian's opening dialogue with the audience, and Tim, Vic and Esther's gentle requests for consent when particularly violent passages are described, contribute to this – spectators are recurrently asked: "Is this okay? Is it okay if I carry on? Do you want me to stop?" (23). Occupying two banks of seats facing one another, like Members of Parliament in the House of Commons, the experience of participation and decision-making capacity is heightened at this point. However, consent is not requested when Tim begins his graphic description of a scene of child abuse, and the cast is instructed to proceed with the performance regardless of voiced protests, silent discomfort and walkouts.[11] The design of spectatorship therefore invokes a community whose power of resistance is eventually nullified by authority and preconceived plans, despite a persuasive rhetoric of equality and concern.

It would be unfounded to read the orchestration of spectatorship in *The Author* as exclusively driven by a critique of contemporary processes of governance and participation. However, strong resonances with the immediate political context in which the play was written, staged and toured in the UK enable such a reading. Alongside references to the unheard public protests against military intervention in Iraq, the spectre of David Cameron's deceptively reassuring slogan since his victory as leader of the Conservative Party in 2005 – "we're all in this

---

[11] As any expression of spectatorial resistance to the description of child pornography is disregarded, audiences also experience being hostage to an unethical and non-consensual relationship with another. This echoes, on a different scale, the many instances of unethical and non-consensual engagements in the fiction, and lays bare the spectators' own vulnerability: our potential to be unheard, not represented, not counted.

together" – runs through Esther's *High School Musical* song. This resonance was particularly prominent during the 2010–2011 tour of *The Author* in the UK, as Cameron's slogan was consistently deployed to veneer drastic austerity measures with the language of social responsibility. Repeated as the central line of the chorus, the words "we're all in this together" simultaneously conjure up a utopian vision of community, the strained cheerfulness of the Disney musical, and the actual withdrawal of community services under Cameron's government. Haunted by its political double, the *High School Musical* song offers further opportunities for an aesthetic problematisation of discourses about community, inclusiveness and participation. Significantly, a song that celebrates togetherness is delivered first by Esther *a capella*. Furthermore, as Crouch has noted elsewhere, "Esther sings in the dark" (2014: 75), visually frustrating the verification of this togetherness. The second time that the song is used in the piece is when Vic verbally relives the moment he attacked Adrian, the character who stands for theatre spectators (see Crouch 2014: 74). On both occasions, spectators – like those who opposed austerity – are disregarded, obscured and subject to injury.

The binary us/them identified previously in the chapter is thus problematised on yet another count. It is not only the case that the helper/victim divide shuns the possibility of self-examination and criticism – that 'we' perhaps have something to do with the violence 'over there'. Neither is it simply that people just like 'us' are capable of taking part in violent acts 'here', as *The Author*'s denouement suggests. It is also that the very notion of 'us' is questioned. The play encourages a self-indulgent, even erotic construction of 'us' throughout, with constant invitations to behold our image: "Look! We're gorgeous! [...] More chance of a snog from one of us than from the Prince of Denmark, don't you think!" (19), "We're all so expectant! We're all being so lovely!!!" (20), "My god, when I think about it, we're incredibly lucky" (31). Yet, the audience's scripted silencing suggests that we may need to take a long hard look at the notions of community invoked by those with authority in the game. As a matter of fact, 'we' might not be in it together.

This reading of spectatorship at the crossover between the seeming failure to intervene in the world and the appearance of participation, however, is not meant to suggest that *The Author* conceives of its audience as inherently powerless; Crouch's exegesis of his own work indeed suggests the opposite (see Bottoms 2009). Gareth White's study of participation in the piece may enable a rapprochement between *The Author*'s theatricalisation of fruitless resistance and participation, and Crouch's interest in an enfranchised experience of spectatorship. For White, "while structured and invited participation fades out of the performance, the intensity of involvement, and implication, of audiences evidently increases" (2013: 189–190). It may be argued that the frustration of meaningful intervention in the piece is precisely what heightens the desire to participate. Politically speaking, *The Author* does not prefigure or represent what a collective based on social justice might look like, or what forms of resistance might work, yet it incites its audiences to disidentify with violent authority, to distrust consensus, and to value consent.

Conclusion

In considering *The Author* in its context of production, this chapter has illuminated its embedded topical critiques, and paved the way for a situated reading of Crouch's trajectory. The play loosely evokes a number of prominent events, discourses and practices in the realms of art, culture and politics between the onset of the War on Terror and the implementation of austerity policy in Britain. The us/them divide, the erasure of history in accounts of violence, and the appeal to reality and representational acts are all called into question. In its more specific critique, *The Author* theatricalises the crisis of democratic legitimacy in the UK. While political discourses insist on celebrating citizens' participation, Crouch's play hints at how dissident public opinion struggles to alter the violent, scripted course of action. The play's implied socio-political context is consistent but ultimately elusive, suggesting that these structures of thought and action are not exclusive to the UK. Similarly, I have argued that the work's non-representational aesthetic allows for the figuration of a universal community on the basis of our shared ontological precariousness. *The Author* is therefore not just about theatre and spectatorship, or consumption and responsibility, as has thus far been argued. It is also about the potential artificiality of consensus, the abuse of authority, and the slippage between intentions, discourses and practices.

Works Cited

Associated Press. 2004. "Islamist Website Shows Beheading". *theguardian.co.uk*, 11 May. <http://www.theguardian.com/world/2004/may/11/iraq> [accessed 8 November 2015].

Angel-Pérez, Élisabeth. 2013. "Back to Verbal Theatre: Post-Post-Dramatic Theatres from Crimp to Crouch". *Études britanniques contemporaines* 45, 30 September. <http://ebc.revues.org/862> [accessed 15 January 2015].

BBC News. 2003. "In Pictures: Army Patrols Heathrow". *BBC News*, 11 February. <http://news.bbc.co.uk/1/hi/uk/2749659.stm> [accessed 26 October 2015].

BBC News. 2004. "British Soldiers Killed in Iraq". *BBC News*, 28 September. <http://news.bbc.co.uk/1/hi/uk/3696978.stm> [accessed 26 October 2015].

Boll, Julia. 2013. *The New War Plays: From Kane to Harris*. Basingstoke and New York: Palgrave Macmillan.

Bottoms, Stephen. 2009. "Authorizing the Audience: The Conceptual Drama of Tim Crouch". *Performance Research* 14.1: 65–76.

Bottoms, Stephen. 2011a. "A Conversation about Dialogue (Symposium Voices)". *Contemporary Theatre Review* 21.4: 423–430.

Bottoms, Stephen. 2011b. "Materialising the Audience: Tim Crouch's Sight Specifics in ENGLAND and *The Author*". *Contemporary Theatre Review* 21.4: 445–463.

Buck, Richard M. 2012. "Democratic Legitimacy: The Limits of Instrumentalist Accounts". *Journal of Value Inquiry* 46.2: 223–236.

Butler, Judith. 2004a. *Precarious Life: The Powers of Mourning and Violence*. London and New York: Verso.

Butler, Judith. 2004b. *Undoing Gender*. London and New York: Routledge.

Butler, Judith. 2005. *Giving an Account of Oneself*. New York: Fordham UP.

Butler, Judith. 2012. "Bodily Vulnerability, Coalitions and Street Politics". In: Marta Kuzma, Pablo Lafuente and Peter Osborne (eds.). *The State of Things*. Oslo: Office for Contemporary Art in Norway/London: Koenig Books. 161–197.

Cortright, David. 2008. *Peace: A History of Movements and Ideas*. Cambridge: Cambridge UP.

Crouch, Tim. 2006. "Tim Crouch's Theatrical Transformations: A Conversation with Caridad Svich". *HotReview.org: Hunter On-line Theater Review*. <http://www.hotreview.org/articles/timcrouchinterv.htm> [accessed 25 April 2014].

Crouch, Tim. 2009. *The Author*. London: Oberon.

Crouch, Tim. 2011a. "Who Do We Think We Are: Representing the Human". Conversation with Dan Rebellato. Department of Drama and Theatre at Royal Holloway, University of London. 19 March. Symposium. <https://www.royalholloway.ac.uk/dramaandtheatre/media/whodowe/timcrouchconversation-web.mp3> [accessed 15 January 2015].

Crouch, Tim. 2011b. "*The Author*: Response and Responsibility". *Contemporary Theatre Review* 21.4: 416–422.

Crouch, Tim. 2014. "Navigating New Patterns of Power with an Audience". Conversation with Aleks Sierz. *Journal of Contemporary Drama in English* 2.1: 63–77.

Delgado-García, Cristina. 2014. "Dematerialised Political and Theatrical Legacies: Rethinking the Roots and Influences of Tim Crouch's Work". *Platform: Journal of Theatre and Performing Arts* 8.1: 69–85.

Delgado-García, Cristina. 2015. *Rethinking Character in Contemporary British Theatre: Aesthetics, Politics, Subjectivity*. CDE Studies 26. Berlin and Boston: De Gruyter.

de Waal, Ariane. 2015. "Staging Wounded Soldiers: The Affects and Effects of Post-Traumatic Theatre". *Performance Paradigm* 11: 16–31.

Felman, Shoshana and Dori Laub. 1992. *Testimony: Crises of Witnessing in Literature, Psychoanalysis and History*. London and New York: Routledge.

Freshwater, Helen. 2011. "'You Say Something': Audience Participation in *The Author*". *Contemporary Theatre Review* 21.4: 405–409.

Freshwater, Helen. 2013. "Children and the Limits of Representation in the Work of Tim Crouch". In: Vicky Angelaki (ed.). *Contemporary British Theatre: Breaking New Ground*. Basingstoke and New York: Palgrave Macmillan. 167–188.

Frieze, James. 2013. "Actualizing a Spectator Like You: The Ethics of the Intrusive-Hypothetical". *Performing Ethos* 3.1: 7–22.

Hopkins, Nick; Norton-Taylor, Richard and Michael White. 2003. "UK on Missile Terror Alert". *The Guardian*, 12 February. <http://www.theguardian.com/uk/2003/feb/12/terrorism.world1> [accessed 26 October 2015].
Hubbard, Wendy. 2013. "Falling Faint: On Syncopated Spectatorship and *The Author*". *Performance Research: A Journal of the Performing Arts* 18.4: 22–29.
Jeffery, Simon. 2003. "UK's 'Biggest Peace Rally'". *The Guardian*, 15 February. <http://www.theguardian.com/uk/2003/feb/15/politics.politicalnews> [accessed 11 December 2014].
Khalid, Maryam. 2011. "Gender, Orientalism and Representations of the 'Other' in the War on Terror". *Global Change, Peace & Security* 23.1: 15–29.
Levinas, Emmanuel. 1989 [1984]. "Ethics as First Philosophy". Trans. Seán Hand and Michael Temple. In: Seán Hand (ed.). *The Levinas Reader*. Oxford: Blackwell. 75–87.
Matthijs, Matthias. 2014. "Mediterranean Blues: The Crisis in Southern Europe". *Journal of Democracy* 25.1: 101–115.
Megson, Chris. 2005. "'This Is All Theatre': Iraq Centre Stage". *Contemporary Theatre Review* 15.3: 369–371.
Nancy, Jean-Luc. 2005. *The Ground of the Image*. Trans. Jeff Fort. New York: Fordham UP.
Radosavljević, Duška. 2013. *Theatre-Making: Interplay Between Text and Performance in the 21st Century*. Basingstoke and New York: Palgrave Macmillan.
Rebellato, Dan. 2013. "Tim Crouch". In: Dan Rebellato (ed.). *Modern British Playwriting, 2000–2009: Voices, Documents, New Interpretations*. London: Bloomsbury. 125–144.
Reinelt, Janelle. 2015. "Performance at the Crossroads of Citizenship". In: Shirin M. Rai and Janelle Reinelt (eds.). *The Grammar of Politics and Performance*. London and New York: Routledge. 34–50.
Thomson, James. 2009. *Performance Affects: Applied Theatre and the End of Effect*. Basingstoke and New York: Palgrave MacMillan.
Townsend, Mark, et al. 2011. "Anti-cuts March Draws Hundreds of Thousands as Police Battle Rioters". *The Guardian*, 27 March. <http://www.theguardian.com/society/2011/mar/26/anti-cuts-march-police-rioters> [accessed 15 January 2015].
Wallace, Clare. 2012. "Uncertain Convictions and the Politics of Perception". In: Mark Berninger and Bernhard Reitz (eds.). *Ethical Debates in Contemporary Theatre and Drama*. CDE Studies 19. Trier: WVT. 55–64.
Wallace, Clare. 2014. "Playing with Proximity: Precarious Ethics on Stage in the New Millenium". In: Mireia Aragay and Enric Monforte (eds.). *Ethical Speculations in Contemporary British Theatre*. Basingstoke and New York: Palgrave Macmillan. 117–134.
White, Gareth. 2013. *Audience Participation in Theatre: Aesthetics of the Invitation*. Basingstoke and New York: Palgrave Macmillan.
Wickstrom, Maurya. 2012. *Performance in the Blockades of Neoliberalism: Thinking the Political Anew*. Basingstoke and New York: Palgrave Macmillan.

Bettina Auerswald
Promises of the Real? The Precariousness of Verbatim Theatre and Robin Soans's *Talking to Terrorists*

Verbatim Theatre: An Introduction

Since the earliest productions in the 1970s, verbatim theatre has been known as a subgenre of documentary theatre that pledges to commit itself to only use spoken evidence or verbatim witness accounts for its playtexts. Traditionally, the prime aim of verbatim plays has been to (re-)tell 'ordinary' people's stories:

> The realisation that you could just have a little bit of space and four performers or whatever – one lighting state, no props, no change of costume – and you could just *tell stories*, and you could *share* narrative was, I contend, a major breakthrough for us. (Rony Robinson qtd. in Paget 1987: 320)

In conversation with Derek Paget, Clive Barker additionally emphasises "the direct communication, or second-hand communication, of lived experience through the actor as instrument" (qtd. in Paget 1987: 318) – the actor is 'reduced' to being a medium for 'real people's' stories, which are both at the centre of the plays and painstakingly preserved and protected from manipulative change. Originally, verbatim theatre was intended to give 'ordinary' people a voice so that they could tell their stories on a public stage through the medium of an actor – and not as a tool to uncover hidden truths or indoctrinate unsuspecting audiences.

Over the last twenty years, many plays have emerged that foreground the use of verbatim techniques as a means to respond (politically) to contemporary issues. This development has made a distinction necessary between plays that follow in the footsteps of first-generation verbatim practitioners and those with a more political mindset. I am basing this distinction on the playwrights' and companies' ideological orientations and intentions – rather than distinguishing verbatim plays solely on the basis of the origin of the source material (tribunal *vis-à-vis* classic verbatim plays) as it has been done so far.[1]

---

[1] The only other reference to the potential existence of two different strands within verbatim theatre that I am aware of was made, in a side note, by Anneka Esch-van Kan, who writes:

I propose the term 'communal verbatim' for plays that include *The Laramie Project* (2000; publ. 2001) by Moisés Kaufman and the members of the Tectonic Theatre Project, and the yet unpublished verbatim production *Counted? A Documentary-Play about British Democracy* by the London-based theatre company Look Left Look Right. Particularly Kaufman's ideology is exemplary and reminiscent of previous practitioners' convictions concerning verbatim theatre's merit and thus responsibility. In his introduction to the play, he emphasises that by "paying careful attention [...] to people's words, one is able to hear the way these prevailing ideas affect not only individual lives but also the culture at large" (Kaufman et al., *The Laramie Project*: v). He further explains that his approach to theatre-making is based on self-reflexivity and on fully embracing his responsibility as an artist towards his community – hence the classification as communal verbatim. On that score, his main concern is:

> What can we as theater artists do as a response to this incident [the brutal, homophobically motivated murder of Matthew Shepard]? And, more concretely, is theater a medium that can *contribute* to the national dialogue on current events? (vi; emphasis added)

Beyond his ambition to actively contribute to political dialogue, Kaufman writes that for every project his two objectives are: "(1) to examine the subject matter at hand, and (2) to explore theatrical language and form [... as a way] to continue to have a dialogue on both how the theater speaks and how it is created" (vi). By implication, Kaufman is not out to pry and expose, but to understand more about how a community will deal with a (potentially troubling) incident, as well as how and why it happened in the first place. Along the same lines, he is interested in his role as an artist and writes candidly about his working methods and ideological interests in the introduction, his author's note (see Kaufman et al., *The Laramie Project*: v–xiv) and in the play itself.[2]

"[O]ne strain of recent documentary plays bonds with naturalism and strives for the uncovering of a hidden truth, the other strain emphasizes the experimental aesthetics of documentary theatre and self-reflexively explores the relationship between representation and reality" (2011: 416).

2 See especially the beginning of the play, where the 'narrator' states: "The play you are about to see is edited from those [over two hundred] interviews, as well as from journal entries by members of the company and other found texts" (Kaufman et al., *The Laramie Project*: 5). Even during the performance itself, Kaufman highlights that the play was edited from interviews by having his actors jump between 'themselves'-as-interviewees and the character they are portraying at that moment. One such instance is 'Greg Pierotti's' account of his interview with Detective Sergeant Hing, in which the actor moves between playing Hing and himself (see 5).

'Political verbatim', in contrast, is marked by a propensity for the working methods of investigative journalism, playing with the notion of 'uncovering hidden truths' (see Esch-van Kan 2011: 414; 416). This promise of new insights and behind-the-scenes, first-hand information is given implicitly through titles and choices of topic such as Richard Norton-Taylor's *The Colour of Justice: Based on the Transcripts of the Stephen Lawrence Inquiry* (1999) or Victoria Brittain and Gillian Slovo's *Guantanamo: 'Honor Bound to Defend Freedom': Taken from Spoken Evidence* (2004), or explicitly in author's notes.[3] Further, these plays lack the ensemble devising process – which used to be a constitutive characteristic of verbatim theatre – as most of the playwrights have primarily journalistic backgrounds. Thus, they are very well trained in journalistic verification methods and interested in investigating the events at hand – and arguably not as much in re-defining their roles and responsibilities as artists or actors, or those of theatre itself.

It is this political strand of verbatim theatre that attracts most criticism. In "Putting the Document into Documentary", Stephen Bottoms criticises David Hare and Robin Soans for their "highly selective manipulation of opinion and rhetoric" (2006: 58) and speaks out for performances which "foreground their own processes of representation in order to acknowledge the problem and encourage audiences to adopt an actively critical perspective on the events depicted", naming Kaufman's *Gross Indecency: The Three Trials of Oscar Wilde* (1997; publ. 1998) "a model of [this] reflexivity" (2006: 61). In terms of my distinction between the two strands of verbatim theatre, Bottoms favours the communal over the political, but, to my knowledge, does not acknowledge their differences. The distinction, however, is necessary because it appreciates that both subgenres act out of responsibility, albeit a responsibility that is placed differently in both strands. Political verbatim is eminently less self-reflexive, because its main concern is to inform its spectators about undisclosed information about a given case (see Kent 2013: 136) and to provoke political debate, a fact both Paget and Janelle Reinelt have discussed in connection with "drama-documentary" and the theatricalisation of everyday life respectively (see Paget 2011: 120 and Reinelt 2006: 74). Margarete Rubik makes a fine point in arguing that, while it would indeed be possible to manipulate theatregoers, it is highly questionable to suppose that audiences are so naïve that they expect to learn 'the truth' about sensitive

---

[3] See David Hare's notorious claim in *Stuff Happens* (2004) that "[t]he events within it have been authenticated from multiple sources, both private and public. What happened happened. Nothing in the narrative is knowingly untrue" (Hare, *Stuff Happens*: author's note) – even though he admits that what happens 'behind closed doors', which, in fact, is the largest part of the play, is taken from his imagination.

political issues on a theatre stage. Critics should rather assess the plays' artistic merits than debate whether the reality that is portrayed on stage is in accordance with the known (or ideologically preferred) 'facts' (see Rubik 2010: 70–71). In harmony with the arguments put forward by Rubik and Reinelt, I believe that by distinguishing between communal and political verbatim, critics may be more likely to turn to assessing the aforementioned merits, because they no longer feel compelled to charge one subgenre with the shortcomings of the other and vice versa.

Promises of 'the Real' and Other Offences: Verbatim Theatre as a Precarious Genre

In this chapter, I want to argue that Judith Butler's view of the human condition as inherently precarious can fruitfully illuminate both communal and political verbatim. Drawing on her paper "Precarious Life, Vulnerability, and the Ethics of Cohabitation" (2012), we can identify various levels of precariousness in verbatim theatre. Although Butler's understanding of precariousness generally transcends Samuel Johnson's definition of it as an uncertainty caused by dependency on others (see Johnson 1968), her account can nevertheless be closely linked to Johnson's. According to Butler, the precariousness of the body is rooted in the realisation that "one's life is also the life of others" which, in turn, "is the condition of being exposed to the other, [...] exposed in ways that sustain us but also in ways that can destroy us" (2012: 141). This condition induces feelings of uncertainty, anxiety, or even threat, as we are dependent on and bound to "those we do not know, and even those we did not choose, could never have chosen" (Butler 2012: 140). For her account of the precarious state, Butler draws on the work of Emmanuel Levinas and Hannah Arendt, concluding that our precariousness is inextricable from our precontractual, unconditional, irrevocable ethical obligations towards all Others at all times, given the thoroughly relational nature of our existence (see Butler 2012: 140–142; 150).

How, now, can the heightened setting of a (verbatim) theatre performance conduce to audiences' sensitivity towards ethical solicitation by the Other? First and foremost, the layout of the theatre space as well as the divide between actors and audience structurally mirrors the state of being called upon by the Other. The described structure also implies the act of witnessing an event, which can be greatly intensified through the verbatim form. Because verbatim theatre takes its material from interviews or (court) transcripts, broadly speaking, audiences witness the distilled essence of 'real' public events and 'real' people's opinions. Particularly when foregrounding issues that are of global interest, such as police brutality and racism (*The Colour of Justice*), homophobia (*The Laramie Project*), or terrorism (*Talking to Terrorists*), verbatim theatre not only exposes audiences to the issues presented, it also subjects them to the respective ideologies that govern the plays – as any form of editing is subjective, let alone the process of staging, which demands further (subjective) decisions as to the *mise-en-scène*, blocking, etc. Thus, by watching a verbatim piece, audiences are likely to experience a state of precariousness when they feel solicited by the Other-as-actor and the 'real' Other through the actor-as-medium. In the verbatim setting, spectators are bound to feel unsettled, or even threatened, when they are exposed to ideas and concepts that challenge or even oppose ideologies and convictions they had previously taken for granted.

In the case of *Talking to Terrorists* (2005), a political verbatim play that lends itself exceptionally well to the study of the issue of precariousness, Soans explains the play's *raison d'être* as the attempt to humanise terrorists:

> Terrorists are, in many cases, demonised. They are seen as bearded devils who squat on Afghanistan hillsides who want to mangle our way of life. That doesn't seem very helpful in telling us who a terrorist is. They're not one-dimensional characters. We needed to humanise them. (2005b)

Confronted with the case of children becoming victims of terrorist attacks, Soans replies that he "would hope that that [child's] relative would think it reasonable for us to try to understand what's going on. How else are we going to prevent somebody else's child being killed?" (2005b). Soans's demand stretches ethical solicitation to its extreme, for example when relatives are tasked to exercise understanding and forgiveness towards their child's murderer. Following Butler's argumentation, it is the discrepancy between one's own self (our wishes, actions, etc.) and that of others (their wishes, actions, etc.) that creates the ineluctable experience of precariousness. Due to the inevitable cohabitation with people we never chose, we (are forced to) open ourselves up to the diversity of their opinions and mindsets concerning issues of morality, religion, personal philosophy and human rights. In my reading of Butler, this process of opening oneself up is, at the same time, also the (gradual) acceptance of boundedness to the Other, a boundedness that constitutes both limitation and adjacency (see Butler 2012: 141), which subsequently requires us to embrace our ethical responsibility towards them. In this sense, verbatim theatre not only addresses issues that foreground the question of precariousness, it also has the power to raise spectators' awareness of their state of precariousness by soliciting them to open themselves onto the world. This can be intensified when audiences are confronted with images that they did not consent to see (see Butler 2012: 136–137). Likewise, the genre also opens *itself* onto the world, especially to criticism about its proximity to manipulation and indoctrination and, more generally, its lack of abstraction, which is why some critics deny verbatim theatre the status of art altogether.

Coming back to Soans's *Talking to Terrorists*, we can find pronounced criticism of its simplification and reduced depiction of reality. Bottoms in particular objects to the fact that the play "simply uses the catch-all label 'terrorism' to imply that the experiences of these individuals are all different kinds of the same thing" (2006: 58). This, of course, is true for the title, and necessarily so, but not for the play itself, which addresses the different points of view of people, most of whom would not call themselves terrorists, but soldiers or freedom fighters. These different groups are likened to each other as representatives of an "ideology of violence" (Soans, *Talking to Terrorists*: 59) rather than of terrorism. Given the temporal constraints most plays are under, playwrights cannot but extensively cut down their (verbatim) material. Bottoms's criticism seems to derive from his disregard for the political verbatim form, which in his view lacks Kaufman-esque self-reflexivity and can thus be faulted with a propensity towards manipulation. Even if this were the case, however, it would not relieve the spectator of his/her duty to deploy critical thinking, because of his/her perdurable ethical responsibility towards the Other.

If we accept Butler's claim that "neither consent nor communitarianism will justify or delimit the range of [global ethical] obligations" (2012: 137), we must likewise accept that there really is no autonomous 'singularity', since we are unconditionally and invariably interconnected with each other. This would lead to the (potentially counter-intuitive) realisation that we thus have the same ethical obligations towards victims as towards perpetrators and everybody in between, "since whatever sense 'our' life has is derived precisely from this sociality" where "the life of the other [...] is also our life" (Butler 2012: 140–141). This concept directly translates into a binding ethical obligation toward the Other, as, following Emmanuel Levinas, "no matter how much one fears for one's own life, preserving the life of the other is paramount" (Butler 2012: 141). And thus, we are not just asked to "try to understand what's going on" (Soans 2005b) – we are at all times ethically responsible, even towards individuals who have hurt us in the past or could hurt us in the future. From this point of view, *Talking to Terrorists* may be said to operate as an instance of "an ethical solicitation" (Butler 2012: 135):

> [W]e are in such moments affronted by something that is beyond our will, not of our making, that comes to us from the outside, as an imposition but also as an ethical demand. I want to suggest that these are ethical obligations that do not require our consent, and neither are they the result of contracts or agreements into which any of us have deliberately entered. (Butler 2012: 135)

These obligations "emerge from the social conditions of political life" and are therefore inescapable, even if Butler acknowledges the fact that implementing them is by no means simple: they are "*ideals* toward which we must struggle" (2012: 150; emphasis added).

Beyond that, it is possible to identify a third level of vulnerability that is particularly relevant to communal verbatim productions. Since this strand of verbatim theatre makes a point of feeding the edited performance text back to the respective communities, the actors subject themselves to heightened levels of precariousness. In his seminal paper "'Verbatim Theatre': Oral History and Documentary Techniques", Paget describes (and defines) verbatim theatre as

> a form of theatre firmly predicated upon the taping and subsequent transcription of interviews with 'ordinary' people, done in the context of research into a particular region, subject area, issue, event, or combination of these things. This primary source is then transformed into a text which is acted, usually by the performers who collected the material in the first place. As often as not, such plays are then *fed back* into the communities (which have, in a real sense, created them), via performance *in* those communities. In Verbatim Theatre, the firmest of commitments is thus made by the company to *the use of vernacular speech*, recorded as the primary source material of their play. (1987: 317)

When the actors returned to Laramie, Wyoming, to perform *The Laramie Project* in November 2000, the likelihood of former interviewees to be sitting in the theatre was considerably high. Knowing that they would eventually return to Laramie, we can assume that each interviewer/actor was particularly diligent in preserving the original meaning of the interviewees' words from the start. With plays such as *Talking to Terrorists*, where the interviews are not taken from one specific community but from topically attractive individuals, this form of 'feeding back' is impossible. Bearing in mind the genre-specific, multi-reflexive devising process that rests upon the collective gathering, rehearsing, performing, and subsequent return to the interview-giving community, and is at the basis of every communal verbatim piece, we can regard this kind of verbatim theatre as considerably more relational than other art forms.

In connection with this, it seems essential to address what is probably the most overlooked aspect of verbatim theatre. In its very distinct make-up, it shares a series of artistic principles with collages – consider for example Kurt Schwitters's *Das Undbild* (1919) – and ready-made art such as Marcel Duchamp's *Fountain* (1917). I would indeed suggest that verbatim theatre uses *mots trouvés* in their unaltered form and turns them into art via the mentioned devising process, during which the selected words are stuck together to yield a bigger picture and finally fayed into the stencil of a playtext. The analogy is, of course, only true as regards the comparable structures. It is the collective aspect of the devising process that constitutes communal verbatim theatre and distinguishes it most clearly from conceptual art. Political verbatim, of course, lacks both the communal as well as the 'feeding back' aspect. Communal verbatim, at the minimum, can be said to be doubly relational – it takes 'real words' from 'real people', turns them into art, and then brings the resulting performance back to those people who gave their stories to the project in the first place. Bluntly speaking: from life to art and back to life.

Here I would like to return to Butler's point about our ethical obligations towards the Other, terrorists or victims, as constituted by their ontological vulnerability. Butler establishes that we cannot ever delimit "the global obligations that form our responsibility" (2012: 137), regardless of our consent:

> [T]he set of ethical values by which one population is bound to another in no way depends on those two populations bearing similar marks of national, cultural, religious, racial belonging. [... W]e are bound to those we do not know, and even those we did not choose, could never have chosen. (2012: 139–140)

Since these obligations are precontractual, every living creature has the same right to exist and nobody has a right to decide with whom to cohabit the earth. Any attempt at that would be genocidal practice (see Butler 2012: 143; 150). Likewise, our claims for autonomy are void because of our unavoidable "global connectedness" (Butler 2012: 138). After all, our claim that we are autonomous comes from the vulnerability we feel through our exposure to the Other. This may go some way towards explaining the reserve with which some critics and audience members approach verbatim theatre, particularly in instances where it confronts them with their own precariousness.

This exposure is both the reason why we need more theatre companies that practise communal verbatim, as well as the reason why it attracts so much criticism. When verbatim theatre presents its version of the reality of an event, incident or topic, and it clashes with our own understanding of it, we have to face up to our precarious state, both in Butler's terms as well as Johnson's state of uncertainty due to dependency on an Other's perspective. The feeling of precariousness derives from the fact that we are all unavoidably connected (see Butler 2012: 138; 140–141), and so there is no way for us to opt out of engaging with whichever events or issues are presented to us. If the version of a given reality that is portrayed clashes with our own, the latter will be exposed as constructed. To take Soans as an example again, when a play presents 'talking to terrorists' as the only solution to the problem and we oppose this view, we are not forced to accept it, but we still cannot forbear to open ourselves up onto it. Qua its existence, it automatically becomes part of our own world.

Generally, verbatim theatre aims for a coherent representation of a subject matter that can be complex and can contain many different points of view. As already discussed above, every depiction of reality must necessarily be reduced through the use of an inevitably subjective filter and thus, no piece of (documentary) art or even scientific research can ever claim unassailable, absolute, objective truth; no serious artist, scientist or scholar would suggest otherwise; and no audience should be fooled by opposite claims or (play)texts that deploy emotional manipulation in order to elicit audience reactions.[4] Thus, verbatim theatre's offer of its point of view can be accepted by spectators or not, as audiences are not only welcome, but expected to make up their own minds.

Lastly, I would like to address the issue of verbatim theatre's relation to 'the real'. As opposed to common belief, I argue that this relation is highly overrated. As much as some political verbatim promises the 'uncovering of hidden truths' (see Esch-van Kan 2011: 414; 416), verbatim theatre in general does not seek to assume the role of journalism even though it sometimes borrows its research techniques. According to Nicholas Kent, one of the main reasons for the use of verbatim theatre is that it is "a way of making plays to deal with certain issues" and that "[y]ou can respond more quickly with verbatim than you can with a fictional drama" (2013: 152). This is not to say that fictional drama is never fed by 'real' events or people. The main difference from verbatim theatre is the latter's endeavour to preserve the real material in its original form, i.e. in verbatim. As any artist involved in verbatim theatre will undoubtedly be aware, this form of theatre can only ever present one version of reality and so what it can achieve through editing is to keep the collaged pieces of the material visible, thus fusing the 'real' with the fictional. Of course, what in the visual arts would look unmistakeably collage-esque is lost in the uniform font and layout of the playtext. However, the higher the degree of self-reflexivity of the verbatim play, the more the stitches of the devising and editing process remain visible, as noted above in the case of *The Laramie Project*, in which Kaufman makes an effort to regularly point to the play's devising process. Likewise, even though the spoken words are preserved in their original wording, the long process of interviews, editing, rehearsal and performance invariably leads to a multi-layered diffraction of verbatim theatre's assumed immediacy.

---

4 Consider particularly Jessica Blank and Erik Jensen's *The Exonerated* (2002; publ. 2004) and their personal take on their responsibility as artists: their prime motive is to bring about social change through compassionate listening and emotional involvement "on an immediate, human level" (Blank and Jensen 2010). They are thereby rather lax when it comes to adhering to verbatim theatre's 'protocol': "*With a few exceptions*, each word spoken in this play comes from the public record" (Blank and Jensen 2006: 8; emphasis added).

The Precariousness of (not) Talking to Terrorists

As already noted above, verbatim theatre's main aim is not to pry or expose, but to understand. Kaufman explains that "[t]he idea of *The Laramie Project* originated in my desire to learn more about why Matthew Shepard was murdered, about what happened that night, about the town of Laramie" (Kaufman et al., *The Laramie Project*: vi). Likewise, with *The Power of Yes: A Dramatist Seeks to Understand the Financial Crisis* (2009), Hare is out to do the same thing. This goes back to Peter Weiss, who postulates that documentary theatre cannot merely show a state of affairs, but that it should portray the reasons for it and then illustrate how it could be remedied (see 2011: 518). Similarly, *Talking to Terrorists* does not merely demonstrate that terrorism is a menace, but offers suggestions for how we might try to tackle it – seeing that *not* talking to terrorists has, so far, not yielded the desired effects. Aleks Sierz's criticism that the play missed the point because "it is precisely the terrorists that won't talk to us that are the problem" (2011: 72) may be partly true, but it is void of any suggestion as to how, that being the case, we should deal with terrorism.

Concerning the two strands of verbatim theatre that I introduced above, *Talking to Terrorists* borrows from both with a slight orientation towards political verbatim. Even though there are instances where political verbatim is used to elicit a desired emotional response from the spectator – which is what Blank and Jensen deliberately do in *The Exonerated* and which can be said of Brittain and Slovo's *Guantanamo* as well – most plays have the goal of arriving at some kind of understanding of specific events. Kent, who co-directed the original production of *Guantanamo*, openly admits that the play "was blatantly a campaigning piece of work, yes, against the injustice of holding people indefinitely in detention without trial and without any charge" (2013: 150). With every verbatim piece he himself is involved in, his "attempt, in using verbatim, is always to get as near to the truth as you can" (2013: 153). Kent is surely aware of the fact that presenting a *version* of reality is all verbatim theatre can do, regardless of the playwright's motive and/or motivation. Hare, Kaufman, and Soans all claim in some way that they use their (research for the) play to try to understand the phenomenon under examination in order to arrive at some *form* of truth – about the financial crisis (*The Power of Yes*), homophobia (*The Laramie Project*), and terrorism (*Talking to Terrorists*) respectively.

Talking to Terrorists offers an excellent ground for the application of Butler's understanding of precariousness. Just like our vulnerability is not chosen, but given, so is our ethical obligation toward the Other (see Butler 2012: 136–140). The issues Butler raises during her inquiry into an ethics of the Other can be pushed to their limits if applied to Soans's play. Soans asks us to recognise terrorists as equally vulnerable beings for whom we are ethically responsible – we, quite literally, "find ourselves invariably joined to those we *never chose*" (Butler 2012: 134; emphasis added). Butler is critical of communitarian positions that "tend to figure ethical relations as binding upon those whose face we can see, whose name we can know and pronounce, those we can already recognize, whose form and face are familiar" (2012: 135). Soans's play can be seen as an attempt to challenge these communitarian views by asking spectators to acknowledge that 'even' terrorists solicit us ethically.

Of course, verbatim theatre cannot facilitate an actual ethical encounter. However, it is probably as close as we can get to terrorists explaining their doings to us. Terrorism most certainly falls into the category of "something that is beyond our will, not of our making, that comes to us from the outside, as an imposition but also as an ethical demand" (Butler 2012: 135). These ethical obligations are precontractual (see Butler 2012: 135), regardless of the Other's physical proximity. If we are only bound to those who are close to us, then our ethics are "invariably parochial, communitarian, and exclusionary. If I am only bound to those who are 'human' in the abstract, then I avert every effort to translate culturally between my own situation and that of others" (Butler 2012: 138). This aspect is exactly what lies at the heart of the "ideology of violence", which is addressed thus in *Talking to Terrorists*:

> EDWARD: The key to the ideology of violence is to see your enemy as sub-human. They're only Jews, gays, blacks, not normal in any sense of the word.
> N.R.A.: Think of them as animals... look at them... they speak a different language, they're dark, black, and very evil. Think of them as scary things... you'll find it much easier to kill them. (59–60)

By dehumanising terrorists, we can categorically condemn their actions. By dehumanising their victims, terrorists find it easier to kill. Both strategies yield ethically undesirable results. As a reason for his play, Soans explains that he is "not in the job of condoning or excusing these people at all". Rather, his "point is to try and find out more about them. Isn't it responsible to do that? Isn't it good that the theatre can do that?" (Soans 2005b).

Kent's insight that verbatim theatre's *forté* is its ability to respond (see 2013: 152) resonates with Levinas's philosophy of the Other and Butler's demand for "answerability" (Butler 2012: 141; see also 135–137 and 142). In addition, Jacques Derrida's later work is, of course, occupied by questions of response and responsibility (see Silverman 2007), while Hans-Thies Lehmann speaks of an 'aesthetic of response-ability' (see 2006: 185). By honouring its response-ability, verbatim theatre can elicit compassion and 'culturally translate' (see Butler 2012: 138) between the spectator's situation and that of the characters portrayed. It can thus help audiences to recognise and deal with their own precariousness by offering an attempt at a "global response", an "ethical recognition and connection" that strives to safeguard "something of the reality of the event" (Butler 2012: 138). By encouraging the 'talking to terrorists' and by doing it himself, Soans acknowledges his responsibility for a suffering he did not make (see Butler 2012: 135). Wherever we can trace this responsibility in verbatim plays, verbatim theatre is "accepting and negotiating the multilocality and cross-temporality of ethical connections" (Butler 2012: 138), not least because in its devising process it reverses proximity and distance by bringing one community's stories to the performance space of another, where this Other is, in turn, ethically solicited by the performance imposed upon him or her – imposed, because audiences might be confronted with images they did not deliberately choose to see (see Butler 2012: 135–137). At the same time, verbatim theatre cannot transcend the "obdurate thereness" (Butler 2012: 137) of the original interviews given in Laramie, London or any other place, from where they were transported to a rehearsal space and then to a multitude of public stages. Likewise, verbatim theatre can never fully transcend its own precariousness.

Conclusion

In her version of the theory of cohabitation, Butler states that we never have a choice as regards with whom we cohabit the earth, as much as we can never be relieved from our ethical obligations towards the Other:

> [S]ince we do not choose with whom to cohabit the earth, we have to honor those obligations to preserve the lives of those we may not love, those we may never love, do not know, and did not choose. (2012: 150)

Therefore, my ethical relation to another can never rely on reciprocity or, in the case of terrorism, on the idea that my life is equally valued by the Other. Quoting Levinas, Butler establishes that "reciprocity cannot be the basis of ethics, since ethics is not a bargain" (2012: 140). However, she criticises Levinas's "exclusionary assumptions", insisting "upon a certain intertwinement between that other life, all those other lives, and my own – one that is irreducible to national belonging or communitarian affiliation" (2012: 140). From her point of view, "individual life makes no sense, has no reality, outside of the social and political framework in which all lives are equally valued" (2012: 143):

> In my view (which is surely not mine alone) the life of the other, the life that is *not* our own, is also our life, since whatever sense 'our' life has is derived precisely from this sociality, this being already, and from the start, dependent on a world of others, constituted in and by a social world. (2012: 140–141)

As ethical beings, we can choose with whom we wish to surround ourselves, what we see or consume but, under the same premise, we cannot eradicate all that we have not chosen. Analogously, we can decide not to talk to terrorists and not to watch verbatim plays about them, but we nevertheless should not question these plays' right to existence, and condone the artists' points of view or their choice of artistic representation or genre.

This essay has introduced a distinction between the communal and political strands of verbatim theatre and applied Butler's concept of precariousness to show that both strands can go a long way towards meeting her demand on us to fulfil our ethical obligations towards all Others who cohabit the earth with us. Political verbatim can counter communitarian tendencies by facilitating a (mediated) encounter with Others beyond distance and proximity. Communal verbatim can train critical thinking and emancipation through its distinctive self-reflexivity. Siding with Rubik, I argue that audiences are not so naïve as to expect all truths to be revealed in a theatrical performance. However, because verbatim theatre vouches to only use 'real' spoken evidence, the events and issues presented have a direct significance for our lives. All the more are audiences therefore advised to fulfil their role as emancipated spectators, whereby they are to "learn from as opposed to being seduced by images" (Rancière 2011: 4). The self-reflexivity of communal verbatim is a helpful tool along the way, and the polarising tendencies of political verbatim are a useful testing ground for the state of our emancipation. With its particular ability to both respond ethically to an issue by putting it on stage, and to elicit an ethical response from its spectators-as-witnesses, verbatim theatre lends itself to being a tool of education, both in terms of the reception process, as well as by lending a voice to diverse points of view – may they come from a community, like the people of Laramie, or may they 'just' be individuals who wish to have their story heard on a public stage, like the former terrorists in Soans's play. In this way, verbatim theatre assumes a responsibility towards both its audiences and its subject matter, as well as towards theatre itself through its doubly 'response-able' process.

Works Cited

Blank, Jessica and Erik Jensen. 2006 [2004]. *The Exonerated*. London: Faber.
Blank, Jessica and Erik Jensen. 2010. "Verbatim Theatre: The People's Voice?" *guardian.co.uk*, 15 July. <http://www.guardian.co.uk/stage/theatreblog/2010/jul/15/verbatim-theatre-aftermath> [accessed 1 February 2015].
Bottoms, Stephen. 2006. "Putting the Document into Documentary: An Unwelcome Corrective?" *TDR* 50.3: 56–68.
Brittain, Victoria and Gillian Slovo. 2004. *Guantanamo: 'Honor Bound to Defend Freedom': Taken from Spoken Evidence*. London: Oberon.
Butler, Judith. 2012. "Precarious Life, Vulnerability, and the Ethics of Cohabitation". *Journal of Speculative Philosophy* 26.2: 134–151.
Esch-van Kan, Anneka. 2011. "The Documentary Turn in Contemporary British Drama and the Return of the Political: David Hare's *Stuff Happens* and Richard Norton-Taylor's *Called to Account*". In: Sibylle Baumbach, Birgit Neumann and Ansgar Nünning (eds.). *A History of British Drama: Genres – Developments – Model Interpretations*. Trier: WVT. 413–428.
Hare, David. 2004. *Stuff Happens*. London: Faber.
Hare, David. 2009. *The Power of Yes: A Dramatist Seeks to Understand the Financial Crisis*. London: Faber.
Johnson, Samuel. 1968 [1755]. *A Dictionary of the English Language*. London: W. Strahan. Repr. Heidelberg: Olms.
Kaufman, Moisés. 1998. *Gross Indecency: The Three Trials of Oscar Wilde*. New York: Vintage.
Kaufman, Moisés and the members of the Tectonic Theatre Project. 2001. *The Laramie Project*. New York: Vintage.
Kent, Nicholas. 2013 [2008]. "Nicholas Kent". Interview with Will Hammond and Dan Steward. In: Will Hammond and Dan Steward (eds.). *Verbatim Verbatim: Contemporary Documentary Theatre*. London: Oberon. 133–168.
Lehmann, Hans-Thies. 2006 [1999]. *Postdramatic Theatre*. Trans. Karen Jürs-Munby. London and New York: Routledge.
Look Left Look Right. 2010. *Counted? A Documentary-Play about British Democracy*. Dirs. Steve Bottoms, Ben Freedman and Mimi Poskitt. Debating Chamber, County Hall, London, 15 April–22 May. Theatre production.
Norton-Taylor, Richard. 2014 [1999]. *The Colour of Justice: Based on the Transcripts of the Stephen Lawrence Inquiry*. In: Victoria Brittain, et al. (eds.). *The Tricycle: Collected Tribunal Plays 1994–2012*. London: Oberon. 291–415.
Paget, Derek. 1987. "'Verbatim Theatre': Oral History and Documentary Techniques". *New Theatre Quarterly* 3.12: 317–336.
Paget, Derek. 2011. *No Other Way to Tell It: Docudrama on Film and Television*. 2nd ed. Manchester and New York: Manchester UP.
Rancière, Jacques. 2011 [2008]. *The Emancipated Spectator*. Trans. Gregory Elliott. London and New York: Verso.
Reinelt, Janelle. 2006. "Toward a Poetics of Theatre and Public Events: In the Case of Stephen Lawrence". *TDR* 50.3: 69–87.
Rubik, Margarete. 2010. "Documentary Drama: David Hare". In: Merle Tönnies (ed.). *Das englische Drama der Gegenwart: Kategorien – Entwicklungen – Modellinterpretationen*. Trier: WVT. 65–80.
Sierz, Aleks. 2011. *Rewriting the Nation: British Theatre Today*. London: Methuen Drama.

Silverman, Hugh J. 2007. "Response-abilities for Legacies: Jacques – on vous suit à travers vos texts". *Mosaic* 40.2: 297–306.
Soans, Robin. 2005a. *Talking to Terrorists*. London: Oberon.
Soans, Robin. 2005b. "Should Terrorists Be Given a Voice?" Interview with Dominic Cavendish. *telegraph.co.uk*, 23 April. <http://www.telegraph.co.uk/culture/theatre/drama/3640875/Should-terrorists-be-given-a-voice.html> [accessed 29 April 2013].
Weiss, Peter. 2011 [1968]. "Das Material und die Modelle: Notizen zum dokumentarischen Theater". In: Peter Langemeyer (ed.). *Dramentheorie: Texte vom Barock bis zur Gegenwart*. Stuttgart: Reclam. 511–518.

José R. Prado
Spaces for the Construction of Community: The Theatre Uncut Phenomenon

> Aha! Now I know how to deal with you. What a fool I was not to think of it before! You can't take away the knowledge you gave me. You said I had a finer ear than you. And I can be civil and kind to people, which is more than you can. (Shaw, *Pygmalion*: 113)

In *Pygmalion* (1941), Bernard Shaw articulates a form of relational politics in the final quarrel between Eliza and Higgins. In her final discovery and transformation, from dependent to autonomous woman, Eliza resorts to the trope of knowledge as the good that Higgins has given her and that cannot be taken away from her once she has acquired it. Her independence is the consequence of the exchange of what political philosophers such as Nussbaum (see 1986, 2010) have termed 'immaterial' or 'relational' goods. Knowledge presupposes the act of sharing and thus disrupts the ideology of individualism and self-profit. It is a transaction that does not involve material goods and whose outcomes are not material benefits, but immaterial ones that must, however, be realised by the participants, since they cannot be enjoyed without the active transformation of the force or potential that they inscribe in us. Thus, the act of sharing involved in education and the transmission of knowledge opens the in-between space that Jean-Luc Nancy (see 1991) has described as community and Hannah Arendt (see 2005: 93) has defined as 'the political'. Equally, Eliza's self-awareness springs from affects, that is, her anger and indignation at not being given credit for her share in the relational process involving teacher and pupil. It is from this encounter (Spinoza's *occursus*) that the relational situation emanates, prompting affect and finally the emergence of relationality through the channelling of such affects, as Gilles Deleuze points out in his account of Spinozist theories (see Deleuze 1978–1981).

Eliza seeks affects, but she is forced to move into the realm of individualism, which Higgins aptly identifies as middle-class morality. In terms of immaterial or relational goods, the end product is transformed during the process, and most importantly, it constitutes itself in the process of becoming and when the potential spaces that have been opened are adopted as one's own. Material goods, however, cannot go through the final process that activates difference and individuality and which emanates from an act of relational community.

My contention in this chapter is that the Theatre Uncut phenomenon can be explained and understood as a successful attempt at political engagement that relies on the mobilisation of relational goods (see Donati 2014; Uhlaner 2014) and political affects (see Castells 2012; Deleuze 1978–1981; Nussbaum 2010). From a relational perspective (see Nancy 1991; Arendt 2005), it may be argued that Theatre Uncut articulates the contradictions inherent in engaged, politically committed artistic ventures, making those contradictions work in its favour. Theatre Uncut cuts across categories and divisions so as to challenge the ideological foundations that constitute the nature of neoliberal individualism and its Hobbesian understanding of community: either as an aggregate of individuals, or as a community of interest directed towards self-preservation or defence from outside threats.

In his monumental *The Empathic Civilization*, Jeremy Rifkin describes the millennial youth as developing a dramaturgical consciousness:

> Where privacy was the coveted value of a bourgeois generation which defined freedom in terms of autonomy and exclusivity, access is the most sought after value of the Millennial Generation, which defines freedom in terms of the depth and scope of one's relationships. Exclusivity has become less important than inclusivity, and the competitive ethos is beginning to be challenged – albeit tentatively – by an ethos of collaboration. (2012: 571)

By resorting to relationality, Rifkin directly confronts some of the major tenets of neoliberal ideology, namely, individualism and meritocracy (see Gilbert 2013; Littler 2013), as the engines of social, economic and cultural evolution. Theatre Uncut shares that relational consciousness, which allows its focus to shift from product to process and to posit a decentralised structure where power can be seized and appropriated by participants in the project. This opens a potential artistic space for activism by making the creative material accessible to any person willing to use it for their own particular aims or purposes. Jacques Rancière suggests that

> [the] aesthetic experience has a political effect to the extent that the loss of destination it presupposes disrupts the way in which bodies fit their functions and destinations [...]. It is a multiplication of connections and disconnections that reframe the relation between bodies, the world they live in and the way in which they are 'equipped' to adapt to it. [... I]t allows for new modes of political construction of common objects and new possibilities of collective enunciation. (2009: 72)

Manuel Castells (see 2012: 147) emphasises that the process becomes the product in the network society, since the emergence of fresh patterns of relationality indicates a departure from and transformation of the previous modes of relating to one another and the world.

Relinquishing control of the project and leaving it in the hands of potential participants implies the mobilisation of affects as regards their own political stance, commitment and sympathies. Thus, the Theatre Uncut collective becomes a political subject irrespective of the outcomes and effectiveness of their political act. Not surprisingly, the participatory and assembly-style structure of Theatre Uncut resembles the one developed by social movements of protest such as Occupy or the Spanish 15M 'Indignados'. The major difference lies in the space they inhabit, since Theatre Uncut does not share a common physical location where all members cohabit. Their common ground is rather an immaterial one based on their producing a performance that is presented simultaneously around the world by a number of heterogeneous groups or collectives. The act of engagement acquires, then, a resonance that goes beyond the specific political message of any particular play, configuring itself as a space of relationality that becomes the reality and the principle by which individuals and groups behave (see Bourdieu 1999: 47).

Similarly, Theatre Uncut can bridge the apparent contradiction of the individual and collectivity. From a relational perspective, there would be no contradiction "in believing that the self is made up of the sum total of experiences that an individual is embedded in over a lifetime, and the idea that those same embedded relationships and experiences make one a unique being, different from all others" (Rifkin 2012: 575–576). In the case of Theatre Uncut, there is not, strictly speaking, an individual, but a group, thus the set of relationships opens up into a *mise en abyme* that makes it resistant to solidification or objectification by subverting any traditional hierarchy. Theatre Uncut resists homogenisation in its protest or political practice because the set of relationships arising from each individual project and performance will per force be unique and different from the others, as will the relationships between those and the coordinating nucleus. And equally relevant, they are constituted as ephemeral.

To avoid the emergence of oppressive types of community, it is necessary to acknowledge the precarious nature of relationality in terms of the vulnerability derived from exposure to encounters. Rifkin describes rigid community formations as based on constitutive relations of fear and self-preservation that thwart the transformative potential of precariousness:

> If we fall prey to an undifferentiated global 'we', we may find ourselves back to square one, when we lived in the undifferentiated mythological fog, with little sense of self and only a rudimentary sense of empathic distress built into our biology. (2012: 575)

It could be argued that the present time shows a return to the mythological 'we' by way of a totalising ideology that has become hegemonic and has (apparently) solved the contradiction between the 'we' and the 'individual' by reducing every aspect of existence to economic interpretations and the neoliberal notion of community mentioned above. Again, Theatre Uncut resists any such reductionism by giving the opportunity to reclaim a voice and a narrative that can be built individually and collectively simultaneously. In fact, Theatre Uncut engages successfully with globalisation's strategies: it disseminates power and freedom through 'externalisation' among citizens willing to seize them of their own accord in order to protest. Theatre Uncut mobilises affects in the opposite direction of economic globalisation: individuals coming together and performing acts of sharing in the global community, as opposed to the amorphous 'we' of corporations and economic interests.

Theatre Uncut challenges traditional, non-participatory dramatic modes by opening the theatrical event to the audience in the post-show talks, thus blurring the gap between stage and auditorium and stimulating active spectatorship. As Rancière puts it in relation to what he terms the 'aesthetic community', "all forms of art can rework the frame of our perceptions and the dynamism of our affects. As such, they can open up new passages towards new forms of political subjectivation" (2009: 82). Specifically, the structure of the Theatre Uncut interventions relies on the concept of appeal. A number of committed playwrights volunteer short pieces that tackle a topic suggested by project coordinators, Emma Callender and Hanna Price. In 2013, the prompt was, "Do we become more conservative in times of austerity?". Three of the playwrights who contributed focused on racism and immigration (Tanika Gupta's *Project N.I.G.H.T.*; Neil LaBute's *Pick One*; Mark Thomas's *Church Forced To Put Up Gates After Font Is Used As Wash Basin By Migrants*), while the other four explored the contradictions of political ideologies in times of crisis (Davey Anderson's *True or False*; Clara Brennan's *The Wing*; Kieran Hurley's *Amanda*; Tim Price's *Capitalism Is Crisis*).

This call for participation acts as an interpellation reminiscent of Judith Butler's concepts of solicitation and exposure in relation to precariousness and the ethical obligation:

> We are, despite ourselves, open to this imposition, and though it overrides our will, it shows us that the claims that others make upon us are part of our very sensibility, our receptivity, and our answerability. We are, in other words, called upon, and this is only possible because we are in some sense vulnerable to claims that we cannot anticipate in advance, and for which there is no adequate preparation. (2012: 141)

The acceptance of the call by theatrical companies, social collectives or individuals reveals what Butler defines as 'ethical responsiveness' (see 2012: 142), that is, the prior willingness to engage that is brought to the fore the moment the response is made. In the case of Theatre Uncut, the exposure to the political implied in responding contains also an agentive potential and a subversive role, which Erinn C. Gilson equates with the capacity for resisting dominant oppressive practices:

> By responding, we speak directly to a problem by addressing its conditions. [... A] response does not operate as a resolution to a problem, but expresses and gives voice to the problem itself, making the depth of the difficulty appear to us. (2014: 88)

Taking control over one's protest can only result from accepting the unpredictability of encounters. In that sense, the Theatre Uncut project draws on the precariousness of the participators' position in relation to their political claims. Additionally, its organizational structure fosters opportunities for those encounters to occur, which may disclose the vulnerable nature of the enterprise, since the set of relations that are released and developed in the course of such encounters cannot be controlled in advance. The three plays selected for analysis in this chapter, Price's *Capitalism Is Crisis*, Gupta's *Project N.I.G.H.T.* and Brennan's *The Wing*, dramatise precariousness by addressing two of its salient features: exposure to encounters, and the reversibility of any given or fixed social position (see Derrida 2000: 9).

Capitalism Is Crisis shows the failure to articulate encounters between the two main characters, Gemma and Alex, problematising in such a manner their act of protest, while bringing to the fore the difficulties inherent in attempting to establish communities simply on the grounds of a shared physical space. The characters walk in opposite directions regarding their vital experiences at the Occupy encampment. Such reversibility of roles suggests the vulnerable positions they inhabit in the social microcosm of the camp. The fact that Price resorts to the device of synchronising their utterances at certain moments in the play increases the gulf between the characters, and acts as a barrier against any encounter that might bring about a felicitous experience.

Gupta's play articulates the encounter with the Other, in this case the illegal immigrant housekeeper Fauzia, and her master, the racist politician Nigel Johnson. The exposure to this asymmetrical encounter has a positive effect for Fauzia, the *a priori* subaltern. She turns the situation of domination into one of equality by becoming the law-abiding citizen, in contrast with the criminal Nigel. Though the encounter exposes Nigel's contradictions for the benefit of the audience, he remains unaffected by its transformative potential. Nevertheless, his exposure underlines the precariousness inherent in the reversibility of the characters' roles: Nigel's failure to identify such precariousness brings about his downfall, whereas for Fauzia it becomes the source for potential liberation.

In *The Wing*, the transformative potential of encounters is reflected upon through a focus on family ties and the articulation of a positive Foucauldian biopolitics, similar to Butler's notion of unchosen co-habitation (see 2012: 145). Father and daughter are made to negotiate their positions and realign their affects in relation to one another. Accepting the Other through their encounter also means accepting their own vulnerability, which opens up the possibility for a new set of relations to emerge in their engagement with each other and with the world.

Relationality, Precariousness and Community: *Capitalism Is Crisis* by Tim Price

In *Postmodern Ethics*, Zygmunt Bauman resorts to Victor Turner's distinction between 'communitas' and 'societas':

> [T]ravellers must first pass through *communitas*, which in terms of the *societas* is a limbo, a void, a nowhere. [...] If *societas* is characterized by its heterogeneity, inequality, differentiation of statuses, system of nomenclature, *communitas* is marked by homogeneity, equality, absence of status, anonymity. [...C]*ommunitas* melts what *societas* tries hard to cast and forge. Alternatively, *societas* moulds and shapes and solidifies what inside *communitas* is liquid and lacks form. (2004: 117)

In fact, societas is the place where stratification and neoliberal categorisation can and do take place. Communitas, conversely, eludes classification and appropriation. Adopting an in-between position in constant process and transformation, community constitutes a space of relations that become resistant to occlusion from the outside. Once one engages in the network of sharing that is community, it is not possible to claim back that which has been shared and, thus, exposed to the community. Moreover, one has already contributed to the on-going process and transformation of community.

This is, I will argue, what happens to the characters in Price's *Capitalism Is Crisis*. The play exposes the contradiction or paradox of community as a contingent phenomenon in a constant state of transformation or Deleuzian 'becoming'. In both their antithetical processes of transformation, the main characters, Alex and Gemma, undergo mirror experiences with opposite outcomes due to their different contextual origins and points of departure. For Alex, the Occupy experience becomes a liberating one, freeing him from any responsibility in the exercise of his newly acquired autonomy. Conversely, for Gemma, it implies an enhancing of responsibility that raises her level of exigency and critical awareness, ultimately leading to scepticism. In their own ways, both contribute to enlarging the scope of the movement and the audience's understanding and problematisation of the phenomenon, even though, or especially because, their experiences are ambivalent and contradictory. Indeed, their social roles are revealed as precarious, open to change and mutability when exposed to unexpected encounters which undermine any stable ideological stances the characters might have held (see Derrida 2000: 9).

At the flagship performance at the Young Vic (23 November 2013), the staging was as minimal as it was effective in presenting this sense of singularity in community: both actors sat on plastic chairs facing the audience and remained in this position throughout, but for a few moments when they stood. Their lack of interaction depicted their isolation and their epiphanies as personal, individual occurrences, at the same time as it highlighted their inability to find moments of connectedness. Price seems to reflect on the inadequacies of community expressed as failures to engage in acts of sharing (see Gilbert 2013; Nancy 1991) that exchange or produce immaterial goods. Similarly, the Young Vic performance foregrounded the incomplete nature of Alex's and Gemma's respective experiences through their inability to have an actual encounter, even though they share the same physical space. The ending has them interacting in a final dialogue where the possibility of such an exchange is glimpsed, but ultimately fails to materialise: "And I try to think of kissing her, but I can't because all I can see, is me asking her 'what are you for?'" (Price, *Capitalism Is Crisis*: n. pag.).

What appear to be centripetal forces that threaten to tear the Occupy London movement apart provide an element of strength when it comes to avoiding a homogeneous depiction of this protest community. The audience, for its part, may understand this as a valuable problematisation of the contradictions inherent to political activism, thereby rejecting over-simplistic representations of utopianism. The suggestion of a community that is never accomplished and which needs to be worked upon continuously to bypass any danger of solidification follows the logic of the network society (see Castells 2012: 222), self-constructed and based on perpetual connectivity. People who belong to specific networks co-evolve through multiple and permanent interactions, and they do so of their own choice and in terms of their own circumstances (see Castells 2012: 221).

In the case of *Capitalism Is Crisis*, the elements that underpin the network society are laid bare in front of the audience. Even though the physical space necessary for the potential encounter to take place – the Occupy camp, the stage, the theatrical event – has been created, and so have the conditions for relations to emerge, the mental and social spaces the two characters inhabit stand wide apart. This state of affairs reflects Castells's (see 2012: 226) argument, itself reminiscent of Wittgenstein's notion of 'grammars of change' (see Marquis 2014), that social change takes place first in the minds of people. Social movements aspire to empower citizens to participate by discussing their lives, with a view to eliciting the self-trust necessary for them to make decisions about the political establishment.

The audience is asked to apprehend the characters' transformations as unsatisfactory due to the coexistence of contradictory forces at play. Gemma's spiritual death presupposes Alex's birth as complementary opposites. The satisfaction that the audience might derive from witnessing the characters' processes of becoming and learning does not always necessarily result in a positive or gratifying experience. In fact, Gemma's engagement with the abstract world of neoliberal efficiency within the Occupy camp alienates her from the actual force of the protest, based on engaging in human relationships or affective encounters, from which she is estranged by the corrupting influence of money:

> GEMMA: Do you know what we could do with that money, if we just chose one thing? One campaign. Just did one thing really well, and fucked the rest. We could close a fucking power plant. We could sue a corporation. We could bring down the City of London. But they want to spread it around so it has no impact everywhere [sic]. I'm fucking over it. We don't share because it's a good idea. We share because we're too fucking scared of trampling over someone else. So sit around, changing nothing. I am over this bullshit. [...] I am over this fucking Occupation. (Price, *Capitalism Is Crisis*: n. pag.)

Gemma's point about sharing is a powerful and ambivalent one. The relation of sharing emerges, for her, from a negative affect or emotion that she is unable to transform into a positive one that may prompt action, in a projection of the paralysis that she intuits in the protest movement (see Castells 2012; Nussbaum 2010). Additionally, the audience becomes aware of its own limitations as a consequence of the relationships of empathy established while witnessing live the antagonistic transformation of the characters. The constant shift of the audience's capacity to empathise with each of the characters signals their metaphorical longing for Alex's and Gemma's experiences to be compatible and complementary, a possibility that is barred in the text. That impossible space signals to the space of community for the audience, one that must be continuously worked upon under shifting social conditions and is therefore always ultimately precarious.

Precarious Spectatorship: Audience Response in Tanika Gupta's *Project N.I.G.H.T.*

Gupta's play dramatises the precariousness of identity through the encounter with the foreign Other in a domestic web of relations where Nigel's objectification of the migrant figure blocks any possibility of interpellation on his part.

However, he, the 'host', is turned into 'hostage' in his encounter with his 'guest', Fauzia (see Derrida 2000: 16), who feels the ethical responsibility to act upon the events she witnesses.

Project N.I.G.H.T. places the audience in a dual position whose aim is to make spectators self-aware of their position as such. The device is quite simple, as is the play, a twelve-minute sketch. Nigel Johnson, an anti-immigration politician, is rehearsing a speech to be delivered in front of an audience of sympathisers. His direct appeal places spectators in the role of the intended addressees, thus forcing or hijacking them into the unasked-for position of attendees to an imaginary political rally. We could call this strategy, by which the audience is made to adopt a role that they might not willingly choose, empathy reversed or negative empathy. Its aim consists in inducing the theatre audience to acknowledge the fragility of any given or stable position they may think they hold by highlighting its relatively straightforward reversibility. A situation that, I will argue, mirrors that of the play's action, where Fauzia's and Nigel's roles are reversed at the end of the piece. And, even though the play's ending is resolved unambiguously by condemning the hypocritical politician, the audience are left in an in-between space where they are asked to consider their own engagement in empathic relations as a solicitation that they cannot reject (see Butler 2012). The dogmatic lack of self-awareness and empathy on the part of Nigel Johnson contributes to enhancing such a perception.[1]

Interaction with non-conventional audiences helps unfold the double nature of the play in terms of audience reception. When performed in front of a prison audience consisting mostly of Spanish offenders, identification rested with Nigel Johnson. Questions in the pre- and post-show talks with the male and female inmates focused on the politician, with a Spanish inmate of Romani/gypsy ethnic origin stating that he would like to perform his part, in what constituted a strong case of identification with the anti-immigration ideas that are parodied in the text. An inmate of Maghrebi origin with a limited understanding of Spanish identified with the message as victim, fearing the possibility of being deported as a consequence of the politician's words, and had to be reassured by the prison teachers that the show was critical of anti-immigration policies. In this case,

---

[1] The following discussion draws on the performances of the play carried out by an amateur theatre group in the city of Castellón, Spain, with which the author was involved as part of the cast. The choice of venues and audiences was not targeted in any way; it was the result of the group's contacts and the accessibility offered by the venues themselves. Comments on audience response are derived from the workshops and the pre- and post-show talks. As such, they reflect the immediate, on-site reactions of audiences and performers alike.

the living reality of this person made him perceive the play as factual account rather than fictional or artistic experience.²

A performance for a group of African migrant women of mixed ethnic and religious condition at Cáritas, a Catholic social organisation, shifted audience identification towards the woman character in the play, Fauzia, a Muslim migrant from Albania who acts as cleaner for Nigel Johnson. In this case, the women, in spite of all the cultural limitations concerning speaking in public, peer pressure by own group and the presence of a male actor in the discussions, spoke openly of how the role of Fauzia was felt as authentic as opposed to the politician's, investing their own living experiences in the fictional woman character. In the play, Fauzia rebels against her master and takes the active role of a good citizen in the community in a comic reversal of fortunes. The final words she addresses to Johnson are enlightening: "You have nothing to fear if all you have done is legal" (Gupta, *Project N.I.G.H.T.*: 5).

As regards what could be termed more sophisticated theatre audiences, that is, spectators who attend theatre performances regularly and are trained to decode them in artistic terms, both reactions above are combined in reverse: intellectually, they are compelled to reject the xenophobic message, in a gesture that does not challenge their pre-established beliefs. On the other hand, the play's strategy seems to indicate that such a response would be insufficient if it is not complemented with the adoption of an informed opposition that can tackle directly Nigel's claims: Nigel has no problem living with the contradiction of demonising migrants, while, at the same time, profiting from them as cheap labour. His totalitarian ideological stance must be challenged, then, through a dual process that comprises raising indignation in the first instance, to moving beyond it by shifting the focus from ideologies to human relations. The response of a small audience of about twelve persons in a pub performance, who were sympathetic with the play's political message, suggested that such was the case. One person mentioned that she could not see the point of Nigel's diatribes, no matter how ridiculous they sounded, until Fauzia took action in her hands at the end of the play. This audience's laughter was of a nervous type, which revealed how uncomfortable they felt about the mixture of humour with issues invested with seriousness and drama. *Project N.I.G.H.T.* was not chosen for performance at the Young Vic in November 2013. But I would claim audience

---

2 The workshop before the performance included the actor taking up the part of Nigel Johnson transforming from casually dressed, average person into sophisticated politician wearing a suit, hair gel, etc., so as to try and create a certain alienating effect. The treatment of text and performance as farce might account for the effects of audience identification, due to farce's strong reliance on suspension of disbelief.

reactions to the other plays tackling racial matters – LaBute's *Pick One* and Thomas's *Church Forced To Put Up Gates After Font Is Used As Wash Basin By Migrants* – were parallel to the one just described. Such reactions speak of the important role played by the piece's comic element in highlighting Nigel Johnson's grotesque, monstrous nature.

The political message in *Project N.I.G.H.T.* springs from the spectator's ability to recognise a racist stereotype as inhabiting the social landscape of European countries. The exposure of the hypocrisy and lack of foundation of anti-immigration policies, as well as the inconsistencies of politicians, stands in open contrast with the emerging humanity of displaced migrant collectives, thus providing a powerful statement against mechanistic, profit-led positions that rest on exploiting them. Additionally, the play's focus on audience response, as shown in the above examples, discloses the precariousness of the theatrical contract entered upon by the spectators. The interpellation posed by the piece acts upon received notions of migration and xenophobia, either as empowerment (migrant audiences) or decentring (left-wing progressive ones) respectively. The play's demand for an active, critical attitude stresses the precariousness of social roles vis-à-vis external exposure.

The Politics of Affect as Precarious Cohabitation in Clara Brennan's *The Wing*

The flagship performance of Brennan's *The Wing* at the Young Vic in November 2013 showed Mick, the male character, reading from the script during performance, which added to the strategy of blurring the boundaries between art and politics, as well as to the feeling of immediacy and urgency of the performance. The fact that an actor delivers a dramatic reading while his counterpart, Kerry, performs her part disrupts conventional theatrical and artistic categories and what might be acceptable for a paying audience. I would even go as far as to suggest that, had it been included as a directorial choice rather than as an effect derived from the lack of time for longer rehearsals and memorising, it would have constituted a strong alienating element. In *The Wing*, Brennan fudges reality and fantasy by adopting an almost realistic style that is challenged by the surreal image of an actual wing growing on Mick's right arm. The show is conceived as a debate between a young, university-educated daughter, Kerry, and a middle-aged, working-class father, Mick, with left- and right-wing roles stereotypically assigned. While Kerry uses her body as labour by selling her nudity to a right-wing tabloid in order to pay for her education, she also uses her pregnancy as a weapon to denounce the sexist, voyeuristic attitudes of readers who might get aroused by a naked body, but would be disgusted or morally shocked when learning that it is a pregnant one. In that way, Kerry contrasts the still picture of nudity with one of dynamic life, the image of waste versus production, and subverts normative perception and categories by disclosing their patriarchal ideology.

The play revolves around the traditional definition of political commitment and seeks a different engagement with the political that lies closer to the display of affects and people's exploration of living in the world. At the end of their quarrel, Mick must drop any sort of ideological sympathy and accept his daughter, his daughter's black boyfriend and his mixed-race grandchild, to the point of offering them his house, that is, sharing their living space. The validity of ideologies is put to the test by confronting them with practical problems. And those are concerned with real people as human beings having to relate and interact with other human beings in actual living situations. Mick's evolution and physical transformation attests to it; and it is such conditions that open the potential for empathic relations, which Mick develops through listening to his daughter's circumstances and by giving up any racial or conservative prejudices. Consequently, the initial image of a wing growing on Mick's right arm acquires a paradoxical meaning when he states, "And what? Take flight! Maybe I will, maybe I'll turn full bird and migrate myself, eh? I've been trying to work out what I am... first I thought, swallow? Then no... starling, is it? Knowing my luck I'm turning fucking pigeon!" (Brennan, *The Wing*: 10–11). Mick, that is, acknowledges the bird's freedom through its ability to migrate, so his transformation into a bird could be for the better or, as he also admits, for the worse, if he becomes a street pigeon and has to live in precarious urban conditions. His reactions are not consciously articulated as political, unlike Kerry's. However, by building up a father-daughter relationship, the play enables the potential space for politics to be developed.

The various notions of female sexuality, politics and racism explored throughout the play are contested in the face-to-face encounter enacted by the characters. Replacing their safe ideological havens with the uncertainties derived from plunging into the realm of affect defines theirs as a precarious relationship based on learning to cohabit. This state of affairs can and does only arise from their actual physical encounter, placing the act of interpellation at the level of the body and affects, prior to any kind of intellectualisation, and subjected to precariousness and vulnerability.

In sum, this is a political play where a different kind of politics is insinuated, away from traditional ideologies and antagonisms and moving instead towards affects that may culminate in the emergence of relations that cut across differences without cancelling them. Thus, shifting the emphasis to the in-between spaces that constantly spring from situations of contact and exposure may constitute a subversive act. Differences may remain, but the potential for cohabitation opens up with Mick's newly acquired family – a family he has not chosen, and with which he must learn to coexist so as to realise such potentiality.[3] The process described above replicates the Theatre Uncut spirit, its heterogeneous nature glued together by affects, in this case empathy. Emma Callender, co-artistic director of Theatre Uncut, puts it as follows:

> But not everyone we work with shares my beliefs. Our rehearsal rooms are full of questions and arguments, of research and learning. We may not agree – that's the joy – but we always return to the core ingredient needed to create a piece of theatre: empathy. (2013)

Conclusion

In this chapter, I have tried to examine the Theatre Uncut project by linking it to the social movements that have emerged in response to the financial economic crisis and the ideology of neoliberalism. By resorting to relational and affective politics, Theatre Uncut creates community formations that defy the traditional definitions associated with proximity, shared spaces or even common objectives. Such notions are replaced by action: the performance of plays that react against the hegemonic neoliberal ideology. The participating theatre groups that engage in the project do not share the same focus or reasons for taking up action, neither do they target similar audiences. Moreover, the outcomes differ in each context of performance. As a project, it is decentralised and ephemeral, cutting across categories and becoming horizontal in nature. An elusive community is united by 'pure' action, symbolically defying rules and laws, such as artistic compartmentalisation. Theatre Uncut conceives the theatrical act as the precarious space where encounters occur. Consequently, precariousness, understood as the positive, transformative experience capable of challenging established categories of entertainment and artistic political commitment, figures prominently in the project's aspiration at destabilisation and protest.

Opening spaces for action and collaboration by making theatrical tools accessible to participants reveals that the project can be successful when it comes to mobilising affects, rather than subjects or individuals. That potentiality

---

3 This is an example of positive affects and immaterial goods springing up, though one should be aware that it is also possible for negative affects to derive from similar situations, as reality shows us on a daily basis. That the ties are fragile, uncertain and anxiety-ridden is a prerequisite for the play to advance its political message: the transformation of negative affects into positive ones that have the potential for empowerment and agency.

also opens a path towards the exploration of modes of politicisation that rely on immaterial goods. In fact, the self-conscious feeling that something, whether material, symbolic or affective, is being built and shared by lending one's capabilities to the enterprise helps overcome some of the pitfalls of virtual communities, such as the atomised nature of participation and the illusion of communication that would bar, according to Bauman (see 2001), ethical responsibility or commitment. By focusing on the accomplishment of a material task, the performance also triggers the immaterial act of learning. Thus, the act of social protest becomes simultaneously a learning process, understood as the set of relations that are produced and dismantled in the course of each performance at a specific venue. As such, the performance becomes an elusive archive of lived experience. Deciding to participate in the Theatre Uncut project becomes an ethical choice, since responding to such a call implies acting – including political action or activism – in a relational manner. As Gilson points out regarding Foucault, "An ethical response is one that responds to [social norms] as well as responding to others in their relation to them; it confronts the social context – its normative pressures, its hierarchies – in a way that allows self and others to transform themselves" (2014: 96).

To conclude, the definition of alter-globalisation put forward by Barry Freeman and Catherine Graham in relation to performances by Canadian theatre companies aptly describes Theatre Uncut too:

> They have chosen not to organize their work around international markets, but to experiment with new spaces, networks, modes of consumption, and participatory processes [...]. Both the show and the networks forged [...] represent an invitation to the kind of participatory democracy that rejects leaving political decision-making to professionals and creates opportunities to take part in discussions of how we want to organize our collective life. (2014: 6)

Reclaiming public spaces creatively transforms us into active social participants, that is, citizens, while foregrounding the vulnerability derived from these direct interventions in the world. It is such a journey from feigned security towards precariousness that inspires Theatre Uncut, and that practitioners who decide to engage with their project feel compelled to endorse.

Works Cited

Arendt, Hannah. 2005 [1956–1959]. *The Promise of Politics*. Ed. Jerome Kohn. New York: Schocken Books.
Bauman, Zygmunt. 2001. *Community: Seeking Safety in an Insecure World*. Cambridge: Polity.

Bauman, Zygmunt. 2004. *Postmodern Ethics*. Oxford: Blackwell.
Bourdieu, Pierre. 1999 [1994]. *Razones prácticas: Sobre la teoría de la acción*. Barcelona: Anagrama.
Brennan, Clara. 2013. *The Wing*. Theatre Uncut. Unpublished.
Butler, Judith. 2012. "Precarious Life, Vulnerability, and the Ethics of Cohabitation". *Journal of Speculative Philosophy* 26.2: 134–151.
Callender, Emma. 2013. "Theatre Uncut Asks: Do We All Get More Right-Wing in Hard Times?". *The Guardian*, 18 November. <http://www.theguardian.com/culture-professionals-network/culture-professionals-blog/2013/nov/18/theatre-uncut-questions-right-wing> [accessed 23 May 2014].
Castells, Manuel. 2012. *Redes de indignación y esperanza: Los movimientos sociales en la era de internet*. Madrid: Alianza Editorial.
Deleuze, Gilles. 1978–1981. "Lecture Transcripts on Spinoza's Concept of *Affect*". <https://www.gold.ac.uk/media/deleuze_spinoza_affect.pdf> [accessed 30 October 2014].
Derrida, Jacques. 2000 [1999]. "Hostipitality". Trans. Barry Stocker with Forbes Morlock. *Angelaki: Journal of the Theoretical Humanities* 5.3: 3–18.
Donati, Pier Paolo. 2014. "Relational Goods and their Subjects: The Ferment of a New Civil Society and Civil Democracy". *Recerca: Revista de pensament i anàlisi* 14: 19–46.
Freeman, Barry and Catherine Graham. 2014. "Imagining Alternative Globalisations through Performance". *Canadian Theatre Review* 157: 5–6.
Gilbert, Jeremy. 2013. "What Kind of Thing Is 'Neoliberalism'?". *New Formations: A Journal of Culture, Theory and Politics* 80–81: 7–22.
Gilson, Erinn C. 2014. "Ethics and the Ontology of Freedom: Problematization and Responsiveness in Foucault and Deleuze". *Foucault Studies* 17: 76–98.
Gupta, Tanika. 2013. *Project N.I.G.H.T.* Theatre Uncut. Unpublished.
Littler, Jo. 2013. "Meritocracy as Plutocracy: The Marketising of 'Equality' under Neoliberalism". *New Formations: A Journal of Culture Theory and Politics* 80–81: 52–72.
Marquis, Nicolas. 2014. "Utopia in a Liberal World Facing Crisis: Analysis of the New 'Grammars of Change'". *Culture, Language and Representation* 12: 87–112.
Nancy, Jean-Luc. 1991 [1986]. "The Inoperative Community". Trans. Peter Connor. In: Jean-Luc Nancy. *The Inoperative Community*. Ed. Peter Connor. Theory and History of Literature 76. Minneapolis: U of Minnesota P. 1–42.
Nussbaum, Martha C. 1986. *The Fragility of Goodness: Luck and Ethics in Greek Tragedy and Philosophy*. Cambridge: Cambridge UP.
Nussbaum, Martha C. 2010. *Not for Profit: Why Democracy Needs the Humanities*. Princeton: Princeton UP.
Price, Tim. 2013. *Capitalism Is Crisis*. Theatre Uncut. Unpublished.
Rancière, Jacques. 2009 [2008]. *The Emancipated Spectator*. Trans. Gregory Elliott. London and New York: Verso.
Rifkin, Jeremy. 2012. *The Empathic Civilization: The Race to Global Consciousness in a World in Crisis*. Cambridge: Polity.
Shaw, George Bernard. 1990 [1941]. *Pygmalion*. Hardmondsworth: Penguin.
Uhlaner, Carole J. 2014. "Relational Goods and Resolving the Paradox of Political Participation". *Recerca: Revista de pensament i anàlisi* 14: 47–72.

Adina Sorian
Living in Liquid Times: Precariousness and Plasticity in Forced Entertainment's *Tomorrow's Parties*

> Ontologies of the present demand archaeologies of the future, not forecasts of the past.
> (Jameson 2002: 215)

If the overriding concern of much of late twentieth- and early twenty-first century theatre was with memory, trauma, and the capacity of theatre to serve as a vehicle for post-traumatic experience (see in particular Wald 2011; Jürs-Munby 2009), British theatre of the new decade might be said to demonstrate a shift to a concern with the present moment, a conspicuous interest in the 'here and now' that moves beyond the obsession with the past apparently central to late twentieth-century theatre. In his contribution to Vicky Angelaki's 2013 volume on *Contemporary British Theatre*, Chris Megson identifies "a metaphysical turn in British theatre, grounded in the performative evocation of the moment, and which is constitutive of a reach for new values, new possibilities of living, beyond the grip of capitalism, religion and exhausted ideology" (2013: 34).[1] Forced Entertainment's 2011 performance piece *Tomorrow's Parties* represents this tendency most forcefully with its distinctively ethical interest in the present moment – a metaphysical concern in Megson's sense, which in *Tomorrow's Parties* interestingly crystallizes around questions about the future, the piece's more readily apparent content.[2]

In this essay, I argue that by exploring various options about what the future may hold for us, *Tomorrow's Parties* effectively engages in broader, ethical reflection on our present social and political situation. In particular, the piece contemplates what some of the most astute thinkers of our time have been referring to as the 'precariousness' of our contemporary situation, that is, the fragility and vulnerability of today's globalized, post-ideological world, a notion articulated, in various contexts, by theorists from Jean-Luc Nancy to Jacques Derrida to Zyg-

---

[1] The *Oxford Dictionary of English*, which Megson quotes (2013: 34), defines metaphysics as "the branch of philosophy that deals with first principles of things, including abstract concepts such as being, knowing, identity, time, and space" (Soanes and Stevenson 2006: 1104).
[2] In conjunction with the UK premiere of the performance, the University of Sheffield held a one-day symposium entitled "In Imagination: The Future Reflected in Art and Argument", featuring speakers from performance and academic contexts and devoted to exploring the "use of the theatre as a tool to speculate, predict, and conceptualise" ("In Imagination" 2013).

munt Bauman and Judith Butler. I argue further, taking my cue from Catherine Malabou's rereading of Hegel's concept of temporality (Malabou 2005), that *Tomorrow's Parties* offers a more optimistic, lighthearted perspective on our present and future than that produced by the discourse of precariousness so far.

Zygmunt Bauman has perhaps been the most outspoken critic of the precariousness of our condition, referring to our post-industrial, post-ideological era as 'liquid modernity' to define it as a period of constant fear and uncertainty. A few years after Bauman published his book *Liquid Modernity* (2000), the precariousness of life itself became the concern of Judith Butler's work. Drawing on Emmanuel Levinas's notion of the face, her 2004 book *Precarious Life: The Powers of Mourning and Violence* vigorously argued for the possibility of a new, post-9/11 community that is based on, rather than fatally compromised by, the inevitable interdependence and vulnerability of our lives. *Tomorrow's Parties* dovetails with this current discourse on precariousness, conjuring issues like the ecological crisis, the results of the biogenetic revolution, global terrorism, and the explosive growth of social divisions. However, the piece's response to the problems of our time, I will argue, deviates significantly both from a stance such as Butler's, which deems our lives as being radically at the mercy of anonymous others, and the pessimistic view of our culture as doomed to fail to respond adequately to the challenges of our time, such as held by Bauman. Looking at the representation of precariousness in *Tomorrow's Parties* from the point of view of concepts put forward by Malabou and Hegel, the chapter hopes to demonstrate that the piece instead explores what will be described here as an 'ethics of plasticity'.

The 'Here and Now' in Forced Entertainment

An ensemble of six artists formed in Sheffield in 1984, experimental theatre group Forced Entertainment have always been concerned with the dramatic evocation of the 'present moment'. The interest in the theatrical, but also actual, 'here and now', evident from their early work to their most recent projects, owes both to theatre and live art practice, as the group state on their webpage (see Forced Entertainment 2011).[3] As part of the latter movement, Forced Entertainment, today widely recognized as one of Europe's leading experimental companies, are engaged in a search for new artistic forms with which to describe contemporary urban life, as well as relating self-reflexively to the nature, dramat-

---

[3] The group's interest in the 'here and now' is clear from any analysis of their work. See in particular Helmer and Malzacher (2004).

ic and non-dramatic, of their own distinctive performance style. Although no single definition can account for the diversity of their work – which spans theatre and performance through gallery installation, digital media, video, sound, and graphic art – what unifies such variety is described by the group as "the aim to make vital interventions in the form of culture, reflecting on the world that surrounds us, [...] engaging audiences in compelling and provocative ways" (Forced Entertainment 2011). While in the twenty years since their formation, Forced Entertainment have also continually been concerned with the exploration of structures of subjectivity (see Gritzner 2008: 337), employing such conventional forms as narrative and dialogue increasingly in their work of the new millennium – "a new departure" for the group, as Karen Jürs-Munby (2009: 21) has pointed out – the interest in the present moment has not waned in their recent work.

Tomorrow's Parties is a case in point. Undergirded by the title, the 2011 production announces itself as a piece about what the future may hold for us, but in fact uses the concept of future as a point of departure for creative reflection on distinctively *contemporary* issues, issues that have been occupying centre stage in sociological and philosophical debates about the precariousness of our current condition. *Tomorrow's Parties* is a show constituted by the different predictions and speculations about the future expressed by two performers on a stage that is bare except for a wooden platform and a chain of multicolored lights. Standing side by side on the platform, framed by the chain of lights, performers Terry O'Connor and Robin Arthur (in alternative combination with the duo Cathy Naden and Richard Lowdon) take it in turns to offer different possible versions of what tomorrow might bring.[4] In opposition to other Forced Entertainment productions, such as their 1993 durational performance *12 am: Awake & Looking Down*, a 6 to 11-hour show where "the audience are free to arrive, depart and return at any point" (Forced Entertainment n.d.), *Tomorrow's Parties* is an intimate piece, which maintains a high level of closeness to the audience through its staging in small venues and its use of unamplified, direct speech. At the heart of the piece is the idea of a radically ambivalent, uncertain future – a motif that is accentuated by the style of the performance, a composition in seemingly aleatoric, improvised statements about futures possible and impossible. Using the phrase 'or in the future' as a means to constantly shift the other performer's propositions about the future, the performers of *Tomorrow's Parties* carry the audience

---

4 All subsequent references to this piece are based on the performance DVD, where Terry O'Connor and Robin Arthur are performing the play; in the anniversary performance of *Tomorrow's Parties* that I attended at the Studiobühne Köln on 16 May 2014, the piece was staged with Forced Entertainment's Richard Lowdon and Cathy Naden.

through a range of utopian and dystopian visions, science fiction scenarios, speculations on posthuman evolution, and politically absurd fantasies.

Yet to take an audience on a journey into imaginary future worlds is not to catapult them away from the 'here and now', and *Tomorrow's Parties*' relentless, almost neurotic circling around questions about the future indeed confirms that a very topical *Zeitgeist* is operative in the piece. Clearly, the restless and questioning mode of the production resonates with what Zygmunt Bauman has referred to as 'liquid fear', that is, the "insecurity of the present and uncertainty about the future" (2006: 128) that he believes characterizes the current stage of our civilization. Bauman terms this stage 'liquid modernity', defining it in opposition to both modernity and postmodernity. As he argues in *Liquid Modernity*, modernity was supposed to be the time in human history when human beings were enabled to take control of their lives and master the forces of the social and natural worlds, but at the beginning of the new millennium, the most technologically equipped stage of human history, we live again in a time of endemic uncertainty, haunted by the constant fear that incalculable dangers could strike at any moment (see Bauman 2000: 29). Be it in the sense of fear of natural disasters, fear of environmental catastrophes, or fear of terrorist attacks, our culture, according to Bauman, is one of fear and, as a consequence, control.

Obviously, *Tomorrow's Parties* manages to deal with this issue mostly humorously, but sometimes it does so also with a poignantly real discomfort. When, for example, eight minutes or so into the show, performer Terry O'Connor articulates the scenario, "Or in the future everything will be on CCTV, all of the time, which, in a way, will also be for your protection" (Forced Entertainment 2013: 07:57–08:03), it is easy to forget that the production was commissioned for the Festival Belluard Bollwerk International as a project dealing with "hope" (Festival Belluard Bollwerk International 2011). And yet, despite the occasional presence of uneasiness and pessimism in the piece, faith in the positive potential of our liquid or precarious situation is eventually vindicated. While what Bauman calls liquid fear prompts his conclusion that the pervasive uncertainty emblematic of our culture leads us to behave without consideration for the future consequences of our actions (see 2006: 128–129), *Tomorrow's Parties* remains upbeat about our human capacity to imagine and even create a better world. Indeed, by foregrounding, in typical contemporary performance art fashion, the creative power of aleatoric performance practice and the seemingly endless repository of human imagination, *Tomorrow's Parties* suggests that the always-uncertain future might be viewed as something which we are radically enabled to shape – in much the same way that the performers of *Tomorrow's Parties* can be seen to shape the futuristic scenarios that constitute the content of the piece.

Malabou, Hegelian Temporality, and *Tomorrow's Parties*

The idea that the future doesn't exist somewhere else, ready to be conquered like a far-off world, but is something that is constantly being shaped in the present is not new but has been proposed among others by G.W.F. Hegel, whose concepts of time and temporality have been recently reinterpreted by French philosopher Catherine Malabou. Key to Malabou's rereading of Hegel is the concept of 'plasticity'. Plasticity is defined by Malabou as an "*entre-deux*" ['between-two'] (2008: 82), designating activity as well as passivity, ability to shape as well as to be shaped. In Hugh J. Silverman's helpful summary, the term "is a kind of deconstructive 'indecidable' between flexibility and rigidity, suppleness and solidity, fixedness and transformability, identity and modifiability, determination and freedom" (2010: 93).

In her book *The Future of Hegel*, Malabou takes the concept of plasticity as a lens for a substantial reevaluation of Hegelian temporality. She argues that for Hegel time is "not only the name given to a pre-formed form, that is, to the sequence of nows. Rather, it *forms* that succession" (2005: 191). Time, says Malabou, is understood by Hegel as 'plastic' in the sense that, just like a form in the plastic art of sculpture, it is something that allows for modulation. Malabou concludes from this that Hegel propounded a concept of future in which the future is radically open – everything can still happen to it. However, she also points out that the concept of future in Hegel has an element of rigidity. Because Hegel believed that the future is always determined by tendencies already in existence (see Malabou 2005: 192), his concept of temporality implies a sense of closure as well – a sense that, even if it is indefinitely postponed from the point of view of our lived present, in a way the future is already accomplished. For Malabou, plasticity, poising between determination and freedom, openness and closure, is therefore the term that best describes Hegelian temporality: "Plasticity designates the future understood as a future within closure" (2005: 192). It is "the possibility of a closed system to welcome new phenomena, all the while transforming itself" (2005: 193).

In the concluding part of his 2012 book *The Year of Dreaming Dangerously*, Slavoj Žižek describes a similar double meaning inherent in the term future, drawing attention to the two French words for 'future': *avenir* and *futur*. He explains that in French,

> *Futur* stands for 'future' as the continuation of the present, as the full actualization of tendencies already in existence; while *avenir* points more towards a radical break, a discontinuity with the present – *avenir* is what is to come (*a* [sic] *venir*), not just what will be. (2012: 134)

Malabou's between-two, plastic concept of future is, in fact, illustrated by the concepts of *futur* and *avenir* when seen together as a paradoxical unity.

It is my contention that much of the typical to and fro-style of undecidability in *Tomorrow's Parties* hinges on precisely this paradox inherent in the notion of future noted by both Malabou and Žižek. Thus, in some parts, the piece suggests that the future is continuous with the present, an "actualization of tendencies already in existence" (Žižek 2012: 134). This is exemplified by Robin Arthur's fast-forward glimpse of what our geopolitical situation might look like in the future if the worst predictions for climate change come to pass:

> Or in the future, the whole world will heat up. And the rising sea levels will create displacement of populations, scarcity of resources, and this in turn will lead to geopolitical conflicts. And governments will have to get stronger and stronger. And the governments will need to be strong in order to impose the sort of rationing of food and fuel that will be necessary to keep those shifting populations in some kind of delicate balance. (Forced Entertainment 2013: 10:19–10:56)

In common with all dystopian narratives, this one encourages audiences to reflect on their contemporary society rather than forget it. Temperature changes, coastal flooding, and resource competition are all tendencies already existing in reality, and reports on their expected effects are well broadcast throughout the media. However, rather than making the future look so grim that we are grateful for our world as it is, in the way that some of the more absurd scenarios in *Tomorrow's Parties* actually do, such realistically dystopian look ahead acts as a warning of what our future might be like if no action is taken. The possibility that things will simply go on as they do now is again explored a little later in the performance, though this time with the implicit assumption that nature will stay the same, too:

> In the future, everything will be like this, really. [...] People will still have jobs. People will still get married. They'll still have a flat. They'll still have kids. [...] People will still be snobs. There'll still be a class system. There'll still be money, guns and bombs – and culture. [...] Things will be pretty much the same. I mean, one or two things may change, but basically it'll all be the same. (Forced Entertainment 2013: 22:12–25:10)

As the first of the scenarios in the piece to evoke a future in which no radical change will have taken place at all, this statement effectively recalls the critical verdict of leftist academic Russell Jacoby, who, writing in 1999, was not to be deluded by the discourse of radicalism that has traditionally surrounded the left: "Today, socialists and leftists do not dream of a future radically different from the present. To put it differently, radicalism no longer believes in itself" (1999: 10). *Tomorrow's Parties* toys with this disillusioned view of the future once more later on in the show, when performer Terry O'Connor speculates, in a comparatively long, three-minute monologue, that possibly

> in the future things will be pretty much like they are now. There'll still be a huge imbalance between poor countries and rich countries. [...] There'll still be friction between one community and another or one religion and another. [...] There'll still be machines that break down. Or computers that freeze, or die, or just fuck things up by losing information. [...] People will still fuck each other up. People will still fuck their kids up. And brothers and sisters will fuck each other up. And couples will still fuck each other up. And people will still resent foreigners. [...] I mean, some things might change. Some things might shift around a bit, but, basically, things will stay the same. (Forced Entertainment 2013: 50:05–53:14)

Such a downbeat statement does not go unchallenged within the competitive, polyphonic logic of the performance, however, and the next proposition about the future, coming from Robin Arthur, immediately provides some comic relief in the form of a satirical sketch of our entertainment culture. Much in the fashion of Suzanne Collins's young adult novel *The Hunger Games* (2008), this envisions a society ruled by reality television shows and brutal governments:

> Or, in the future, capital punishment will be so common that it won't be enough just to kill criminals anymore but the killings will just have to get more and more theatrical. So, you know, murderers, for example, might in their turn be murdered as part of some very complicated reality TV programme with, you know, a very complex plot and lots of sort of characters that are also played by people who are minor celebrities. (Forced Entertainment 2013: 53:22–53:56)

Managing to evoke laughter at regular intervals, *Tomorrow's Parties* constantly pits against each other gloomy and hilarious scenarios, clear-eyed and playful perspectives, the worst political nightmares and the most radically utopian dreams. Similarly, the piece maintains a stance of undecidability regarding the duality of *futur* and *avenir* (or determination and freedom, to use Malabou's terminology). The above excerpts imply a concept of futurity that suggests a continuation of the same in the sense of *futur*, imagining worlds that are probable or at least possible. Other parts, however, are much more 'science-fictional', presupposing a concept of future that is best described by the notion of *avenir*, as that which comes to us from what is ahead, something that is not explainable on the basis of what went before it.

When, in the final moments of the piece, for instance, the performers speculate about how in the future time will literally become mutable, first expanding and then accelerating until in the end people's life spans will last only for one hour, the underlying notion is that of a future understood as an *avenir* that marks a complete break with what has been up to that point (although when read metaphorically, this scenario is uncannily close to home, and I will return to this point). The aesthetic finesse of the concluding part of *Tomorrow's Parties* lies in the way in which, as the performers evoke the scenario of a shrinking of time, this fictional time 'shrunken' to one hour seems to coalesce with the actual time of the performance – we realize at this point that the performance of *Tomorrow's Parties* has also lasted about one hour. The impression of fictional time collapsing into actual time is corroborated and emphasized by the lighting: as the performers utter their concluding sentences, the cone of light that had illuminated them during the show up to that point shrinks and then disappears, along with the lighting of the chain of lights, leaving the performers standing on the stage in complete darkness as the play ends. Apparently injecting the virtual, 'shrunken' future conjured up by the performers into the space of the actual present of the performance, the final futuristic vision evoked in *Tomorrow's Parties* reflects back on what the performance, in a truly self-reflexive manner, is making us experience in actual fact – the limitation of time (the time that audiences and performers have shared by the end of the performance) to one hour. This self-reflexive play with virtual and actual theatrical time, and so in this instance with the relationship between future and present, not only profoundly disturbs the widely held notion of a consecutiveness of present and future but, in a very Hegelian way, suggests that "time in itself is in its concept eternal" (Hegel qtd. in Hoffmeyer 1994: 5). Indeed, making the future virtually *present* in the present, the concluding section of *Tomorrow's Parties* offers a very literal take on Hegel's assumption that, as "true time", time consists in the simultaneity of past, present, and future (qtd. in Hoffmeyer 1994: 66).

Precariousness and the Ethics of Plasticity

"Prediction is very difficult, especially about the future", physicist Niels Bohr once said (qtd. in Hillson and Murray-Webster 2007: 3). Today, predicting the future is usually also an ethico-political thing to do: it depends on how we see the world, and on how we assess the challenges that face us. Living at the beginning of the twenty-first century, how do we estimate and interpret the extent of climate change, the imbalances within the economic system, the biogenetical revolution, and the continued growth of social ruptures? Our answers to these questions all have a direct effect on how we imagine the future. In the arts, the key issues and developments of our era have of late excited a surge of dystopian novels and films that, by providing us with various worst-case scenarios, implicitly hope to jolt us up to try and prevent those scenarios from eventually happening in real life. Similarly, in the intellectual world, predictions about the future are implicitly or explicitly political. A good example for the latter is Slavoj Žižek, who, predicting in his book *Living in the End Times* that "the global capitalist system is approaching an apocalyptic zero-point" (2010: x), calls for a new world order that will be able to face up to the challenges of a world that has radically changed.

No such explicit political agenda underpins *Tomorrow's Parties*, but even so, the piece contains a rather clear ethico-political dimension, I would argue. By showing us the future not simply as a moment in time but as something malleable and constantly open to change through our interpretation and intervention, *Tomorrow's Parties* sends the message that "the future is not someplace we are going to, but one we are creating", as John Schaar (1989: 321) once put it. In the following, I shall call the logic that underlies the piece explicitly one of plasticity. As Malabou specifies in *What Should We Do With Our Brain?*, where she uses the concept of plasticity to replace the old neurological model of the brain as a machine, the logic of plasticity is delineated by three dimensions: an aesthetic, an ethical, and a political one. Plasticity's "aesthetic dimension" is described by Malabou by terms such as "sculpture" and "malleability"; the ethical one as a dimension of "solicitude, treatment, help, repair, rescue"; while the political one is related by Malabou to the "responsibility [that rests] in the double movement of the receiving and the giving of form" (2008: 30). Turning to *Tomorrow's Parties*, one should perhaps rethink the central notion of precariousness in this precise context. Indeed, viewed through the perspective opened up by Malabou, *Tomorrow's Parties* suggests a surprisingly close correlation between precariousness and plasticity itself: where in most contexts (especially in those referring to Butler) precariousness is understood as a shared human experience of vulnerability, and particularly vulnerability to violence, the sense of precariousness reflected in *Tomorrow's Parties*, rather, takes on the meaning of what Malabou describes as plasticity, the "double movement of the receiving and giving of form".

This logic of plasticity/precariousness, as I contend, is present in the piece in its full tripartite dimensionality of the aesthetic, the ethical, and the political. The aesthetic dimension of sculpturing and malleability is reflected in the constantly self-transforming movement of the piece: whether through counter proposals or word association, the leitmotiv phrase "or in the future", far from merely being used by one performer to take over from the other one, shifts the meaning of the latest proposition every time it is used, introducing a scenario that strikes us as radically unexpected, irreducibly new, appearing to be sculpted on the spot in the here and now.[5] Drawing on Žižek, the arrangement of sentences around the word 'or' can thus be seen to performatively demonstrate how, in the piece, 'future' refers not only to a logical-consequential outcome of present circumstances in the sense of the French *futur*, but also, and perhaps more so, to the advent of a disruptive, radically Other *avenir*, a quality that, like each of the performers' replies, displays emergent structures that cannot be predicted in any way, nor be traced back to their antecedents (on which they nonetheless depend).[6] That granted, one need not look far in the piece for the ethical and political dimensions of plasticity: not only does the logic of malleability drive the aesthetic manoeuvre of *Tomorrow's Parties*, but it is also obviously used in the piece to make a case for the 'real-life' possibility (or responsibility) of intervention. In its ethical dimension, this might be understood, following Malabou, as the margin of freedom to think about what she summarizes as "solicitude, treatment, help, repair, rescue" (2008: 30), and in its political dimension, as the responsibility to organize, to give form to, collective action aimed at the transformation of existing circumstances which are considered precarious in the most common, negative sense of the term.

Corroborating the latter point, hope in change for the better is once more manifested in the concluding section of *Tomorrow's Parties*. However, playing on the notion of precariousness in a connection that is reminiscent of Hartmut Rosa's idea of 'social acceleration' (see 2005), this happens somewhat unexpectedly here. Although, as already noted, the final scenario may at first sight seem melancholic, indeed dystopian, evoking a future in which our life spans, as a result of a continuing 'shrinking of the present', last only for an hour, looking beyond the obvious, one is likely to find that the piece finishes with a glimpse of hope in a seemingly bleak situation. While pointing out the fragile perishability of flowing time and so our precarious position in a world where, as a result of continued technological acceleration, time seems to flow incredibly fast, the ending of the performance may well work to instill in audiences the incentive to appreciate every moment as if it were their last – to live their lives to the fullest. Indeed, I would argue that by slowly bringing the flow of association that constitutes the piece to a halt and concluding with a moment of intensified presence, the finale of *Tomorrow's Parties* works in a similar way as what Jill Dolan

---

[5] As Forced Entertainment have explained in an interview, when devising *Tomorrow's Parties* the group worked precisely through improvisation, even though the text for the piece was finished and fixed in rehearsal (see Lowdon and Naden 2013).

[6] In a personal conversation after the performance of *Tomorrow's Parties* at the Studiobühne Köln on 16 May 2014, Lowdon asserted that the piece was inspired by the logic of a game, or aleatoric composition.

has called 'utopian performatives'.[7] In her book *Utopia in Performance*, these are defined as

> small but profound moments in which performance calls the attention of the audience in a way that lifts everyone slightly above the present, into a hopeful feeling of what the world might be like if every moment of our lives were as emotionally voluminous, generous, aesthetically striking, and intersubjectively intense. (2005: 5)

Based on Dolan's argument, my contention is that with its insistence on the present moment, the conclusive vision in *Tomorrow's Parties* isolates and makes available for us a moment in time that acts as a space in which we "connect more fully with the complexities of our past and the possibility of a better future" (Dolan 2005: 5), thus becoming a utopian performative in Dolan's precise sense. She emphasizes that the utopias evoked by utopian performatives are not (necessarily) enacted or shown in the performance, but rather "spectators might draw a utopian performative from even the most dystopian theatrical universe" (2005: 8). Such, I would argue, is the case with the conclusive scenario of *Tomorrow's Parties*: affectively experiencing the urgency of now, spectators of the piece are encouraged to turn the dystopia of a radically limited time into the utopia of a life lived with a radical intensity.

This essay has argued that *Tomorrow's Parties* engages with the discourse of precariousness by contemplating topical concepts such as uncertainty, vulnerability, and fluidity through reference to a remarkably ambivalent concept of futurity, one that reflects, in a seemingly contradictory unity of openness and closedness that Malabou calls plasticity, the ability to shape as well as to be shaped, contingency as well as necessity, freedom as well as determinism. The concept of future in *Tomorrow's Parties* demonstrates qualities of what Žižek refers to as both *avenir* and *futur*: the openness of *avenir* is manifested in the improvisational, aleatoric style of the piece, which constantly takes the performers' speculations in various, unpredictable directions, while the closedness of *futur* is conveyed through the emphasis on the continuity or even coexistence of present and future, detectable in the striking analogies the piece establishes between some of the future scenarios it evokes and our shared present.

In *Liquid Modernity* and *Liquid Fear*, Bauman defines our times as precarious, because they are radically uncertain, ungraspable in their consequences, resulting in a cultural climate that he believes stifles or discourages any genuine ethical discourse. While this leads Bauman to conclude that what he terms the

---

[7] In connection with Dolan's discussion of utopian performatives, see also Mireia Aragay's chapter in this volume.

fluidity of our present and future renders us morally helpless and politically powerless,[8] my reading of Forced Entertainment's *Tomorrow's Parties* has instead drawn attention to an interest in what Malabou terms the *plasticity* of present and future, an interest in the *hopeful* notion that the future, precisely because it is irreducibly fluid and radically malleable, is also radically in our hands, always open to change, which might at any moment be introduced in the here and now, the experiential moment of presence on which the piece's emphasis is placed.

Works Cited

Bauman, Zygmunt. 2000. *Liquid Modernity*. Cambridge: Polity.
Bauman, Zygmunt. 2006. *Liquid Fear*. Cambridge: Polity.
Butler, Judith. 2004. *Precarious Life: The Powers of Mourning and Violence*. London and New York: Verso.
Dolan, Jill. 2005. *Utopia in Performance: Finding Hope at the Theater*. Ann Arbor: U of Michigan P.
Festival Belluard Bollwerk International. 2011. "Call for Proposals". *archives.belluard.ch*. <http://archives.belluard.ch/en/node/622> [accessed 22 November 2014].
Forced Entertainment. 2011. "Tomorrow's Parties: Information Pack". *forcedentertainment.com*. <http://www.forcedentertainment.com/> [accessed 28 November 2014].
Forced Entertainment. 2013. *Tomorrow's Parties*. Performance DVD.
Forced Entertainment. n.d. *12am: Awake & Looking Down*. forcedentertainment.com. <http://www.forcedentertainment.com/project/12am-awake-looking-down/> [accessed 4 February 2015].
Gritzner, Caroline. 2008. "(Post)Modern Subjectivity and the New Expressionism: Howard Barker, Sarah Kane, and Forced Entertainment". *Contemporary Theatre Review* 18.3: 328–340.
Helmer, Judith and Florian Malzacher (eds.). 2004. *Not even a Game Anymore: The Theatre of Forced Entertainment*. Berlin: Alexander Verlag.
Hillson, David and Ruth Murray-Webster. 2007. *Understanding and Managing Risk Attitude*. 2nd ed. Aldershot: Gower.
Hoffmeyer, John F. 1994. *The Advent of Freedom: The Presence of the Future in Hegel's Logic*. Cranbury: Associated University Presses.

---

8 "[P]resent day men and women differ from their fathers and mothers by living in a present 'which wants to forget the past and no longer seems to believe in the future'. But the memory of the past and trust in the future have been thus far the two pillars on which the cultural and moral bridges between transience and durability, human mortality and the immortality of human accomplishments, as well as taking responsibility and living by the moment, all rested" (Bauman 2000: 128–129).

"In Imagination: The Future Reflected in Art and Argument". 2013. University of Sheffield. 4 October. Symposium. <http://www.eventbrite.co.uk/e/in-imagination-the-future-reflected-in-art-and-argument-tickets-7224064371> [accessed 28 November 2014].

Jacoby, Russell. 1999. *The End of Utopia: Politics and Culture in an Age of Apathy*. New York: Basic Books.

Jameson, Fredric. 2002. *A Singular Modernity: Essay on the Ontology of the Present*. London and New York: Verso.

Jürs-Munby, Karen. 2009. "'Did You Mean Post-traumatic Theatre?': The Vicissitudes of Traumatic Memory in Contemporary Postdramatic Performances". *Performance Paradigm* 5.2: 1–33. <http://www.performanceparadigm.net/wp-content/uploads/2009/10/jurs-munby-posttraumatic-postdramatic-final-copy-with-images.pdf> [accessed 22 November 2014].

Lowdon, Richard and Cathy Naden. 2013. "Q&A with Forced Entertainment". *Arnolfini*. <http://www.arnolfini.org.uk/blog/q-a-with-forced-entertainment/> [accessed 17 September 2015].

Malabou, Catherine. 2005. *The Future of Hegel: Plasticity, Temporality and Dialectic*. Trans. Lisabeth During. London and New York: Routledge.

Malabou, Catherine. 2008. *What Should We Do With Our Brain?* Trans. Sebastian Rand. New York: Fordham UP.

Megson, Chris. 2013. "'And I was struck still by time': Contemporary British Theatre and the Metaphysical Imagination". In: Vicky Angelaki (ed.). *Contemporary British Theatre: Breaking New Ground*. Basingstoke and New York: Palgrave Macmillan. 32–56.

Rosa, Hartmut. 2005. *Beschleunigung: Die Veränderung der Zeitstrukturen in der Moderne*. Frankfurt a.M: Suhrkamp.

Schaar, John H. 1989. *Legitimacy in the Modern State*. New Brunswick: Transaction Publishers.

Silverman, Hugh J. 2010. "Malabou, Plasticity, and the Sculpturing of the Self". *Concentric: Literary and Cultural Studies* 36.2: 89–102.

Soanes, Catherine and Angus Stevenson (eds.). 2006 [1998]. *Oxford Dictionary of English*. Oxford: Oxford UP.

Wald, Christina. 2007. *Hysteria, Trauma and Melancholia: Performative Maladies in Contemporary Anglophone Drama*. Basingstoke and New York: Palgrave Macmillan.

Žižek, Slavoj. 2010. *Living in the End Times*. London and New York: Verso.

Žižek, Slavoj. 2012. *The Year of Dreaming Dangerously*. London and New York: Verso.

Verónica Rodríguez
Bridging Precariousness and Precarity: Ecstasy and Bleeding Across in the Work of David Greig and Suspect Culture

One of the most widely accepted meanings of the term 'ecstasy' – from the Greek word έκσταση – is 'being out of oneself'. According to Judith Butler, "[t]o be ecstatic means, literally, to be outside oneself, and thus can have several meanings: to be transported beyond oneself by a passion, but also to be *beside oneself* with rage or grief" (2004: 24). This chapter explores the creative and ethical energies and potentialities behind the manifold manifestations of 'the self outside the self' – or 'out-of-body experiences' – in the work of David Greig and Suspect Culture by placing it in its political and theatrical contexts.

The notions of 'self' and 'body' are used in this chapter rather indistinctively, given, for instance, Anthony Giddens's observation that "the reflexivity of the self *extends to the body*" (2000: 253). Although such conceptual blurring might seem disorientating, it may actually cast some light on the "e/affects" (Thrift 2008: 11) of ecstasy, for the surface of the body, figuratively pierced by ecstatic or reaching-out experiences, undergoes a (temporary) dissolution of its contours, with bodies 'extending' to other bodies in a profoundly relational sense of space that triggers a confounding sense of bleeding across.[1] Propelled both by passion and grief, the impulse to reach out, which is persistent in Greig's and Suspect Culture's work, draws acute attention to the self's rigid immanence under globalization and therefore reveals, judging from its pervasiveness and abruptness, "political rage" (Butler 2004: 24) against this normative limit and its negative consequences.

More elaborately, in relation to Butler's first meaning of ecstasy, the work under discussion seems to pursue ecstasy in the sense that it foregrounds a passion, or even a lust, for connection. That is, out-of-body experiences, either attempted or achieved, and whether they are positive or negative, suggest Greig's and Suspect Culture's work's intimate desire for oneness. As far as Butler's second meaning is concerned, this chapter argues that attempts at or instances of

---

[1] 'Reaching out' is a common motif in Suspect Culture's work, as Dan Rebellato has consistently argued (see, for instance, 2003 and 2013). The present chapter links that motif to Greig's work via the concept of ecstasy.

ecstasy in the work under discussion are simultaneously driven by an urgent need to express rage at violence and injustice.

The present chapter has two main sections: the former focuses on a brief theoretical framework and the latter, considerably longer, examines some specific instances of ecstasy and bleeding across in the work of Greig and Suspect Culture. The theoretical section begins by contextually exploring why it is the case that the work under discussion seems interested in ecstasy and bleeding across. This is then linked with theatre criticism, with a particular (but not exclusive) emphasis on the impact of ecstasy on characterization, and subsequently on how ecstatic characterization shapes the work's e/affects through the generation of a sense of bleeding across. The theoretical section ends with the formulation of a possible rationale – suggested by the chapter's title – for Greig's and Suspect Culture's work's insistent focus on ecstasy and bleeding across.

Policed Self vs. Impossible Interiority

In *Liquid Fear*, Zygmunt Bauman argues that "[i]n the liquid modern society of consumers, each individual member is instructed, trained and groomed to pursue individual happiness by individual means and through individual efforts" (2006: 48). This chapter suggests that Greig's and Suspect Culture's explorations of 'the self out of the self' constitute a move against this instruction, training and grooming. Crucially, Bauman states that "[t]he boundary between the body and the world outside is among the most vigilantly policed of contemporary frontiers" (2000: 184), while on the other hand, as Jacques Derrida has it, ontologically and ethically the self "is open before I make a decision about it" (1997).

Following on from both those observations, this chapter reads instances of transgression of the border between the body and the world as practices of resistance in the age of globalization. In a statement that spells out the connection between Bauman's critique of the policing of the body-world boundary and Derrida's notion of the openness of the self, Butler argues:

> We can think about demarcating the human body through identifying its boundary, or in what form it is bound, but that is to miss the crucial fact that the body is, in certain ways and even inevitably, unbound – in its acting, its receptivity, in its speech, desire and mobility. *It is outside itself*, in the world of others, *in a space and time it does not control.* (2009: 52; emphasis added)

Theorists such as Nigel Thrift and Sara Ahmed seem to adhere to Butler's ontology of the unbound body. The former opines that "bodies can and do become overwhelmed" (2008: 10), while the latter refers to the "unfolding of bodies into worlds" (2010: 30). Furthermore, in his seminal essay "The Inoperative Community", Jean-Luc Nancy posits the "rejection of an impossible interiority" (1991: 4).

Taking these notions on board, this chapter understands moments of ecstasy in Greig's and Suspect Culture's work, or even mere yearnings for reaching out, as triggers that may eventually coalesce into instances of unbounded bodies and spaces, thus generating a sense of bleeding across. To Butler, this foregrounds an ethical dimension: "[W]hen I act ethically, I am undone as a bounded being" (2012: 142). In this light, then, it is suggested that the ethical dimension of Greig's and Suspect Culture's work is inseparable from its presentation to the spectator of characters that attempt to cross the line between themselves and the world, and thus may become undone beings. The pervasive presence of unbounded bodies produced by ecstatic characterization – echoed by comparable elements at other levels of formal construction – fosters a sense of bleeding across, that is, the e/affect of confounding bodies, spaces and worlds that characterizes Greig's and Suspect Culture's work.

Characterization under Globalization: Unbounded Bodies

According to Giddens, "[r]ather than talking in general terms of 'individual', 'self' or even 'self-identity' as distinctive of modernity, we should try to break things down into finer detail" (2000: 252), contrary to globalization's persistent aspiration to keep an individualized narrative of the self in place.[2] If "[t]he global individual" resists the 'perceptual safety' offered by this rounded narrative of the self, for instance via the discourse of consumerism, s/he "is doomed to be *exiled from himself*" (Bourriaud 2009: 76–77; emphasis added). However, perhaps the self does not need to be either confined within the body's limits or eternally exiled. In that connection, this chapter is interested in exploring how in Greig's and Suspect Culture's work the contemporary, globalized self or body becomes temporarily unbounded and undelimitable, and with what particular resonances.

The idea of unbounded bodies can be traced in theatre criticism. Dan Rebellato has argued that while state-of-the-nation plays "focus on specific, fully realized individual characters" (2007: 248), plays under globalization display characters that undergo a process of "evaporation of singularity" (2009: 76). Rebellato exemplifies the process by reference to the gradual disappearance of Samuel Beckett's characters, from proper names in *Waiting for Godot*, to the "more formalized" characters in *Happy Days*, through to the reduction to gender

---

2 In this connection, see also Giddens's *Modernity and Self-Identity* (1994).

markers in *Play* and bodily truncation in *Not I* (2009: 76). On to the era of globalization, he adds that "Sarah Kane followed the Beckettian trajectory by moving from Ian and Cate in *Blasted* to A, B, C, and M in *Crave* [...], and in her final play, *4.48 Psychosis* [...], no characters are indicated at all" (2009: 76). In his introduction to Kane's *Complete Plays*, Greig already referred to "the intoxicating release of Kane's writing as the borderlines of character evaporate entirely" (2001: xiv). On her part, Cristina Delgado-García defines character as "any figuration of subjectivity in theatre, regardless of how individuated or, conversely, how unmarked its contours might be" (2015: 14), a view that is compatible with both Rebellato's argument about plays in the era of globalization and with the notion of poststructuralist subjectivity, which, as Liz Tomlin crucially notes, "no longer recognizes an 'authentic' [...] self or 'essential' self" (2013: 14). By reference to a series of Suspect Culture shows, Wallace has noted that they engage with "a 'dispersed idea of self'" (2013: 25). Greig's and Suspect Culture's "sustained engagements with characterization [...] mirror the constructed nature of contemporary selfhood" (Tomlin 2013: 101), thus confirming that, like postdramatic theatre, "dramatic theatre can also deconstruct representational practice" (Tomlin 2013: 13). Indeed, among other elements, it is through this experimentation with character and its potential e/affects that the work under analysis punches a hole through its representational practice and bursts into the real.

Deconstructing the Representational: Attempts at Bridging

The main thesis of this chapter is that attempts at and instances of ecstasy and bleeding across – most commonly found in characterization mechanisms – express a dramaturgical and theatrical bridging between precariousness and precarity that ultimately seems to aim at suggesting the connection of all existence. In Butler's demarcation of the two concepts, while "lives are by definition precarious: they can be expunged at will or by accident", precarity, on the other hand, "designates that politically induced condition in which certain populations suffer from failing social and economic networks of support and become differentially exposed to injury, violence and death" (2009: 25). Nicolas Bourriaud, in tune with Bauman's understanding of precariousness as the contemporary, liquid condition of "until-further-noticeness" (2000: 14; 162; 2006: 140), defines 'the precarious' as "a right of use that could be revoked at any time" (2009: 79).

Through exploring moments of ecstasy and potentially producing senses of bleeding across, the work of Greig and Suspect Culture seems to foreground instances of ontological precariousness in ways that simultaneously register a preoccupation for political precarity. In other words, their work's experimentation with character suggests that precariousness and precarity are intricately interwoven, which conveys a sense of "commitment to the existence of a real world" (Rebellato 2014). Specifically, the work under discussion craftily locates damage in the bodies of those usually less exposed to injury, violence and death for politically induced reasons and dis-locates precarity, that is, places precarity where it is usually not. Through instances of ecstasy and the potential sense of bleeding across they generate, Greig's and Suspect Culture's work confers materiality to the intertwined nature of precariousness and precarity, eventually insisting that precariousness is to a large extent precarity in disguise – particularly bearing in mind that precarity is unevenly distributed between the globe's 'desirables' and 'undesirables', the latter, in Bauman's lexicon, corresponding to the category of *homines sacri* of failed consumers in a neoliberal economy (see 2005: 101).[3]

Ultimately, then, Greig's and Suspect Culture's work talks about the real and to the real. It deconstructs the representational by suggesting a dramaturgical and theatrical interconnectedness between precarious bodies that are less exposed to precarity and equally precarious bodies that are more exposed to precarity. It does so by exploring the aforementioned ontology of unbounded bodies through experimentation with character and characterization. Speculatively, this might infuse spectators' own bodies with a sense of porosity, unboundedness and interconnectedness.

Instances of Ecstasy and Bleeding Across

In this chapter, ecstasy names an experience or phenomenon that emerges on a large number of occasions and in a range of different shapes. Indeed, "affective practices which are too often neglected [such as] seeing visions, praying [and] crying" (Thrift 2008: 196) are here considered ecstatic. Examples of those pervade Greig's plays – respectively Claire in *The Events* (2013), Marie in *San Diego* (2003) and Robert in *Outlying Islands* (2002). Expanding on Thrift's vindication, practices such as nail biting, having an orgasm, vomiting, extreme pain or suffering, breathing out, or even meditating and loving something or someone also constitute instances of ecstasy in so far as they instantiate ways of being outside the body and transgressing its boundaries. Thus, John's throwing up in

---

3 As Bauman puts it, "[e]ach model of spatial order divides humans into 'desirables' and 'undesirables', under the code names of 'legitimate' (allowed) and 'illegitimate' (not allowed)" (2010: 169). Greig has also used the term 'undesirables' in an article on architecture (see 2011b).

Greig's *One Way Street* (1995) is an instance of ecstasy. What is interesting in this particular case is that the content of John's stomach (the inside) intermingles with the space outside in such a way that he can describe the shape of and the lumps in his vomit as a map of his life. This open understanding of ecstasy, which oscillates from spiritual to physical as in John's case, shows that it connotes not only an *immaterial* but also a *material* being out of oneself. The interest in expressing ecstasy materially might be connected with globalization's emphasis on materiality in the context of the "financialization of everything" (Harvey 2006: 24).

Other examples of ecstasy and bleeding across in Greig's work include Dorothy, Leo Black's daughter in *The Architect* (1996), who wants to smash her skull against the wall of a house: "Smack it and feel the bricks cut me. / Feel my skull smack" (Greig, *The Architect*: 118). An attempt, perhaps, to break open the delimitable self that prevents her from experiencing existence outside herself. Simultaneously aware of the futility of this act yet perhaps reliant on the potentiality of breaking out, she pictures herself crashing her skull on the wall repeatedly: "Slide down half conscious. / Pick myself up and do it again" (118).

Another early instance of ecstasy in Greig's work appears in *The Speculator* (1999), which includes a narrative about "the cautionary tale of John Law, the Scot whose scheme to move away from a gold standard of currency made him, for a time at least, the richest and most powerful man in Europe" (Scullion 2007: 69). In the play, the terms St Antoine uses to describe his realization that something is not for sale are highly significant:

> ST ANTOINE: I walk
> Away from my wife. Away from my child.
> DEALER 3: I shouldn't be telling you.
> DEALER 1: I said no – it's for the misuse.
> ST ANTOINE: And suddenly I found that I felt something –
> DEALER 1: Not for sale.
> DEALER 2: I'm giving you – for a deposit of three thousand.
> DEALER 3: There are thirty ships – fitted – sitting in Le Havre.
> ST ANTOINE: I felt a feeling as though my skin had been peeled from me – (Greig, *The Speculator*: 18–19)

Several senses of ecstasy can be extricated from this passage. Firstly, they include St Antoine's rebirth into a new life as he walks away from his past life. Secondly, and related to the first, there is a graphic example of that rebirth whereby he feels his skin has been peeled off from him. Thirdly, Dealer 3 and 1 give the impression of taking over St Antoine's voice, with the result that his lines bleed out into theirs – "I shouldn't be telling you" and "Not for sale" respectively. The sense of "uncertain identities" (Rebellato 2002: 14) put forward by the example of a character's lines ecstatically running into those of another character finds theoretical articulation in Rebellato's idea that "the ideological shifts of the last twenty years have rendered it difficult to decide where one person stops and another ends" (2002: 14). In that sense, we seem to bleed across each other, to be trespassed by each other.

An even earlier, perhaps more radical, example of ecstasy occurs in *Timeless* (1997), a piece about four friends who attempt to recapture the joy of a past communal experience, where the skin, instead of being peeled off as in *The Speculator*, is traversed by a 'new' Stella:

> You are stuck in your own body. Your own life. Whatever you've done or not done. You can't even run away. You know? So the only thing I think when I look at that situation is I imagine owning some kind of car and just getting into it and driving off to the furthest place away I can think of. Like fucking Russia or fucking Alaska and my skin's going to crack open like one of those snakes or lizards or something and a new Stella's going to slide out of my skin and fall onto the snow. (Greig, *Timeless*: 154)

Towards the end of the play, Stella recounts her violent rebirth, which involves an 'out-of-body experience' in space – "I'm watching the snow turn red as I slide out of my body onto it. / And I can't hear my own shouting over the sound of the wind and... / I am the wind. / I am the fucking wind" (181). Stanton B. Garner's remark, in relation to Bertolt Brecht's theatre, that "the desiring, suffering body was 'taken out of itself' and refigured as an element" (1994: 163) might stand as an apt description of Stella's ecstasy and sense of bleeding across. After that, she awkwardly bursts into the place where Martin is, throws him against the window and then picks the glass out of his eyes and wipes his blood. Building upon Rebellato's claim that "[t]he quest for a true sense of self draws [Greig's] characters towards seeking some purer, more natural state" (2002: 5), this chapter argues that, if anything, a 'true' sense of self is crucially and "inevitably" (Butler 2009: 52) also outside itself, and that the natural state Rebellato refers to is related to a desire to convey global interconnectedness. The sense of a self enclosed within the body's enveloping skin is also a confinement characters seek to trespass both in *Timeless*, through "the repetition of [...] words [...] and phrases that signal a shared [...] language" (Wallace 2013: 24), and in *Lament* (2002), in this case through spiritual yearning and ritual.

The idea of the self-sufficient self is underpinned, among other elements, by language(s) and past experience(s). Greig's and Suspect Culture's work engages with blurring a sense of individual 'linguistic' and 'experiential' selves. In Suspect Culture's *Airport* (1996), although characters do not know each other, sometimes they speak the same line or give the impression of having had the same past experience, and in so doing transgress their immanent selves, thus momentarily becoming, in Charlotte Thompson's terms, "transpersonal" (2011) entities. Ecstasy also operates at the level of gestural movement in *Airport*, among other Suspect Culture shows. Graham Eatough points out "gestural motifs of reaching out, longing and so on" (2013: 12) that visually articulate and reinforce the reaching outs signalled in the narrative.

Furthermore, stage design can also be read in terms of ecstasy in, for example, Suspect Culture's *Mainstream* (1998), a show about two strangers who meet in a seaside hotel and attempt to communicate (see Greig n.d.). As Rebellato notes, in this play "[t]he stage is organised in four quarters, one item of furniture indicating each of the rooms the relationship passes through" (2013: 308). This notion of 'the relationship passing through' space leads to further 'traversing' as "particular actions and lines of dialogue bleed across these zones, overflowing the spatial boundaries of the narrative" (Rebellato 2013: 308). Moreover, the intertwining of the textual and the visual in *Mainstream* highlights ecstasy even more powerfully, so that "[t]he whole encounter seems to *exceed the bodies of the particular actors*, transcending its material representation, intensifying and sharpening the difference between what we see and what we feel to be happening", which generates "a shimmering, *undecidable sense of character transcending the individual*" (Rebellato 2013: 308; emphasis added). Ultimately, the formal strategy whereby stage design and narrative jointly suggest a sense of character/actor that exceeds individuality may be read as gesturing at Butler's unbounded ontology of the body. The overflowing of boundaries – this time in terms of gender – is intensified by lines being delivered indistinctively by two male and two female performers.

Mainstream also points out another way to question the boundary between the body and the world, namely, through the allusion to meditation and sex. The play reads, "[s]tay still. / Stay absolutely still. / Think of me. / Imagine me. / Conjure me up. / Touch yourself" (Greig, *Mainstream*: 241). In *On Touching – Jean-Luc Nancy*, Derrida suggests that what is at stake is "*se toucher toi* and not *se toucher soi*" (2005: 290) – that is, touching 'you' when I touch 'me' not due to a transposition between 'you' and 'I', but due to the possibility that 'I am you too', that interiority is always-already exteriority. This, in turn, foregrounds the connective, invisible fabric that joins "the vast spillage of *things*" (Thrift 2008: 9) or "worlds, bodies and their in-betweens" (Gregg and Seigworth 2010: 4) – in other words, the 'bleeding across' between and through bodies and worlds. On the other hand, staying still brings to mind what could be considered the opposite of ecstasy, namely stasis.[4] However, in this chapter, stasis or allusions to it in Greig's and Suspect Culture's work are viewed as manifestations of ecstasy – thus, in *Mainstream*, the desire to stop movement is inseparable from the desire to seek to merge with the outside. The phrase "moving into stasis", used by the network Inside/Outside Europe (2013), helpfully illuminates the phenomenon.[5]

Greig's *San Diego* (2003) is a play about global labour, immigration and illness, where one of the various jobs of the immigrants Pious, Innocent and Daniel is to process minced meat, while Laura shares her self-mutilated flesh with her lover David. This extreme form of sharing and material ecstasy, whereby both Laura and David brutally undo and redraw the frontier between a delineated self and the world through mutilation and cannibalism, might be read as a radical expression of rage at the utter lack of bodily unboundedness. Additionally, the presence of the author's persona in the play, in the form of a character called 'David Greig', together with other 'Davids' also present in the play, reinforces an ecstatic notion of being 'out of the self'.

In this connection, it is not only that the playwright is in some cases outside or beyond himself, but a character on stage is always somehow out of himself or herself too. Greig has stated that "character floats around the actor's body", and the only thing the actor can do is "express or present that ungraspability" (2007: 54) – a notion that is arguably influenced by Brecht's epic theatre, where "an actor should reserve for himself the possibility of *stepping out* of character artistically" (Benjamin 1999: 150; emphasis added). Such an emphasis on the fluidity of the actor-character relationship constitutes another example of ecstasy, graspable, for instance, in plays such as *The American Pilot* (2005), *San Diego* or *Mainstream*, where actors stay on stage throughout the performance, even when they are not taking part in a particular scene, therefore ecstatically 'stepping out' of themselves as characters. Thus, in relation to *The American Pilot*, Clare Wallace points out "[t]he double nature of the pilot – as a person [and] a body on stage" (2013: 141).

Highlighting the need for bodily unboundedness can also occur through accounts of hyperbolic boundedness, as in "[t]he theory of Japanese rope bondage"

---

[4] The word 'stasis', from Ancient Greek στάσις, means lack of movement. Its Modern Greek equivalent, στάση, designates from a bus stop to the coming to a halt of a process, among other meanings.

[5] One of the outcomes of the workshops conducted by Inside/Outside Europe is the book *Performances of Capitalism, Crises and Resistance: Inside/Outside Europe* (2015), where Marilena Zaroulia's chapter, "At the Gates of Europe: Sacred Objects, Other Spaces and Performances of Dispossession", contains a reference to stasis (see 209–10).

(Greig and McIntyre, *Midsummer*: 53) expounded in Greig's and Gordon McIntyre's *Midsummer* (2009):

> the tighter your / Body is bound, the more restricted your bodily movement / And the more your mind feels like it's transcending the / Physical and you find your mind floating free on a sea / Of endorphins – / Time slows down – you lose your inhibitions – the border / Between you and the world seems to melt away – you feel / Like you're one with the universe. (53)

In this example, the body mentally spills over itself into the world. As is discernible in this quote, being out of oneself has the desirable but unpredictable effect of cosmic connectedness or oneness.

In *Fragile* (2011), a play that addresses the cuts to public spending in the UK introduced by the Coalition government formed by the Conservatives and the Liberal Democrats as well as the Arab Spring which overthrew several oppressive regimes in the Middle East and Northern Africa (both starting in late 2010), the mental patient (Jack) of a health care worker (Caroline) – a role that is performed by the audience via a PowerPoint presentation due to austerity measures – can be argued to move outside himself in two ways. Firstly, in the sense of his mental illness, and secondly, in his expressed will to be out of himself by setting himself alight. That potential act – we do not know whether he eventually commits suicide or not – fuses his body and Mohamed Bouazizi's – whose suicide is generally perceived to have ignited the Tunisian revolution – into one, linked not only by Jack's idea of perpetrating the same act as Bouazizi but also by the narrative's fusing of the revolution in Tunisia and the demonstrations in London. Thus *Fragile* shows how bodies, violence and acts of protest are bound together in a tightly interwoven globe, and throws light on the strong connection between precariousness and precarity through the ecstatic dramatic and theatrical practice described above and the potential sense of bleeding across bodies and spaces that is thus produced. Additionally, spectators who go along with the injunction to stand in for Caroline also find themselves putting their singular voices out, which reinforces the sense that selves are being merged together. Through the act of doing something collectively (or trying to) by performing Caroline, they generate a sense of what might be called 'dissonant assonant voice' that evaporates their singularity as individual spectators, while simultaneously they create Caroline's unbounded body through voice.

In *The Events* (2013), a play that evokes the massacre perpetrated by Anders Behring Breivik in Norway on 22 July 2011 and explores how communities attempt to cope with trauma after extremely violent events, the Boy, the 'character' that plays the massacre's perpetrator, embodies a host of other 'characters' by going out of himself to become other people in the story, including Claire's girlfriend Catriona, Claire's psychologist, the Boy's father, the Boy's friend and the leader of an extremist right-wing party whose meetings the Boy attended. Consequently, in terms of character, he engages in successive acts of ecstasy, which not only interrogates the events from many different angles but also distributes the task of understanding and perhaps also instances of responsibility across various agencies.

Claire, the massacre's survivor, also goes out of herself in many ways. She does so, firstly, when she becomes various 'Claires' in a number of possible worlds in order to seek understanding and arguably cope with trauma.[6] Secondly, we also learn she experiences ecstasy when she says that the moment she knew she was going to die, she felt her soul was leaving her body. Thirdly, she leads an ecstasy-searching shamanic exercise performed by the Choir in an attempt to get out of a self that is depressed and traumatized and rise above it and outside it, albeit momentarily, so as to achieve partial healing. The spectator may also be argued to be impelled by the play to experience ecstasy under the effects of the simultaneously defamiliarizing and life-affirming use of music and the real choirs performing every night in *The Events*.

Conclusions

This chapter has aimed at finding a rationale behind Greig's and Suspect Culture's insistence in depicting unbounded bodies through ecstatic characterization that produces a confounding sense of bleeding across. It has been argued that, in so doing, their work illuminates the connection between precariousness and precarity, and therefore, ultimately, the connectedness of all existence. By offering a series of non-immanentist versions of the body through ecstasy and

---

[6] Possible worlds theory has been productively used in postmodern literature criticism. One of the forms that it has taken in postmodern narrative points to a "[f]ascination with the scenarios of counterfactual history and creation of fictional universes in which the real and the possible exchange places. (In such worlds characters may ask: 'What would have happened if Hitler had not won the war?')" (Ryan n.d.). In Greig's *The Events*, this takes the form of the multiple questions Claire ponders, whose possible answers morph in the play into different scenes. The questions include, 'what if I kill him?', 'what if he had had a different childhood?' and 'what if I had killed him just after being born?', which lead respectively to Claire describing how she will torture the Boy and eventually kill him, Claire and Catriona adopting a youngster (the Boy), and a nurse (Claire) killing a newly-born baby (the Boy) just after birth. Greig's interest in possible worlds theory has been noted by Wallace (see 2013: 25–26) in connection to *Mainstream*, and is further explored in my PhD thesis, "Globalisation in David Greig's Theatre: Space, Ethics and the Spectator".

its productive e/affects, the work under discussion moves against the grain of globalized culture, which, among other things, would seek to maintain an artificial separation between categories that incessantly bleed across each other, such as the individual and the communal or precariousness and precarity, among others. In criticizing such immanentology, Greig's and Suspect Culture's work shatters the sense of a unique interiority that prevents the self from experiencing an unbounded ontology of body and space.

This chapter has aimed at exploring how an unbounded "ontology of the body serves as a point of departure for [...] a rethinking of responsibility" (Butler 2009: 33), while stopping short of dismissing the concept of the self altogether. In answer to Elinor Fuchs's question whether "identity consist[s] of continuously changing personae with no inherent self" (1996: 6), it may be claimed that this is only partially the case, for an evaporation of singularity (see Rebellato 2009: 76) and "an intensification of self-reflexivity" (Clough 2007: 3) need to remain in dialectical tension in order to leave some leeway for alternative constructions of the self at the theatre and elsewhere. By highlighting the constructed nature of the self, Greig's and Suspect Culture's work may contribute to engendering a perception and a projection of a different sense of selfhood, one that is *also* crucially outside, touching and being touched, and in constant movement – thus the vital importance of space. Their work puts forward a sense of self that, by blurring any immediate, rational graspability of the location of bodies and spaces, highlights both dramatically and theatrically the interconnections and interdependencies between human beings, as well as human beings and the world at large. Greig's and Suspect Culture's work achieves this through the e/affects generated via instances of ecstasy and bleeding across, which potentially leave the spectator with a sense of unboundedness in relation to their perception and understanding of bodies and space.

Although instances of ecstasy in Greig's and Suspect Culture's work are usually steeped in violence and seem to suggest a lack of hope, they sometimes hint at fragile acts of re-composition, such as the beauty refracted by *Aiport*'s repeated attempts to connect, Laura eventually not committing suicide (*San Diego*), the audience collectively generating 'Caroline' (*Fragile*), or ecstasy as an experience driven, for instance, by the need to understand (*The Events*). Although the experience of ecstasy is a crucial step towards Butler's renewed sense of unbounded responsibility, it must be highlighted that ecstasy is not merely a question of multiple beings individually experimenting "ekstasis from an immanent self" (Nancy 2007: 73), but of them being in ecstasy, *open*, without the need to eclipse singularity or interiority. Indeed, a sense of bleeding across only retains its significance when presences are understood "as disposed together and exposed to each other" (Nancy 2007: 73). Greig has claimed that, "[t]he more art that is available to us, the larger the imaginative space available for us to inhabit. The more space we inhabit, the more we can locate ourselves. The more we can locate ourselves, the easier it is to navigate, to find our way out of ourselves and towards new possibilities" (2013e: 16). A theatre that highlights the connection between precariousness and precarity by producing moments of ecstasy and bleeding across is not the destination, but just a small contribution towards the beginning of the equal consideration of all presences.[7]

Works Cited

Ahmed, Sara. 2010. "Happy Objects". In: Melissa Gregg and Gregory J. Seigworth (eds.). *The Affect Theory Reader*. Durham: Duke UP. 29–51.
Bauman, Zygmunt. 2000. *Liquid Modernity*. Cambridge: Polity.
Bauman, Zygmunt. 2005. *Liquid Life*. Cambridge: Polity.
Bauman, Zygmunt. 2006. *Liquid Fear*. Cambridge: Polity.
Bauman, Zygmunt. 2010. *44 Letters from the Liquid Modern World*. Cambridge: Polity.
Benjamin, Walter. 1999 [1950]. *Illuminations*. London: Pilmico.
Bourriaud, Nicolas. 2009. *The Radicant*. Trans. James Gussen and Lili Porten. New York: Sternberg P.
Butler, Judith. 2004. *Precarious Life: The Powers of Mourning and Violence*. London and New York: Verso.
Butler, Judith. 2009. *Frames of War: When is Life Grievable?* London and New York: Verso.
Butler, Judith. 2012. "Precarious Life, Vulnerability, and the Ethics of Cohabitation". *Journal of Speculative Philosophy* 26.2: 134–151.
Clough, Patricia Ticineto and Jean Halley (eds.). 2007. *The Affective Turn: Theorizing the Social*. Durham: Duke UP.
Delgado-García, Cristina. 2015. *Rethinking Character in Contemporary British Theatre: Aesthetics, Politics, Subjectivity*. CDE Studies 26. Berlin/Boston: De Gruyter.
Derrida, Jacques. 1997. "Politics and Friendship: A Discussion with Jacques Derrida". Centre for Modern French Thought, University of Sussex. 1 December. Discussion. <http://livingphilosophy.org/Derrida-politics-friendship.htm> [accessed 27 April 2014].
Derrida, Jacques. 2005 [2000]. *On Touching – Jean-Luc Nancy*. Trans. Christine Irizarry. Stanford: Stanford UP.
Eatough, Graham. 2013. "An Interview with Graham Eatough". Interview with Dan Rebellato. In: Graham Eatough and Dan Rebellato (eds.). *The Suspect Culture Book*. London: Oberon. 9–36.
Fuchs, Elinor. 1996. *The Death of Character: Perspectives on Theater after Modernism*. Bloomington: Indiana UP.

---

7 Special thanks to my thesis supervisor Mireia Aragay, and to Enric Monforte and Pilar Zozaya, three inspirational mentoring figures during my period as postgraduate researcher at the University of Barcelona (2010–2014), to whom I am deeply indebted.

Garner, Stanton B. 1994. *Bodied Spaces: Phenomenology and Performance in Contemporary Drama*. Ithaca: Cornell UP.
Giddens, Anthony. 1994. *Modernity and Self-Identity*. Cambridge: Polity.
Giddens, Anthony. 2000. "The Trajectory of the Self". In: Paul Du Gay, Jessica Evans and Peter Redman (eds.). *Identity: A Reader*. London and New Dehli: Sage. 248–266.
Gregg, Melissa and Gregory J. Seigworth (eds.). 2010. *The Affect Theory Reader*. Durham: Duke UP.
Greig, David. 1996. *Airport*. Typescript.
Greig, David. 1998. *One Way Street*. In: Philip Howard (ed.). *Scottish Plays: New Scottish Drama*. London: Nick Hern Books. 227–259.
Greig, David. 1999. *The Speculator*. In: David Greig and Lluïsa Cunillé. *The Speculator/The Meeting*. London: Methuen. 1–119.
Greig, David. 2001. "Introduction". In: Sarah Kane. *Complete Plays*. London: Methuen. ixx–viii.
Greig, David. 2002a. *The Architect*. In: David Greig. *Plays 1: Europe, The Architect, The Cosmonaut's Last Message to the Woman He Once Loved in the Soviet Union*. London: Methuen. 91–201.
Greig, David. 2002b. *Outlying Islands*. London: Faber.
Greig, David. 2007. "Physical Poetry". Interview with Caridad Svich. *PAJ: A Journal of Performance and Art* 29.2: 51–58.
Greig, David. 2010a. *The American Pilot*. In: David Greig. *Selected Plays 1999–2009: San Diego, Outlying Islands, Pyrenees, The American Pilot, Being Norwegian, Kyoto, Brewers Fayre*. London: Faber. 341–418.
Greig, David. 2010b. *San Diego*. In: David Greig. *Selected Plays 1999–2009: San Diego, Outlying Islands, Pyrenees, The American Pilot, Being Norwegian, Kyoto, Brewers Fayre*. London: Faber. 1–121.
Greig, David. 2011a. *Fragile*. In: Hannah Price (ed.). *Theatre Uncut*. London: Oberon. 47–64.
Greig, David. 2011b. "Weekend Scotsman – Architecture Article" <http://www.front-step.co.uk/wp-content/uploads/2011/05/Architecture-article-for-Scotsman.pdf> [accessed 14 October 2013].
Greig, David. 2013a. *The Events*. London: Faber.
Greig, David. 2013b. *Lament*. In: Graham Eatough and Dan Rebellato (eds.). *The Suspect Culture Book*. London: Oberon. 247–297.
Greig, David. 2013c. *Mainstream*. In: Graham Eatough and Dan Rebellato (eds.). *The Suspect Culture Book*. London: Oberon. 188–246.
Greig, David. 2013d. *Timeless*. In: Graham Eatough and Dan Rebellato (eds.). *The Suspect Culture Book*. London: Oberon. 107–187.
Greig, David. 2013e. "Hunting Kudu in Streatham". In: Allan Gillis (ed.). *Edinburgh Review: Haggis Hunting: Fifty Years of New Playwriting in Scotland* 137: 7–17.
Greig, David. n.d. "Suspect Culture: *Mainstream*". <http://www.front-step.co.uk/mainstream/> [accessed 21 October 2013].
Greig, David and Gordon McIntyre. 2009. *Midsummer (A Play with Songs)*. London: Faber.
Harvey, David. 2006. *Spaces of Global Capitalism: Towards a Theory of Uneven Geographical Development*. London and New York: Verso.

Inside/Outside Europe. 2013. "Performances of Capitalism, Crises and Resistance: Notes on Stasis (2)". *insideoutsideeurope.wordpress.com*, 29 October. <http://insideoutsideeurope.wordpress.com/2013/10/29/notes-on-stasis-2/> [accessed 12 May 2014].

Nancy, Jean-Luc. 1991 [1986]. "The Inoperative Community". Trans. Peter Connor. In: Jean-Luc Nancy. *The Inoperative Community*. Ed. Peter Connor. Theory and History of Literature 76. Minneapolis: U of Minnesota P. 1–42.

Nancy, Jean-Luc. 2007 [2002]. *The Creation of the World or Globalization*. Trans. François Raffoul and David Pettigrew. New York: State U of New York P.

Rebellato, Dan. 2002. "Utopian Gestures: David Greig's Texts for Theatre". <http://www.danrebellato.co.uk/utopian-gestures/> [accessed 7 June 2012].

Rebellato, Dan. 2003. "'And I Will Reach Out My Hand with a Kind of Infinite Slowness and Say the Perfect Thing': The Utopian Theatre of Suspect Culture". *Contemporary Theatre Review* 13.1: 61–80.

Rebellato, Dan. 2007. "From the State-of-the-Nation to Globalization: Shifting Political Agendas in Contemporary British Playwriting". In: Nadine Holdsworth and Mary Luckhurst (eds.). *A Concise Companion to Contemporary British and Irish Drama*. Oxford: Blackwell. 245–263.

Rebellato, Dan. 2009. *Theatre & Globalization*. Basingstoke and New York: Palgrave Macmillan.

Rebellato, Dan. 2013. "Suspect Culture: Reaching Out". In: Graham Eatough and Dan Rebellato (eds.). *The Suspect Culture Book*. London: Oberon. 299–329.

Rebellato, Dan. 2014. "Keeping it Real: Stories and the Telling of Stories at the Royal Court". *Contemporary Theatre Review: Interventions* <http://www.contemporarytheatrereview.org/2014/keeping-it-real-royal-court/> [accessed 10 August 2014].

Ryan, Marie Laure. n.d. "Possible-Worlds Theory". <http://www.log24.com/log05/saved/050822-PossWorlds.html> [accessed 22 April 2015].

Scullion, Adrienne. 2007. "Devolution and Drama: Imagining the Possible". In: Berthold Schoene (ed.). *Contemporary Scottish Literature*. Edinburgh: Edinburgh UP. 68–77.

Thompson, Charlotte. 2011. "Beyond Borders: David Greig's Transpersonal Dramaturgy". In: Anja Müller and Clare Wallace (eds.). *Cosmotopia: Transnational Identities in David Greig's Theatre*. Prague: Litteraria Pragensia. 103–117.

Thrift, Nigel. 2008. *Non-Representational Theory: Space/Politics/Affect*. London and New York: Routledge.

Tomlin, Liz. 2013. *Acts and Apparitions: Discourses on the Real in Performance Practice and Theory 1990–2010*. Manchester: Manchester UP.

Wallace, Clare. 2013. *The Theatre of David Greig*. London: Bloomsbury.

Zaroulia, Marilena. 2015. "At the Gates of Europe: Sacred Objects, Other Spaces and Performances of Dispossession". In: Marilena Zaroulia and Philip Hager (eds). *Performances of Capitalism, Crises and Resistance: Inside/Outside Europe*. Basingstoke and New York: Palgrave Macmillan. 193–210.

Elżbieta Baraniecka
Precariousness of Love and Shattered Subjects in Dennis Kelly's *Love and Money*

> JESS: [...] sometimes you think that the only reason we do anything at all, anything, is to reach out and touch
> just touch, just to
> feel
> something (Kelly, *Love and Money*: 279)

Dominated by money and consumerism, the world represented in Dennis Kelly's play *Love and Money* (2006) is an emotionally vacuous place where, as Jess, a character in the play, observes, real connection or feeling have become true rarities, as what is often mistakenly deemed as the safer consumerist desire has replaced the far more precarious experience of love and true connection.

Precariousness, according to Judith Butler, is the unavoidable dependency of our lives on factors that are beyond our control, introducing uncertainty and fear into our existence. It is an intrinsic quality of human life, anchored in the embodied nature of our being: "the body", as Butler argues, "implies mortality, vulnerability, [and] agency: the skin and the flesh expose us to the gaze of others, but also to touch, and to violence, and bodies put us at risk of becoming the agency and instrument of all these as well" (2004: 26). Our bodies open us to the possibility of both experiencing and inflicting pain upon others. Most unsettlingly, perhaps, inherent in our embodiment is the prospect of our death: "To live is always to live a life that is at risk from the outset and can be put at risk or expunged quite suddenly from the outside and for reasons that are not always under one's control" (Butler 2010: 30). Precariousness, therefore, injects tenuousness and insecurity into our existence, qualities which we, and the characters in the play, do not readily welcome, particularly in the absence of control.

Love, as Jean-Luc Nancy points out in his essay "Shattered Love", is often considered to be the force that protects our lives from precariousness by endowing them with a sense of meaning, purpose and the prospect of immanence. According to Nancy, "we [often] think of love in the guise of a substitute or transfiguration of these things that our imaginary figures as realities that we would have possessed, then lost: religion, community, the immediate emotion of the other and of the divine" (1991: 93). Love is often expected to make up for this sense of loss and to fill in the gap that the decline of such realities in the modern world has brought about.

And yet, as Nancy insists, love does not conquer death or lead the subject to fulfilment or immanence. Neither is it an effacement of the subject in a self-sac-

DOI 10.1515/9783110548716-012

rificial gesture. Rather, he claims, love overcomes the opposition between love of the Other, "in which I lose myself without reserve", and self-love, "in which I recuperate myself" (1991: 96). The result of this overcoming is, as Nancy puts it, the joy of presence that comes from the sensation of shared being and transformation of the subjects in love. "*Self* that joys", according to Nancy, "joys of its presence *in the presence of the other*" (1991: 107).

For the recuperation of the self and sharing of being to occur, however, the subjects in love need to first expose themselves to one another and give up their desire for fulfilment, wholeness and immanence "without reserve" (Nancy 1991: 96). Or as Nancy also puts it, they need to be "shattered" and "broken":

> I do not return to myself *from* [love], and consequently, something of *I* is definitely lost or dissociated in its act of loving. [...] *I* return broken [...]. [H]e, this subject, is touched, broken into, in his subjectivity, and he *is* from then on, for the time of love, opened by this slice, broken or fractured, even if only slightly. (1991: 96)

Love, in other words, exposes an opening, a point of vulnerability in the subject, through which the subject and the Other, or, simply, love, can enter and depart (see Nancy 1991: 98). Without this opening there is no love or possibility of joy from shared being, which, as Nancy further defines, is a constant motion or "e-motion" (1991: 88) of "the incessant coming-and-going" (1991: 98). It is a movement that cuts across the subject's heart: "The other comes and cuts across me, because it immediately leaves for the other: it does not return to itself, because it leaves only in order to come again. This crossing breaks the heart" (1991: 98).

As the subject's exposure to the Other, love is defined by Nancy as an experience that is, therefore, rooted in vulnerability. In order to feel love and experience its joy, the subject must let go of its subjectivity, of the prospect of fulfilment and wholeness, and allow for its boundaries to be penetrated. What the experience of love thus reveals is that the subject "doesn't belong to himself, and he doesn't come back to himself: he is shared, like the joy he shares" (Nancy 1991: 108). The same movement, however, that opens the subject to joy and even ecstasy creates a situation that is also particularly susceptible to precariousness, potentially putting the subject in a highly unstable position.[1] As the

---

[1] Nancy uses the term 'ecstasy' when he discusses the concept of community, arguing that the two ideas are inseparable from one another. "Ecstasy", according to Nancy, "implies no effusion, and even less some form of effervescent illumination [...]. [I]t defines the impossibility, both ontological and gnosological, of absolute immanence [...] and consequently the impossibility either of an individuality, in the precise sense of the term, or of a pure collective totality"

subject can neither predict nor control the Other's response, or the way it will be transformed by it, the vulnerability of love may also be a cause of great anxiety and result in self-protective or even aggressive rather than open behaviour.

The characters in Kelly's play all seem to long for the raptures of love and the joys that the moment of sharing brings about, but are at the same time unwilling to expose themselves to the intensified precariousness that is also inherent in the movement of crossing that love creates. Expecting love to exclusively provide them with a sense of belonging and safety, they are sooner or later disillusioned, for love, as Nancy argues, is no guarantee of those things. Many of them turn away from love and choose consumerism instead, as the latter seduces them with promises of instant gratification of their desires. Partly responsible for generating those desires in the first place, it may seem as if the consumerist system was indeed offering a more reliable form of happiness. Such happiness, however, is of the consumerist kind and, therefore, wholly always-already defined and controlled by the system itself.

The play describes the marriage of Jess and David, both of whom have extremely idealistic attitudes towards love and are equally disappointed in their high expectations – Jess in her assumption that love will give meaning and purpose to her existence, and David in his belief that it obliges him to renounce his own needs and sacrifice himself completely in order to save his wife and his marriage from financial crisis. Jess suffers several breakdowns and ultimately attempts to commit suicide but botches it. David, who has now become part of the consumerist system that he used to disdain so passionately, actually finishes the job by pouring alcohol down her throat.

In the following, rather than focusing on the history of Jess and David's marriage, I will first explore the e-motion of love, with all its vulnerable and precarious moments of coming-and-goings. For that purpose, I will analyse the beginning of the play, which shows an email exchange between David and his new love interest, Sandrine, whom he met at work and spent a night with. With David's shy and anxious attempts at making first contact, opening himself and pulling back, taking a risk and withdrawing again, the play's initial scene is a vivid illustration of the vulnerability, shattering and dispossession that subjects in love live through. What it also manifests is how daring and risky such an exposure of the self may turn out to be, as making yourself vulnerable to the Other does not guarantee the Other's unconditional reciprocity and may end in rejection, leaving the subject shattered without the joy of sharing and being shared.

(1991: 6). Ecstatic being is, therefore, a being that transgresses its individuality, a being that is outside of itself.

In the remaining part of the essay, I will focus on the anxiety that the vulnerability of the subject in love causes, in the context of two of the play's female characters – Jess, David's wife and Val, his ex-girlfriend. Both characters fear the heightened precariousness that love brings about and both try to escape it by turning to money – Jess by excessively spending it and Val by excessively earning it. Whereas Val consciously rejects the whole experience and joys of love in favour of safety, apparently without any regrets, and becomes an extremely confident but also cruel and lonely person in the process, Jess remains torn between two choices: experiencing love with both its raptures and risks, or playing it safe by satisfying her desire with consumerist goods. Incapable of bearing the tension that this ambivalence creates, and finding the consumerist answer unable to satisfactorily resolve it, Jess attempts to take her own life.

David

The fact that love can be dangerous is clearly illustrated in the email correspondence between David and Sandrine. The email exchange is initiated by David, who, after plucking up his courage, contacts Sandrine first, clearly aware that he is risking rejection or ridicule. Communication through emails has often been considered to be more superficial than an actual encounter with the Other in real life. As Zygmunt Bauman, for instance, observes, "Once face-to-face contact is replaced by a screen-to-screen variety, it is the surfaces that come into touch. [...] What has suffered as a result is the intimacy, the depth and the durability of human intercourse and human bonds" (2010: 19). Looking at a screen rather than facing a real person may seem to be easier, more secure and less vulnerable, as there is nobody to throw the punch, and no eyes filling with tears in response to a cruel remark. With no immediate, physically palpable consequences, we may feel less answerable for the effects of our actions and words. Because the situation feels less intimate, it may seem much easier to break off a conversation, ignore an uncomfortable question, or post a venomous remark. And yet, as Nancy argues, writing can also be a form of very intimate communication with the Other: "touching the body (or some singular body) with the incorporeality of sense" (2008: 11). In a context of real feelings and true appeal to the Other, the incorporeal communication puts the vulnerable subject at an even greater risk than a real encounter. Though perhaps there is no immediate danger of bodily harm, the potential for misinterpretation, public ridicule or even abuse of our words is just as real and just as painful, leaving permanent scars. With the decrease of our answerability and receptivity to the

Other in a screen-to-screen 'relationship', there is an increase in precariousness and in the possibility of real emotional injury.

It is therefore hardly surprising that there is a visible tension in David's writing, which he clearly experiences as a moment of his self-exposure and vulnerability. Moving between reaching out for more intimate connection and hiding behind the surface of meaningless words, his writing continuously oscillates between desperate longing for love and human touch and fear of putting himself in a very precarious position in the process. The stakes are, in fact, very high, for David is guarding a dark secret about himself, which makes opening himself like this even more risky – a fact which is revealed to Sandrine and the audience only much later in the scene.

His emails to Sandrine reveal David's longings and anxieties through the motions of reaching out and withdrawing that can be seen in his writing, removing the distance between the I and the Other, then putting it back in place again. Unsurprisingly, David's exposure begins very cautiously, as if carefully testing the waters, opening with a very shy:

> Hello
> How are you? Just thought I'd email you to say hello.
> Hello.
> *Beat.* (Kelly, *Love and Money*: 209)

Being the first to initiate contact, even if it is 'only' by email, and even if it is only by what would seem to be with such a risk-free, noncommittal, innocent word as 'hello', is a step which is ridden with a great sense of anxiety if the stakes are high. In such a context, the unavailability of the physical person and their immediate response may make the situation of prolonged anticipation of an answer truly unbearable.

In order to minimize the fearful sensation caused by the possibility of the risk and the vulnerability that such an initial moment of exposure through his 'hello' may create, in the next passage David immediately withdraws again into his safety zone, putting a protective distance between himself and Sandrine by hiding behind a more official tone:

> Just wanted to say thanks for a really instructive couple of weeks and we hope that you learnt as much from us as we did from you. I can honestly say that despite our differing sales strategies (perhaps you found us a touch aggressive?) your customer service recommendations will have a very real impact on the way we do business. However, you will have to forgive me if I maintain a healthy British scepticism regarding your optical relaying systems. It'll never work!
> *He laughs. Beat.* (209)

He then switches to a humorous, witty style in a renewed attempt to establish contact, while still avoiding making himself really vulnerable by resorting to flirting this time:

> Hope the Eurostar was okay. Are you missing our English food? If the pain gets too much my suggestion is have a look behind the fridge, find something brown, stick it in between two slices of bread, et voila! The taste of England.
>
> Beat. (209)

Flirtation, according to Georg Simmel, structures communication as a "simultaneity of implicit consent and refusal" (qtd. in Allan 2010: 202) and, as such, includes both the possibility of invitation and rejection, "hint[ing] at consent and denial [yet] without letting the interaction come to either" (202). The light, flirtatious tone thus offers David the option of an immediate withdrawal by dismissing his email as a merely insignificant trifle without losing face, should the situation take a turn in the wrong direction.

David's longing for real connection seems, however, to go beyond such tentative motions typical of flirtation. The latter, also defined as "purposiveness without consequence" by Thomas S. Henricks in his analysis of flirtatious behaviour (2006: 121), is unable to accommodate David's desire to make himself vulnerable and surrender to the Other "without reserve" (Nancy 1991: 96), though such desire may still be instinctive rather than intentional at this point. Gradually winning him over, the yearning for shared being makes David take risks again and again, and expose himself further and further. Abandoning both the official and the joking tone, he again moves a little closer towards Sandrine and out of himself, in a tentative, circling motion outwards and then back again, from 'hi' to 'hi':

> And as well, I just wanted to say Hi. From me.
> So hi. (209)

The somewhat awkward, insecure phrases mark yet another rather abrupt change in his style. The fragmented sentences indicate the shattering of David's unity as a subject, slowly but surely exposing the ontological fissure in the heart that Nancy speaks about (see 1991: 96). Or to refer to Butler's description of such an exposure of the self, David's fractured writing manifests the workings of the desire for shared being in him, opening him to the Other and instigating an instinctive awareness in him that

> I am not, as it were, an interior subject, closed upon myself, solipsistic, posing questions of myself alone. I exist in an important sense for you, and by virtue of you. If I have lost the conditions of address, if I have no 'you' to address, then I lost 'myself'. (2005: 32)

Perhaps it is this fracturing and the instinctual pull towards the 'you' which the fracturing facilitates, as tentative as it still is at this stage, that allow David to finally gather his courage and quickly say how he feels, even if he is still too afraid to address Sandrine directly at this point:

> I had a great time. And I don't just mean that (but that was great). So I thought I'd just email you coz... I just thought it was sort of...
> Special. (209)

Blurting the last word out like this is reminiscent of quickly pulling off a bandage, which David does:

> There. Said it. Now I feel a twat.
> David. (209)

David's gesture of reaching out, as cautious and as protected by all kinds of walls on all sides as it is, pays off, at least initially. Sandrine does respond, drawing David out of his safety zone more and more with her very direct, fearless candour about their feelings, openly admitting her affection for him, manifesting the joyful side to the crossing undertaken by subjects' hearts:

> I am happy to hear for you today. I ask to myself for this ten days 'Why does this cunt not email me (very British, yes?) Perhaps there is not a feeling that I thought?' But I forgive you because of your delicious sandwich, so thanks. (210)

Tearing down David's protective walls in the process, Sandrine demands even more vulnerability and deeper connection. She challenges and exposes his shields, boldly confronting him with his emotional cowardice:

> [W]hy do you tell me of this stupid story about this fat wanker and his sales of high-speed access? Perhaps you believe I am interested so much to the instalment of telephonic lines that I am waiting with an anticipation to see what will happen next? I ask of myself 'is this the same man who told me my hair was smelled of the future and my eyes were hope?' I forgive you, of course, because you are British and a twat, but please, you can talk me of this bullshit of the telecommunications or you can talk me of how you feel, you cannot do both. (211)

Thus encouraged, David finally lets his guard down, opens himself, and tells Sandrine about his feelings. The result is a cataract of emotions:

> Okay.
> How I feel.
> *Beat.*
> I feel confused. I feel happy. I feel frightened. I feel horny. I feel desperate, I feel worthless because I'm not getting a pay upgrade this year, I feel angry because I wrote such a stupid thing to you and I feel inspired because you didn't let me get away with it. I feel honest, you make me feel
> honest and
> I feel
> *Beat.*
> I feel like I'm betraying
> the
> memory
> of my wife. Or something. I dunno.
> *Pause.*
> There. You wanted to know. (212)

David's overwhelming outpouring of feelings shows the liberating effect that the shattering motions of love have on him: a powerful sense of both release from and expansion of the self in the Other. Nancy describes this sensation as a throbbing heart, with its infinite pulsation of "being-nothing-becoming" (1991: 251). Making ourselves vulnerable, exposing ourselves to the Other is only part of the motion of love according to Nancy, who sees in love an alliance of selfless love and self-love (see Secomb 2007: 144). As much as love ruptures the subject in its motion towards the Other, the same motion also allows him or her to come into being, bringing the subject about:

> Love overcomes the opposition between love of the other [...] and self-love [...]. This overcoming is not achieved by subsuming one within the other, through a dialectical sublation but through the actions and effects of love, actions which transform the subject, who, in love, or through love, is broken into, touched and fractured by love. (Secomb 2007: 145)

This situation of liberating and ecstatic vulnerability and fracturing, however, changes abruptly, as it gives way to the darker side of the experience in all its precariousness. As, undaunted, Sandrine finally manages to tease out all of David's secret about pouring vodka down his dying wife's throat to make sure that her attempted suicide is successful, and with her death their debt is wiped out, this turns out to be more than she bargained for. Suddenly the exhilarating sense of intimacy vanishes, and the vulnerability that connected and opened them to one another initially now takes on bleaker tones. The situation becomes too much for Sandrine and makes her withdraw, creating more and more distance between them and finally breaking off contact altogether, leaving David's desperate appeals for response unanswered. The scene ends with an image of David's utter loneliness and dejection, as this time his writing to "say hi" (219) is left unanswered: a desperate figure, obsessively checking his emails, and receiving none.

What the end of this scene foregrounds is the precariousness of self-exposure. Opening ourselves to the Other in an act of narration involves the risk that, as Butler observes, "the account that I give of myself [may] break apart and [...] become undermined" (2005: 38). Narrating the self necessarily leaves out the corporeal element of our being. As Butler further argues,

> There is a bodily referent here, a condition of me that I can point to, but that I cannot narrate precisely, even though there are no doubt stories about where my body went and what it did and did not do. The stories do not capture the body to which they refer. (2005: 38)

David tries to narrate feeding alcohol to his wife, and give an account of himself from that moment to Sandrine. Since, however, such narration eclipses his bodily presence from the situation, Sandrine cannot see the opacity of David's exposure, overlooking the possibility that there might be something missing in his account, such as the possibility that Jess wanted her death. David's motivation may not have been purely greed, as he presents it to her in words ridden with guilt – something which not even David himself may consciously understand, as the self is also partially opaque to itself (see Butler 2005: 39). Forgetting for a moment that it is alcohol that David is forcing into his wife's mouth, and focusing solely on the bodily dimension of David's account of that moment, the image that emerges is one of two people in a very intimate position of one feeding the other. With their faces locked onto one another, looking deeply into each other's eyes, the scene makes David's narration more ambiguous than it may initially sound:

> So I go back to pouring. And it's hard, it's very hard
> and
> her
> eyes
> open.
> And they look at me. With the bottle.
> Really unfocused. But they knew. They look at me with the
> bottle.
> *Beat.*
> And I managed to feed her about another quarter. Her
> eyes looking at mine.
> Looking into mine.
> Looking into mine. (218)

Neither Sandrine nor the audience know how great David's love really was for Jess at this point, as the story begins in *ultimas res*. How much of himself he sacrificed to save their marriage from financial disaster (see 251–252) – leaving his job as a teacher even though he felt passionately about it, humiliating himself in front of his ex-girlfriend and begging her for a job, and perhaps even prostituting himself for money at some point – only becomes gradually revealed in the course of the play, making the audience revisit their initial judgement of David's account and perhaps even re-evaluate it.

Jess

What dominates the structure of Jess's character is her insatiable yearning for a real connection with another human being, a connection through feeling, which, by extension, she perceives as the thing that gives meaning and depth to human life. Having freshly fallen in love with David, she initially conceives human closeness and the possibility of being touched by the Other in extremely positive terms:

> I might be saying this because I'm in love.
> And
> I might be looking for meaning because I'm in love
> and what is that? alright, what
> chemicals
> or
> electric pulses racing, yes, yes, but let me tell you – and I'm not arguing with all that – but let me tell you that what
> I feel is so
> real
> and tangible
> and powerful and honest and torrential it screams through me sometimes and I want to vomit, I want to puke because I'm in love, isn't that fucked, I'm so in love I could puke.
> (280)

She experiences the touch of love as the most real, tangible, powerful and honest moment in her life – a feeling of joy from shared being that she definitely does not want to give up. But she also senses, even if only subtly at this point, that love, too, makes her vulnerable, which her mention of the feeling of nausea may implicitly indicate – the experience of the precariousness of love, the risk of letting love cut across her heart, to use Nancy's terminology, and opening her selfhood with little control over when and how it comes and goes.

The ambivalence of Jess's attitude to the experience of precariousness is even more clearly manifested by a situation in which she is suddenly confronted with it, or as Butler would put it, solicited by it, in another person, a stranger. Walking down Oxford Street in London she witnesses a man being stabbed at a bus stop. Her reaction seems to be instinctive as she immediately attends to the man's needs by putting her hand on his wound to stop the bleeding. This experience leaves her deeply disturbed:

> It was leaking out of him. It was like it was just leaking, just ebbing out of him and you'd see, you know, you could see him shutting down. You know? Like blood is what, I don't know, we are, or something, just this liquid, like we're bags of water walking around and one day someone pokes a hole in the bag, and that's it, you know, end of story, you start leaking and everything starts shutting down until you close, just close down and then that's it. (272–273)

Jess's distressed description of the human body as fragile, a bag of water that can be pierced at any time, is reminiscent of Butler's definition of precarious life as always exposed to the risk of being expunged without warning. Even though she is not paralyzed by the situation, she is nevertheless deeply unsettled by this experience of human injurability and her own impotence in the face of life's frightening contingency.

Considering the depth of her concern for another human being and her strong desire for true connection and love, it may perhaps seem contradictory that Jess becomes so fascinated by the world of money (or rather by excessively spending it) that it leads her marriage to bankruptcy. Her addiction to shopping, however, may be explained precisely as being directly related to her experience of her own precariousness and vulnerability that the e-motion of love and the incident with the wounded man reveal to her.

Her deep concern for the Other and her fear of her own tenuousness lead her to the yearning for a more spiritual world, a world that is 'more than' money and numbers, where she herself is also more fulfilled and whole, and her life less vulnerable. Jess wishes "to reach out with [her] soul and to find out that it's not all just dust and rocks and nuclear explosions in the hearts of stars" (279). This quasi-religious desire for a certain cosmic "design", a "purpose" and a sense of "belonging" (283–284), may be seen as the reason why she lets herself be seduced by consumerism, which exploits this particular yearning.

One of the most successful marketing strategies of consumerism is that of spiritualizing commodities. The strategy is based on the recognition that even though organized religions are in serious decline, the yearning for spirituality and more meaning in life is just as strongly felt as ever.[2] As François Gauthier points out, drawing upon the marketing guru Douglas Atkin's bestselling book *The Culting of Brands* (2004), in view of the unquenchable, most basic human desire for more, brand design amounts to creating religious cults. "Brands are symbols", he argues, "and the economy of consumerism is a 'spiritual' and 'symbolic economy.' [...C]ults and brands answer similar 'urges' for meaning, identity, community, belonging, security and intelligibility. In other words, the branding ideal is to create a nexus of religiosity" (Gauthier 2013: 152).

And even though, as Slavoj Žižek observes in the related context of commodity fetishism, people like Jess "know very well that there is nothing magic about money, that money is just an object which stands for a set of social relations", they nevertheless "act in real life as if [they] believed that money is a magical thing" (qtd. in Mulhern 2007: 482). Attracted by the quasi-spiritual power of the commodity, Jess seems to be fully aware of its illusory effect and yet falls for it nevertheless:

> Last week I was standing in front of this window staring at this bag that I couldn't afford, and – it was a really nice bag, it was – and I felt like, I felt like I couldn't move, I couldn't leave because of the bag, I mean physically I was rooted to the spot and all the hair was standing up on the back of my neck and I felt terrible because I was getting so emotional about a fucking bag and meanwhile there's still no sign of a two-state solution in the Middle East and it suddenly dawned on me that the bag was designed, not to hold things, but to hold me and it was like hearing for the first time and I felt so elated at this discovery that I immediately went in and bought it because it no longer held power over me, and I felt brilliant for the rest of the day. But when I thought about it again that evening it just seemed ... stupid. (245)

The bag, unlike the 'leaking' body of the man stabbed on the street, offers Jess an image of wholeness that is immediate and within her reach. This promise, however, turns out to be extremely fleeting and disappointing. Disillusioned and yet unable to resist her quasi-religious fascination with commodities, Jess suffers a nervous breakdown, "panicking, screaming, actually, real terror" (249).

Falling in love exposes Jess to the precariousness within herself. She experiences herself and her life as porous, leaking – and she tries to fill in the holes with the quasi-religious solutions offered to her by consumerism. Yet her striving for wholeness and fulfilment stands in opposition to her deep concern for the

---

[2] The yearning for spirituality in consumerist culture is a common topic in contemporary plays, as is demonstrated by Chris Megson in "'And I was struck still by time': Contemporary British Theatre and the Metaphysical Imagination", where he identifies a "metaphysical turn" (2013: 33) in recent British drama.

Other and her desire for real connection with it. Overwhelmed by the tension between these opposing needs, Jess attempts to take her own life by overdosing on pills. Her last act may be seen as a final attempt to exert control over her subjectivity and feel at one with herself. The fact that she fails in the attempt and is dependent on another person to fulfil her wish may be seen as the play's implicit commentary on the thoroughly relational nature of our lives.

Val

Unlike Jess, who wants the joy of shared being in her life but is at the same time scared of letting go of her self, of allowing her subjectivity to be shattered, David's ex-girlfriend Val is much less ambivalent with regard to the question of vulnerability and precariousness (both her own and that of others). In the past, Val was deeply hurt and disappointed by her experience of love, which, she felt, was not capable of transcending the differences in beliefs between herself and David. Nor could it save her from the rejection that she experienced from his friends and David himself. Val experienced the painful side of vulnerability inherent in the emotion of love, which, after exposing her to the Other, after cutting across her heart, departed and never returned with the joy of shared being.

Disappointed with love, Val decides to put her trust in what she feels makes her position less precarious from now on, namely:

> Money. I believe in money.
> David.
> That's my thing now.
> David.
> And in the same way that a plant takes oxygen and nutrients and uses the process of photosynthesis to turn sunlight into energy, I take customers and employees and use the process of hard fucking work to produce cash.
> I am a photosynthesist of cash. (237)

A former Christian, Val's new religion is "cash". Money gives her the sense of power and control over herself and her situation that she did not have when she was in love, and which she now embraces whole*heartedly*. When David turns up at her office many years after their break-up, begging for a job, which he desperately needs to save his marriage from financial ruin, Val does not respond to his precariousness and *heart*-breaking vulnerability with empathy, but instead uses the situation to humiliate him with the utmost cruelty, showing her superiority over him and his total dependency on her decision at every possible occasion. For example, she practically makes him beg for a job:

> VAL: Look, I can give you a job, David.
> DAVID: Can you?
> VAL: Yes.
> *Beat.*
> [...]
> VAL: Is that really what you want? A job here?
> DAVID: Only if you have one.
> VAL: In this? Commerce?
> DAVID: Only if you have one, Val, I'm not asking you to make one for me.
> VAL: I don't have one. I'd have to make one for you.
> DAVID: Right.
> VAL: David?
> *Beat.*
> DAVID: Could you make one for me?
> VAL: Of course I can. I could, couldn't I Paul?
> PAUL: Yes, you could. You definitely could.
> VAL: I don't have one, but I could make one for you.
> *Pause.*
> DAVID: Okay then. Look, Val, could you make one for me? (231–232)

Val clearly revels in David's vulnerability and uses it to assert her own position. Her humiliation of him finally reaches its zenith when she suggests that he can always prostitute himself if he is not satisfied with the salary that she can offer him:

> DAVID: Val, I fucking need money.
> *Beat.*
> VAL: [...]
> Have you ever sucked a man's cock?
> DAVID: What?
> VAL: That's a way of making money.
> DAVID: Val —
> VAL: You or Jess could suck men's cocks, take pictures of it and sell them on the internet.
> *He sort of laughs. She doesn't.* (239)

Avoiding precariousness in order to elude the possibility of pain, injury and lack of control turns Val into an extremely cruel person, who will not hesitate to exploit another's vulnerability to assert her own position of power. Her ostensibly safe position seems to come at a price, however. At the end of the scene, which many reviewers have referred to as the most excruciating one to watch, Val suddenly remembers David's mole and wants to have a look at it. "*She reaches out and touches it with her finger. Pushes it. Beat. Licks it. Beat. Goes back to her seat*" (240). This odd behaviour may be seen as another way of asserting herself over

David, but it may also be read as a lingering echo of Val's desire for human contact.

To conclude, as much as Jess wants "a world that is flesh and bone and love" (284), that world is unattainable without precariousness, which Jess is unwilling to welcome into her life, and which ironically leads her to her factual death. Whereas Jess is thus stuck between love and safety, unwilling to forgo either, Val consciously rejects love for the sake of safety, which gives her control over herself and others but results in her emotional death.

Kelly's *Love and Money* shows the ambiguity of the e-motion of love, which stems from human beings' inherently vulnerable nature. Since vulnerability increases in the situation of love due to the latter's constant crossing of the subjects' hearts, such situations, naturally, are more volatile and therefore more open to the negative side of precariousness. This, in turn, causes anxiety in the subjects in love, and it requires a great amount of courage to not give in to the fear and expose themselves to one another – a risk, as the play shows, that not many are willing to take. Love, as Nancy argues and Kelly illustrates, is an ecstatic experience of shared being which liberates the subject from its isolation and makes it move outside of itself. Yet love is no guarantee of happiness in the sense of security or stability, a complication Kelly's characters also experience which makes them look for other means to satisfy their desire for happiness and joy, often turning to the solutions offered by consumer culture instead. The latter, in fact, often capitalizes on the human yearning for spirituality and completeness, presenting itself as an alternative to religious experiences.

Works Cited

Allan, Kenneth. 2010. *Explorations in Classical Sociological Theory: Seeing the Social World*. London: Pine Forge.

Bauman, Zygmunt. 2010. *44 Letters from the Liquid Modern World*. Cambridge: Polity.

Butler, Judith. 2004. *Precarious Life: The Powers of Mourning and Violence*. London and New York: Verso.

Butler, Judith. 2005. *Giving an Account of Oneself*. New York: Fordham UP.

Butler, Judith. 2010. *Frames of War: When Is Life Grievable?* London and New York: Verso.

Gauthier, François. 2013. "The Enchantments of Consumer Capitalism: Beyond Belief at the Burning Man Festival". In: François Gauthier and Tuomas Martikainen (eds.). *Religion in Consumer Society: Brands, Consumers and Markets*. Farnham: Ashgate. 143–158.

Henricks, Thomas S. 2006. *Play Reconsidered: Sociological Perspectives on Human Expression*. Urbana-Champaign: U of Illinois P.

Kelly, Dennis. 2009. *Love and Money*. In: Dennis Kelly. *Plays One: Debris, Osama the Hero, After the End, Love and Money*. London: Oberon. 207–287.

Megson, Chris. 2013. "'And I was struck still by time': Contemporary British Theatre and the Metaphysical Imagination". In: Vicky Angelaki (ed.). *Contemporary British Theatre: Breaking New Ground.* Basingstoke and New York: Palgrave. 32–56.

Mulhern, Francis. 2007. "Critical Considerations on Fetishism of Commodities." *ELH* 74.2: 479–492.

Nancy, Jean-Luc. 1991 [1986]. "Shattered Love." Trans. Lisa Garbus and Simona Sawhney. In: Jean-Luc Nancy. *The Inoperative Community.* Ed. Peter Connor. Theory and History of Literature 76. Minneapolis: U of Minnesota P. 82–109.

Nancy, Jean-Luc. 2008 [2006]. *Corpus.* Trans. Richard A. Rand. New York: Fordham UP.

Secomb, Linnell. 2007. *Philosophy and Love: From Plato to Popular Culture.* Edinburgh: Edinburgh UP.

Clara Escoda
Ethics, Precariousness and the 'Inclination' towards the Other in debbie tucker green's *dirty butterfly*, Laura Wade's *Posh* and Martin Crimp's *In the Republic of Happiness*

The notion of precarity has acquired primary importance, particularly after the 2008 financial crisis, which has put an end to any sense of security in Western societies. Drawing on Judith Butler's reflections on precariousness and on Adriana Cavarero's "Inclining the Subject: Ethics, Alterity and Natality" (2011a), and turning finally to Jean-Luc Nancy's concept of the "*clinamen*" (1991: 3), this chapter explores how contemporary British theatre has responded to the increasing social, political and economic crisis of late capitalism through the analysis of three plays – debbie tucker green's *dirty butterfly* (2003), Laura Wade's *Posh* (2010; publ. 2012), and Martin Crimp's *In the Republic of Happiness* (2012). The main claim that will be made is that the three plays highlight what Butler calls the "unequal distribution" of precarity and dramatize the necessity to (re)structure social bonds according to the condition of "mutual need and exposure" (Puar 2012: 169).[1]

In addition, it is suggested that the three plays seek to activate spectators as witnesses of contemporary precarity and thus impel them to "assume ethical responsibility for the fragile life of the other" (Ridout 2009: 8). Specifically, the plays dramatize the violence and loneliness of what Cavarero has theorized as the "vertical" (2011a: 195), neoliberal self inherited from modernity, understood as a private, Cartesian body that is shut off from the Other. Opposing this view of an isolated self, the plays invite spectators to conceive of subjectivities that "inclin[e]" (Cavarero 2011a: 195) towards the Other, thus "re-energiz[ing] an ethical responsibility towards the body's vulnerability and precariousness" (Fragkou 2012: 25) and showing how precariousness "can become a source of solidarity and 'common cause' among different groups" (Gill and Pratt 2008: 6).

---

[1] This essay follows Butler's distinction between precarity and precariousness. Butler understands precariousness as "an acknowledgement of dependency, needs, exposure, and vulnerability" (Puar 2012: 163) that can entail "a certain way of opening onto the world" (Butler 2011: 2) and the Other. Precarity, on the other hand, is a created, social type of condition, which is being distributed unequally (see Puar 2012: 169).

DOI 10.1515/9783110548716-013

In her article, Cavarero draws on Hannah Arendt's *The Human Condition* (1998 [1958]), and mobilizes Arendt's definition of 'inclination' against the traditional Western ideology of individualism through a focus on relationality and dependence. In *The Human Condition*, Arendt regards human beings as equal, and sees birth or natality as "the naked fact of our original, physical appearance" (1998: 179), that is, as standing for the essential human condition. As Cavarero explains, taking the new-born as emblematic of the fundamental fact of human vulnerability, Arendt asserts that human beings are "constitutively exposed one to the others, beginning with the initial phase of this appearance: birth" (2011a: 199). Cavarero, however, argues for an ethics of dependency, not interdependency, and claims that the figure of the mother, missing from Arendt's account, is indispensable, since "each human being is, first of all, exposed to the mother" (2011a: 199). Thus, she offers the figure of the mother as an archetype for an ethics of care, as "the mother, or whoever occupies her position, is [primarily] accountable for the face of the Other" (2011b: 15). As she puts it, "The mother not only confirms the relational frame of Arendt's ontology, but also, by predisposing it towards an altruistic ethics, cautions against dreams of horizontal reciprocity and compels us to understand it in terms of dependency" (2011a: 199). The classical tradition of individualism, instead, regards the subject as defined by its autonomy and verticality. As Cavarero claims, from Kant, to Hobbes and Descartes, to Canetti, the modern self has been constructed as "transparent or opaque, enthralled by the dream of its own autonomy and integrity" (2011b: 16). Ultimately, therefore, Cavarero expresses the necessity to redefine the subject as being "inclined" (2011b: 17) to the Other and, moving away from feminist critics who have valued interdependency over dependency, such as Carol Gilligan (1892) or Joan Tronto (1993), she chooses the unbalanced, unilateral inclination as a new ethical paradigm.

Cavarero's inclining subject resonates with Nancy's notion of a subject that leans outside itself, "over that edge that opens up its being in common" (1991: 4). In "The Inoperative Community", Nancy reacts against both the failure of Soviet communism and the subsequent advent of neoliberalism, and sets out to question the idea of a homogeneous community, characterized by 'common being', as opposed to 'being-in-common'. However, he also questions the traditional theory of individualism, in that it takes the individual as a self-contained, self-sufficient being, when s/he is, he claims, "merely the residue of the experience of the dissolution of community" (1991: 3). And, he adds, "the individual can be the origin and the certainty of nothing but its own death" (1991: 3). Thus, Nancy describes the 'singular being' as one who, as opposed to the individual, accepts its own finitude, and the community of singular beings as an ethical paradigm. On these terms, "being 'itself' comes to be defined as relational, as non-absoluteness, and, if you will [...] as *community*" (Nancy 1991: 6). In consequence, we are all exposed to others, "always turned toward an other and faced by him or her, never facing [ourselves]" (Nancy 1991: xxxvii–xxxviii).²

From the point of view of the singular being, it is the "existence of being-in-common, which gives rise to the existence of being-self" (Nancy 1991: xxxvii). Like the figure of the mother, the singular being encompasses the Other and understands it as part of its innermost core. Going back to Cavarero, this chapter will thus finally suggest that *dirty butterfly*, *Posh* and *In the Republic of Happiness* evoke the mother as a "figure" (Cavarero 2011b: 16) of openness and inclination towards the Other, thus potentially laying the foundations for an idea of community that is "not the space of the *egos* [...] but of the *I*'s, which are always others (or else are nothing)" (Nancy 1991: 15). In short, the plays invite spectators to work towards an ethics based on a reconfiguration of the human in which it is the "relation to the other that counts", allowing for an "ontology of linkage and dependence to come to the fore" (Cavarero 2009: 21). Ultimately, the complex implications of using woman as a point of departure for a reconstruction of ethical obligation and of what it means to be human will also be discussed.

dirty butterfly and the Face-to-Face Encounter

In *Staging Black Feminisms*, Lynette Goddard claims that tucker green's plays "use stories of abuse in domestic settings to raise broader questions about care and neighbourliness in contemporary societies" and are about how in "an individualistic society one might be more concerned with one's own needs than with helping someone in despair" (2007: 182; 188). debbie tucker green's *dirty butterfly*, which premiered at the Soho Theatre in February 2003, focuses on the precarious lives of four people, Jo and her husband, a powerful off-stage presence, both white, and their black neighbours Amelia and Jason. Jo is a victim of domestic violence, and even though Amelia and Jason, a couple, overhear how she is abused, they do nothing to intervene. Amelia is annoyed that her sleep is being disturbed and Jason stays awake listening through the thin walls, secretly aroused. This analysis is going to focus on the second part or Epilogue,

---

2 The concept of exposure and vulnerability as essential to the human condition chimes in with Butler's idea that precariousness exposes "our sociality, the fragile and necessary dimensions of our interdependency" (Puar 2012: 170). It is also related to Cavarero's definition of vulnerability as stemming from the Latin roots 'vulnus' and 'vel', both alluding "to hairless and smooth skin, to skin which is most exposed" (2011b: 9) and similarly emphasizing the idea of vulnerability as an essential condition.

which no longer features the three characters on stage, but shows Jo, bleeding from a wound inflicted by her husband and from a possible miscarriage, stepping into the café where Amelia works as a cleaning lady and forcing her to confront her situation of abuse.

Critics like Mireia Aragay and Enric Monforte (2013) and Marissia Fragkou (2012), amongst others, have claimed that tucker green's plays seek to awaken the witness in spectators so that they may be able to move towards an ethics of care. In *dirty butterfly*, as Sara Montes has argued, the centrality of witnessing is underscored by the performance taking place in the round and by the close proximity between actors and spectators, which disrupts the fourth wall (see 2012: 51). This chapter further claims that *dirty butterfly* dramatizes the violence and isolation of what Cavarero terms the vertical, private individual of late capitalism and, by casting spectators as witnesses of Jo's physical vulnerability, ultimately appeals to them to conceive the need for subjectivities that 'incline' towards the Other. As shall be seen, *dirty butterfly* invites spectators to imagine the beginnings of a supportive sisterhood based on women's similar experience and on their position within late capitalism.

As mentioned above, Jo's corporeal vulnerability becomes fully exposed in the Epilogue as she steps into Amelia's working space, where she "*soils the pristine floor with blood and vomit*" (tucker green, *dirty butterfly*: 30). As the stage directions put it, "*the café is extremely shiny, clinically clean*" (38). In contrast, "*Jo is weak. She is damaged. She is bleeding. She is wet. She is defiant (She looks a mess)*" (38). As Monforte has argued (see 2015: 324), in this scene Jo confronts Amelia with what Emmanuel Levinas calls the face of the Other, asking Amelia to take responsibility for her wounded body. Amelia, however, remains shut off from her, claiming that she does not want to see Jo, since seeing her might give rise to an empathic response.

Despite her not wanting to see the face, Amelia eventually steps on Jo's blood. This signals the moment when the women's initially separate worlds and spaces become increasingly intertwined and Jo "*becomes part of [Amelia's] problem*" (48). As the stage directions put it, "*Amelia [...] doesn't notice that she has Jo's blood on her own feet so every step makes a bloody footprint*" (48). Jo's injured body metaphorically comes to stand for the damage inflicted by the neoliberal understanding of the self as vertical and shut off from the Other. In the premiere production at the Soho Theatre, the actors' movement was restricted during the first part of the play, which conveyed the absence of empathy and connectedness while also facilitating a focus on language, thus enabling the conditions for spectatorial witnessing (see Fragkou 2012: 27). In the Epilogue, however, the *mise-en-scène* suddenly changed and became hyperrealistic, in stark contrast with the more minimalist, sparser first part. The heightened realism sought to urgently emphasize to spectators the necessity for witnessing. In the 2008 Young Vic production, on the other hand, the stage was very minimalistic throughout, with just an empty, low platform for actors to stand on which was surrounded by benches for spectators, thus directly interpellating them as witnesses.

By positioning spectators as witnesses of Jo's suffering and open, porous body, tucker green invites them to, unlike Amelia and Jason, empathize with Jo. As Monforte puts it,

> [W]hile Amelia and Jason spend the whole play showing no solidarity with Jo, evading their ethical responsibility towards the 'other' and refusing to meet the 'face', tucker green makes spectators look the 'face' in the face [...]. And hold the look." (2015: 324)

Jo stays in the café, risking her own death, so that Amelia will acknowledge her precarious body, thus radically "abandoning her own balance" (Cavarero 2011a: 203). Ultimately, that is, the scene evokes the archetypal figure of the 'inclining' mother as a possible foundation for a new ethics. The footprints, which form a trail of red blood, join the two women's bodies, stressing the connection between them and invoking their shared vulnerability and mutual dependence.

In the contemporary context of extreme precariousness and disposability, Jo uses her body as a surface of representation and communication in order to claim that she, as a precarious, unseen, unacknowledged body, has not yet been "disposed of", in Butler's words (Puar 2012: 168). Thus, overall, *dirty butterfly* evokes the need for a new ontology consisting of "unbalanced and even unilateral exposures" (Cavarero 2011a: 196), evoking the figure of the mother as paradigm or primary instance of a "*care* of the *other*" (Cavarero 2011a: 198).

Posh: A Deconstructive Satire of the Neoliberal Subject

Wade's *Posh* is a two-act play concerning the ten male members of the exclusive Oxford University 'Riot Club', who rent out a country pub's dining room for their termly dinner and, in the course of the night, end up destroying the pub as well as beating up the landlord. Seeing they must take the landlord to hospital, they decide they will pin the blame on Alistair, who ends up in jail, but they all agree that they will make sure they see him right.

As Aleks Sierz has pithily put it in his review of the play, *Posh* is a "timely study of class, power and masculinity" (2012). It was inspired by the "violent antics of the Bullingdon Club" (Cochrane 2012), to which "politicians like James Cameron or Chancellor George Osbourne famously belonged" (Cavendish

2012). Members of the Bullingdon Club were "rumoured to have smashed up all the instruments [...] belonging to the string band they'd hired to play" (Cochrane 2012). As Charles Spencer claims, "the damage the club members inflict on the pub and its employees precisely mirrors the damage the Tories are now doing to Britain with their cuts and their austerity programme" (2012). Indeed, *Posh* shocked audiences because of its harsh criticism of the privileges and snobbery of a class that, having attended a prestigious university such as Oxford, proves to be devoid of any ethics instead of setting a moral example.

In the premiere production at the Royal Court Theatre Downstairs in 2010, the whole play unfolded in the pub, which was located in a basement, thus clearly conveying a strong sense of claustrophobia. In such a setting, spectators were forced to bear witness to the gradual material destruction and degradation not only of the pub but also of humane individuals like Chris, the landlord, and his daughter Rachel. The *mise-en-scène*, indeed, clearly set out to shock spectators out of complacency by presenting them with a frantic escalation of violence, produced by the boys' desire to live up to the highest possible living standard. It sought to lead spectators to experience the contempt of the upper class for the middle and working classes in the context of the financial crisis by showing the boys' relentless desire to provoke and humiliate Chris and Rachel in order to foreground their own power and privilege. *Posh* takes the metaphor of trashing as a central idea, and dramatizes how the Riot Club's veneer of civilization wears out during the night, thus unveiling the violence and abuse that underlie the boys' sense of entitlement.

Described as "incendiary and savage" (King 2013), *Posh* criticizes the neoliberal mind-set and the type of "self-sufficient, impermeable egos it creates" (Cavarero 2011a: 194). In contrast, it invites spectators to witness forms of subjectivity based on dispossession and dependency, values which, in the play, are seen to be the precondition for ethics. This chapter focuses on the second act, and specifically on the moment when the landlord sees the destruction the boys have wreaked in the room and resists their paying their way out of it by bribing him with money. It contends that, through Charlie, the prostitute, and particularly the landlord, who opposes the boys' network of privilege from the start and finally forces them to redefine themselves as powerless and finite, *Posh* invites spectators to encounter their "human sharing in finitude, insufficiency and dependence" (Cavarero 2011a: 195).

In the course of the dinner, the boys dream of doing "drunken skiing" while being forced to admit that "cousins in Greece [are] eating *actual grit* right now" because of the "Debt crisis" (Wade, *Posh*: 18; 57). Through its leitmotif of destruction and exploitation of the Other for individual benefit, which culminates when the boys hire a prostitute and seek to exploit her, the play stands as a critique of "neoliberal frames of privatization" wherein "jobs are being taken away, hopes are obliterated, and bodies are instrumentalized and worn out" (Butler and Athanasiou 2013: 12).

The conversation flows ripe with "misogynist disdain" (Cochrane 2012) and, when the prostitute arrives, they ask her if she can be "under the table" (89) while all of them sit around it. Yet Charlie immediately refuses to satisfy their whims, telling them they have to "talk that up at the agency" and that she does not do "more than two visits in a row without a proper break" (91–92). While the men insist that "one would probably assume we pay you and you do whatever's required", or offer her a "considerable bigger fee, which the agency needn't know about" (91), Charlie confronts them with a network not of privilege but of rights that protect her personhood. The climax is finally reached when Charlie claims that "You could do it yourself – you'll be under the table, a mouth's a mouth" (93).

Later on, they intimidate Chris's daughter, and as she also refuses to satisfy their whims, become increasingly resentful towards her and Chris himself, whom they call "bourgeois" (100) and who, little by little, begin to represent what for them is the new, aspiring social class that does not allow them full freedom to run the country. Finally, then, they become increasingly violent with both Rachel and Chris, ultimately "trashing the room" (126). Once the landlord sees the mayhem in the room, the men offer to give him a huge amount of money that will cover the costs of the repairs, but Chris immediately tells them he is well aware that they are "buy[ing] their way out of everything" (130), and squarely refuses to take the money. It is when Chris tells them that he will sue them for sexual assault given the way they have intimidated his daughter, and reminds them that this is something they cannot pay their way out of, that Alistair, Guy, Harry and Miles punch him until he falls unconscious.

Like tucker green, Wade also explores the mother understood as a figure of dispossession, and thus a "limit to the autonomous and impermeable self-sufficiency of the liberal subject" (Butler and Athanasiou 2013: 2). Like Jo in *dirty butterfly*, Chris "conspicuously abandon[s] [his] own balance" (Cavarero 2011a: 203) in order to "compel the self to renounce its arrogant pretensions of autonomy and independence" (Cavarero 2011a: 199). As Butler and Athanasiou put it, "dispossession can be a term that marks the limits of self-sufficiency and that establishes us as relational and interdependent beings [...] We are dispossessed of ourselves [...] by virtue of being moved and even surprised or disconcerted by [the] encounter with alterity" (2013: 3). Chris offers up his body in order to defend his ethical views and, in a context of unbridled neoliberal capitalism in which lives are rendered "available" and "expendable" (Butler and Athanasiou 2013: 31), his gesture evokes the need for the inclining subject in order to move towards an ethics of care.

In the Republic of Happiness: Witnessing the Ethical Subject

In the Republic of Happiness is divided into three parts, "The Destruction of the Family", "The Five Essential Freedoms of the Individual" and "In the Republic of Happiness". Part One, which opens with a naturalistic stage setting, presents a family during their Christmas lunch as it is interrupted by the visit of Uncle Bob, who has come to say good-bye as he and his wife Madeleine are leaving for another country. Part Two is composed of five speeches, and the "characters' names disappear [as] the cues are randomly attributed to the actors" (Rousseau 2013: 2). Finally, Part Three, which this chapter focuses on, presents Madeleine and Uncle Bob's relationship in the foreign country they were about to leave for in Part One.

In an interview with Crimp, "Martin Crimp in the Republic of Satire", Aleks Sierz claims that "*In the Republic of Happiness* [...] reads like it's his most experimental work since his 1997 masterpiece, *Attempts on Her Life*" (Crimp 2012b). This chapter claims that, in Part Three, both the dialogue and the songs dramatize the loneliness, isolation and violence of the neoliberal self, the limitations of the vertical subject of individualism, and present Uncle Bob as a subject predisposed or inclined towards the Other. It is specifically through Uncle Bob's monologue in Part Three, where he tells Madeleine about the disappearance of his "citizens" (Crimp, *In the Republic of Happiness:* 84), that the play interpellates spectators as "'response-able'" (Lehmann 2006: 185) witnesses of the destruction of solidarity and self-awareness in neoliberal, late capitalist societies.[3]

As Martin Middeke has claimed, "even in those plays that seem fairly grounded in reality, the recipient encounters ambiguous, menacing, often opaque and surreal, never conclusive [...] scenarios, dreamscapes, or frescoes of the skull" (2011: 97). Indeed, for the Royal Court premiere production of *In the Republic of Happiness* in 2012, Crimp and director Dominic Cooke turned the stage into a Magritte-like painting dominated by white walls and an echoing emptiness, thus suggesting to spectators that they found themselves within the

---

3 As Crimp puts it, the starting point for the play was his awareness that society "makes us feel angry and vulnerable even when we are materially prosperous" (2013b). And he adds, "Because the US/UK model of *laissez-faire* liberalism insists that individuals are entirely responsible for their own destiny – while at the same time fabricating needs which – notoriously – can never be met. These voices were the starting point for this play" (2013b).

consciousness of the vertical, individualist, neoliberal subject and, as shall be seen, interpellating them to search for a new ethics grounded instead on dispossession and proximity.

Part Three presents Madeleine and Uncle Bob in the late capitalist 'utopia' they were moving to in Part One, where they have become heads of a republic where both happiness and connectedness are imposed and understood in terms of a technology-ridden, consumerist society of spectacle, and where true contact is replaced by simulation and mediation.[4] In this context, Madeleine wants Uncle Bob to sing the "hundred-per-cent happy song" (85) to the 'citizens', a song that describes a dystopia where the earth has "burned to ash", yet insists that "we're the happiest that human beings / have ever so far been" (89). This uncaring, unequal society of spectacle is conveyed through Uncle Bob's song and speeches, which mould the 'citizens' according to Madeleine's desires. As Madeleine herself puts it, there "must be so many billions of malleable human cells [...] being moulded, Robbie – yes moulded by me through you inside each skull by the sound of each thrilling syllable of our hundred-per-cent happy song" (85).

In an interview with Dan Rebellato, Crimp claimed that Part One of *In the Republic of Happiness* represents the institution of the family, Part Two the institution of the individual, and Part Three the institution of the state (see Crimp 2013a). From this perspective, Uncle Bob's and Madeleine's republic represents the neoliberal governance of the present moment, which "invests – politically, psychically, and economically – in the production and management of forms of life: it 'makes live' [...] while shattering and economically depleting certain livelihoods, foreclosing them, rendering them disposable and perishable" (Butler and Athanasiou 2012: 31) – in other words, radically and unequally precarious.

Uncle Bob, on the other hand, confronts the *laissez-faire*, neoliberal state with his incessant questioning of Madeleine's certainties and by reminding her of his vulnerability. Indeed, before singing the song in Part Three, Uncle Bob expresses his doubts *vis-à-vis* the type of governance he and his wife represent, and portrays a landscape not only of the destruction and precariousness brought about by neoliberal policies, but also of the moral indifference on the part of individuals who have stopped being citizens, that is, responsible, ethical, resistant individuals. His monologue takes the form of a testimony that is offered to Madeleine as well as to the audience to witness:

---

[4] As is well known, in *The Society of Spectacle* (2004 [1967]), Guy Debord claimed that public life was becoming increasingly dominated by the image, which was rendering individuals passive and docile in relation to the social injustices the system itself generated.

> What lectures? Where are the citizens? Why aren't they thronging the staircase? Or using small plastic cups to drink coffee? Why can't I hear the small plastic cups crackle? Is it I'm going deaf? You talk about the world but I listen and listen and I still can't hear it. Where has the world gone? What is it we've done? [...] And of course I'm happy but I feel like I'm one of those characters Madeleine crossing a bridge and the bridge is collapsing behind me slat by slat by slat but I'm still running on – why? What's holding me up? (84)

Uncle Bob expresses himself in a lyrical, indeterminate, metaphorical language, a language that is characteristic of testimonies, and which, as Shoshana Felman and Dori Laub have asserted, is defined by "fragmentation" and "cognitively dissonant" speech modes (1992: 24). He, for instance, portrays the state of anxiety and fear of those who, like himself, lament the loss of ethical structures that can sustain individuals in late capitalist society through the metaphor of the collapsing bridge. His speech seeks to interpellate spectators regarding the atomization of the subject in late capitalism, where forms of community, equality and solidarity are being violently eroded in favor of radical consumerism and inequality.[5]

This kind of defamiliarized language, as Theodor W. Adorno puts it, attempts to "make those things be heard which ideology conceals" (2004: 214) in order to make social contradictions visible. Adorno suggests that "the subjective being that makes itself heard in lyric poetry [...] has, so to speak, lost nature and seeks to recreate it [...] through descent into the subjective being itself" (2004: 215–216). Because the images Uncle Bob uses in order to refer to the socio-political order his wife embodies are highly personal, spectators need to decode them by bringing to bear remnants of their own similar experiences of coercion, thus becoming, in Felman and Laub's words, "double witnesses" (1992: 58) – that is, witnesses to Uncle Bob's act of testimony and to themselves. Through the poetics of testimony, spectators are thus interpellated in their capacity for ethical responsiveness. While the 'citizens' of Uncle Bob's republic have ceased to enact resistance, he urges spectators to envision a new kind of politics and new subjectivities beyond the present moment of capitalism. The dramatization of testimony is part and parcel of a search for a new ethics grounded on dispossession and proximity. This was effectively foregrounded in

---

[5] Madeleine is destabilized by Uncle Bob's testimony and appeal to vulnerability, and seeks to divert his attention by suggesting they could take "a trip" somewhere (86). Their dialogue, at this point, clearly resonates with Richard and Corinne's conversation in *The Country* (Crimp 2005), where Richard seeks to divert his wife's attention after her denunciation of his behaviour by suggesting they could "drive somewhere" (2005: 359). As in *The City* (2008), in *In the Republic of Happiness* it is a woman, however, who occupies a position of power. Regarding Crimp's approach to gender, both plays can be considered to be rewritings of *The Country* and exercises in self-questioning on Crimp's part.

Cooke's production through the Magritte-like emptiness of the stage, the setting where Uncle Bob searches for a more intimate, deeper relationship with Madeleine, which thus became a metaphor for Uncle Bob's desire to incline towards and connect with the Other.

Uncle Bob's sense of dispossession and exposure stands in sharp contrast in the play with Madeleine's verticality. This was emphasized in Cooke's production by the emptiness and whiteness of the room where Uncle Bob kept reaching towards her. Uncle Bob uses a physical language throughout, as if trying to emerge out of the limits of his own finitude. As he puts it, for instance, "I'm opening my mouth now, sweetheart – look at it – look – opening it now – here – my mouth – now – look at it – and I don't know what's coming out" (84). At the same time, when Madeleine orders him to kiss her, he confronts her hierarchical, commanding kiss with a much stronger, almost primeval desire for contact. Like Levinas, *In the Republic of Happiness* redefines ethics not as a pre-existing, normative epistemology, but as stemming from a common human vulnerability, bodily exposure and mutual need. Through the defamiliarization of testimony – reinforced in Cooke's production by the feeling of isolation conveyed by the *mise-en-scène* – spectators are impelled to move towards an ethical framework based on proximity and on what Levinas metaphorically terms the space of the "meeting" (1989: 69) or the face-to-face encounter with the Other.

And indeed, as Butler and Athanasiou put it, dispossession "establishes the self as social, as passionate, that is, as driven by passions it cannot fully consciously ground or know, as dependent on environments and others who sustain and even motivate the life of the self itself" (2013: 4). Madeleine, on the other hand, as mentioned earlier, represents the vertical subject of property, utterly hierarchical and shut off from the Other, that neoliberal capitalism is relentlessly "moulding" (Crimp, *In the Republic of Happiness:* 85), as she herself puts it in Part Three. The precariousness of the neoliberal order that can be gleaned from the conversations the family hold in Part One has not led Madeleine to question the grand narrative of late capitalism. After she interrupts the dinner in Part One, and before leaving, she breaks into a song where she explains that she has "booked a ticket: I'm flying first class / to a cool place thin as a pane of glass / where I just have to swipe a security pass / to swim in the milk of thick white stars" (37), and goes on to complain of what she calls "fixed human relationship[s]" (36). Instead, she simply accepts that, like the fluctuations of an ever changing, unpredictable market, "some people you lose / some people you keep", admitting that "[she] never go[es] deep" (36).[6]

---

6 In Cooke's production for the Royal Court, Madeleine's song was staged as a deeply melan-

In Cooke's production, Part Three created a poetic space that was offered as a possible vehicle of transformation for spectators, triggering their imaginative search for new ethical paradigms. Ultimately, through Uncle Bob's yearning for Madeleine and his openness to her, Crimp evokes the figure of the mother and the need for a "unilateral 'inclination'" (Cavarero 2011a: 195) towards the Other as the basis for a reconstruction of ethics and of a community, in Nancy's terms, of singular beings. Against a neoliberal construction of the self as a self-contained entity/body which "neither exposes itself nor leans out" (Cavarero 2011a: 199), Uncle Bob declares a "congenital vulnerability as his constitutive condition" (Cavarero 2011a: 200). Thus, by representing the dispossessed subject and evoking the figure of the mother, Crimp – as well as Cooke in his premiere production of the play – seek to lay the foundations for a less mediated understanding of identity and community away from the vertical, neoliberal, contemporary self.

Conclusion

In the context of neoliberal capitalism, playwrights like tucker green, Wade or Crimp dramatize the figure of the mother as a figure of dispossession and inclination in order to invite spectators to work towards a new ethics based on the positive value, in Butler's terms, of fragility and precariousness as our "common non-foundation" (Puar 2012: 170). In so doing, their plays seek to break with the consumerist values of acquisition and individualism, and highlight the potential for new subjectivities and new kinds of politics that can evade or exceed capitalist colonization. The possibility of inclination should not, however, be considered as essentially female. Cavarero herself is wary of essentializing 'maternal' inclination as something belonging only to women. As she points out, that is precisely how patriarchy has defined and encased women, i.e. by means of the stereotype of the self-renouncing mother (see Cavarero 2011a: 201). Rather than identify any allegedly specific essence for women, the figure of the mother signals primarily "a predisposition to respond" (Cavarero 2011a: 202). It is in this sense that it presents us with an immediate ethical force.

---

cholic one. As she sang, the stage was progressively flooded by a backdrop of intense red light, creating a highly dramatic, poetic stage picture. Set against Madeleine's light blue dress, the light seemed to emphasize the passion, feeling and vulnerability that the vertical neoliberal subject denies, and functioned as the unconscious or mirror image of the "Hard. Clear. Sharp. Clean" (35) life Madeleine aspires to, precisely urging spectators, instead, to "go deep".

Understood in Cavarero's sense, then, the figure of the mother lays the ground for a rethinking of community in terms of Nancy's notion of the singular being, a being that is fully aware of its own existential precariousness and finitude and therefore acknowledges that "only a being-in-common can make possible a being-separated" (Nancy 1991: xxxvii). As he puts it, "one cannot make a community with simple atoms. There has to be a *clinamen* [...] an inclination or an inclining from one toward the other" (1991: 3). In contrast with the radical and, in Cavarero's terms, vertical individualism dramatized in the plays, the figure of the mother enables the clinamen or inclination between subjects that is indispensable if a community of singular beings is to be attained. The three plays redefine community as "compearance" (Nancy 1991: 29) or as the expression of "finitude itself" (Nancy 1991: 28). In Nancy's words, the "singular being appears [...] at the end (or at the beginning), with the contact of the skin (or the heart) of another singular being, [...] always *other*, always shared, always exposed" (1991: 28). Ultimately, the three plays foreground the body and its impulses and inclinations as the basic locus of our shared vulnerability and exposure and, therefore, of our claim to equality, and redefine subjectivity as always already exposed and encompassing the Other.

Works Cited

Adorno, Theodor W. 2004 [2000]. "Lyric Poetry and Society". In: Brian O'Connor (ed.). *The Adorno Reader*. 3rd ed. Oxford: Blackwell. 212–229.
Aragay, Mireia and Enric Monforte. 2013. "Racial Violence, Witnessing and Emancipated Spectatorship in *The Colour of Justice, Fallout* and *random*". In: Vicky Angelaki (ed.). *Contemporary British Theatre: Breaking New Ground*. Basingstoke and New York: Palgrave. 96–120.
Arendt, Hannah. 1998 [1958]. *The Human Condition*. 2nd ed. Chicago: U of Chicago P.
Butler, Judith. 2011. "Precarious Life, Vulnerability, and the Ethics of Cohabitation". Centre de Cultura Contemporània (CCCB), Barcelona. 11 July. Lecture manuscript.
Butler, Judith and Athena Athanasiou. 2013. *Dispossession: The Performative in the Political*. Cambridge: Polity.
Cavarero, Adriana. 2009 [2007]. *Horrorism: Naming Contemporary Violence*. Trans. William McCuaig. New York: Columbia UP.
Cavarero, Adriana. 2011a. "Inclining the Subject: Ethics, Alterity and Natality". In: Jane Elliot and Derek Attridge (eds.). *Theory After 'Theory'*. London and New York: Routledge. 194–204.
Cavarero, Adriana. 2011b. "Unbalanced Inclinations". Centre de Cultura Contemporània (CCCB), Barcelona. 11 July. Lecture manuscript.
Cavendish, Dominic. 2012. Rev. of *Posh*, by Laura Wade. telegraph.co.uk, 30 November. <http://www.telegraph.co.uk/culture/theatre/theatre-features/9255360/Laura-Wade-on-Posh-rich-boys-having-a-riotous-time.html> [accessed 26 October 2013].

Cochrane, Kira. 2012. Rev. of *Posh*, by Laura Wade. *theguaradian.co.uk*, 16 May. <http://www.theguardian.com/stage/2012/may/16/laura-wade-return-thugs> [accessed 26 October 2013].
Crimp, Martin. 2005. *Plays Two: No One Sees the Video, The Misanthrope, Attempts on her Life, The Country*. London: Faber.
Crimp, Martin. 2008. *The City*. London: Faber.
Crimp, Martin. 2012a. *In the Republic of Happiness*. London: Faber.
Crimp, Martin. 2012b. "Martin Crimp in the Republic of Satire". Interview with Aleks Sierz. *theartsdesk.com*, 10 December. <http://www.theartsdesk.com/theatre/interview-martin-crimp-republic-satire> [accessed 16 May 2015].
Crimp, Martin. 2013a. "Dialogue with Martin Crimp". Interview with Dan Rebellato. "Dealing with Martin Crimp". Department of Drama and Theatre at Royal Holloway, University of London, and University of Birmingham. 1 January. Conference.
Crimp, Martin. 2013b. "Interview with Martin Crimp, Author of *In the Republic of Happiness*". *Aesthetica Online Magazine*. <http://www.aestheticamagazine.com/blog/interview-with-martin-crimp-writer-of-in-the-republic-of-happiness> [accessed 17 July 2014].
Debord, Guy. 2004 [1967]. *The Society of Spectacle*. Trans. Donald Nicholson-Smith. Detroit: Black and Red.
Felman, Shoshana and Dori Laub. 1992. *Testimony: Crises of Witnessing in Literature, Psychoanalysis, and History*. London and New York: Routledge.
Fragkou, Marissia. 2012. "Precarious Subjects: Ethics of Witnessing and Responsibility in the Plays of debbie tucker green". *Performing Ethos* 3.1: 23–39.
Gilligan, Carol. 1982. *In a Different Voice: Psychological Theory and Women's Development*. Cambridge: Harvard UP.
Gill, Rosalind C. and Andy Pratt. 2008. "In the Social Factory? Immaterial Labour, Precariousness and Cultural Work". *Theory, Culture & Society* 25.7–8: 1–30.
Goddard, Lynette. 2007. *Staging Black Feminisms: Identity, Politics, Performance*. Basingstoke and New York: Palgrave Macmillan.
King, Alison. 2013. Rev. of *Posh*, by Laura Wade. *theindependent.co.uk*, 22 May. <http://www.independent.co.uk/arts-entertainment/theatre-dance/features/laura-wade-queen-of-theatres-brat-pack-7771214.html>[accessed 26 October 2013].
Lehmann, Hans-Thies. 2006 [1999]. *Postdramatic Theatre*. Trans. Karen Jürs-Munby. London and New York: Routledge.
Levinas, Emmanuel. 1989 [1963]. "Martin Buber and the Theory of Knowledge". In: Seán Hand (ed.). *The Levinas Reader*. Oxford: Blackwell. 59–74.
Middeke, Martin. 2011. "Martin Crimp". In: Martin Middeke, Peter Paul Schnierer and Alex Sierz (eds.). *The Methuen Drama Guide to Contemporary British Playwrights*. London: Methuen. 82–102.
Monforte, Enric. 2015. "The Theatre of debbie tucker green: A Dramaturgy of the Border". In: Núria Santamaria and Francesc Foguet (eds.). *De fronteres i arts escèniques*. Lleida: Punctum. 319–332.
Montes, Sara. 2012. "Witnessing, Testimony and Ethics: The Theatre of debbie tucker green". MA Dissertation. University of Barcelona.
Nancy, Jean-Luc. 1991 [1986]. "The Inoperative Community". Trans. Peter Connor. In: Jean-Luc Nancy. *The Inoperative Community*. Ed. Peter Connor. Theory and History of Literature 76. Minneapolis and London: U of Minnesota P. 1–42.

Puar, Jasbir (ed.). 2012. "Precarity Talk: A Virtual Roundtable with Lauren Berlant, Judith Butler, Bojana Cvejić, Isabell Lorey, Jasbir Puar and Ana Vujanović". *TDR: The Drama Review* 56.4: 163–177.
Ridout, Nicholas. 2009. *Theatre & Ethics*. Basingstoke and New York: Palgrave.
Rousseau, Aloysia. 2013. "Martin Crimp's *In the Republic of Happiness:* Reinventing the Musical?" *Études britanniques contemporaines* 45: 1–5. <http://ebc.revues.org/877> [accessed 10 April 2014].
Sierz, Aleks. 2012. Rev. of *Posh*, by Laura Wade. *thestage.co.uk*, 24 May. <https://www.thestage.co.uk/reviews/2012/posh-review-at-duke-of-yorks-theatre/?> [accessed 26 October 2013].
Spencer, Charles. 2012. Rev. of *Posh*, by Laura Wade. *thetelegraph.com*, 16 April. <http://www.telegraph.co.uk/culture/theatre/theatre-reviews/7597617/Posh-Royal-Court-review.html> [accessed 26 October 2013].
Tronto, Joan. 1993. *Moral Boundaries: A Political Argument for an Ethic of Care*. New York: Routledge.
tucker green, debbie. 2003. *dirty butterfly*. London: Nick Hern.
Wade, Laura. 2012 [2010]. *Posh*. London: Oberon.

Martin Riedelsheimer
Vulnerability and the Community of the Precarious in David Greig's *The Events*

Before David Greig's *The Events* premiered at the Edinburgh Fringe Festival in 2013, there had been concerns that the play might somewhat inappropriately turn mass murder into a musical (see Campbell 2013). While such worries turned out to be unfounded, it is certainly true that *The Events* uses unusual theatrical means, most striking among them a full-scale choir on stage, to address a delicate topic: it portrays the consequences of a violent irruption into communal life – a gunman's attack on a multicultural choir – so as to remind the theatre-going public of the risks of living in an open, liberal society. The play is therefore concerned with what Judith Butler has termed the "condition of primary vulnerability" (2004: 31) all humans are subject to and it reflects on responses to this precarious state of being. Both the fragmentary structure of Greig's play and his protagonist Claire's encounters with her multiple Others in her search for an explanation for the traumatic 'events' serve to engender the precarious aesthetics of *The Events*, which is reinforced by the use of strategies of contingency in performance practice. While thus an air of precariousness – both in Butler's sense and, when it comes to the face-to-face encounter between the victim and the shooter, in the sense of Emmanuel Levinas's ethics – prevails in Greig's play, it also projects a potential community of the precarious, the choir, as its response to this vulnerable condition.

My understanding of precariousness is based on Samuel Johnson's definition in his famous *Dictionary of the English Language*, where the 'precarious' is described as that which is "dependent; uncertain, because *depending on the will of another*; held by courtesy; changeable or alienable at the pleasure of another" (1968; emphasis added). As a word of warning to writers (and presumably also critics) engaging with the precarious, Johnson adds that "[n]o word is more unskilfully used than this with its derivatives. It is used for uncertain in all its senses; but it only means uncertain as dependent on others" (1968). It seems that this definition still underlies most, if not all, philosophical and theoretical uses of 'precariousness' and allows for a lucid approach of the precarious in contemporary theatre. In her detailed analysis of the semantics of the precarious, Katharina Pewny (see 2011: 25–37) identifies the aspects of revocability, of being uncertain, or at risk, and of being delicate or fragile as defining elements of the precarious. The meaning of 'precarious', she concludes with a pun, is *"ungesichert"* (2011: 36), which means both 'uncertain' and 'insecure'. De-

DOI 10.1515/9783110548716-014

spite the semantic vagueness of the term, the crucial aspect of precariousness is, as Johnson insists, that the state of uncertainty is caused by the dependence on an Other. In this sense, precariousness is always rooted in an encounter with the Other, which explains why the term has been fruitfully used both in political and in ethical discourse.

Thus Emmanuel Levinas describes the face, a notion that is central to his work, as precarious. The face is that which makes an encounter with the Other "straightaway ethical" (Levinas 1985: 87). This is because of the unprotectedness and nudity of the face (see 1985: 86) – it is that part of the body which ultimately cannot be covered, which remains bare skin. It therefore allows for a direct, unmitigated confrontation, face to face with the Other. It is in this encounter with the Other that the precarious nature of the face becomes apparent:

> The proximity of the other is the face's meaning, and it means from the very start in a way that goes beyond those plastic forms which forever try to cover the face like a mask of their presence to perception. But always the face shows through these forms. Prior to any particular expression and beneath all particular expressions, which cover over and protect with an immediately adopted face or countenance, there is the *nakedness and destitution* of the expression as such, that is to say extreme exposure, defencelessness, *vulnerability itself.* (Levinas 1989: 82–83; emphasis added; see also Levinas 1996: 167)

The primary condition of the Levinasian face, then, is that of defencelessness and vulnerability, where the Other is at my mercy – a perspective that is crucial to Levinasian thought. For in Levinas's ethics, there is a primacy of the Other over my self, that is, the Other has replaced my self at the centre of ethical consideration (see Ridout 2009: 52–53). Thus, Levinas does not focus on my vulnerability at the hands of a hostile Other, but rather on the vulnerability of the Other who is encountered by me. The Other as demanding care rather than an object of contemplation (or even confrontation) is at the core of his philosophy (see 1996: 166–167). For it is precisely from this condition of vulnerability that the ethical appeal of the face arises, because through its destitution, "the face summons me, calls for me, begs for me, and in so doing recalls my responsibility, and calls me into question" (Levinas 1989: 83). This means that the encounter with vulnerability demands the ability to respond ethically, to resist any impulse to, as it were, prey on the defencelessness of the Other. This is expressed in Levinas's frequently quoted enigmatic statement, "The face as the extreme precariousness of the other. Peace as awakeness to the precariousness of the other" (1996: 167). The face exposes the vulnerability of the Other, who in this state of vulnerability is dependent on me – hence precarious – and out of this precariousness demands a response from me, demands that I be awake to the vulnerability of the Other and to abstain from violence.

In her essay collection *Precarious Life* (2004), Butler relies on Levinas's ethics, and in particular on his concept of a fundamental condition of vulnerability, as a basis to analyse reactions to the 9/11 attacks. She diagnoses an ontological state of human vulnerability that we are reminded of whenever we suffer injuries (for example in terror attacks) and "sees in these events a reminder of the reality of persistent insecurity rooted in a constitutive and persistent vulnerability" (Watkins 2008: 188). For Butler, this condition of vulnerability is both *universal*, in that everyone is subject to it (see 2005: 34–35; see also Watkins 2008: 188), and *irrecusable*, because "one cannot will [it] away without ceasing to be human" (Butler 2004: xiv; see also 19; 29). Our injurability highlights the fact that we are dependent on others, who may commit acts of violence against us and even kill us (see Butler 2004: xii).[1] This dependence on others, with its implication of insecurity and being at risk, is what makes our lives precarious. For this reason, Butler arrives at her "broad existential claim, namely, that everyone is precarious" (2012: 148). It is a precariousness that is caused by our ontological vulnerability and that we are reminded of whenever we suffer an injury.

Such an insight into our "primary vulnerability" (Butler 2004: xiv) cannot be without consequence for our living together. Indeed, for Butler, it requires a rethinking of our way of life, both on the level of society, or politics, and on the level of community. This leads Butler to the following question:

> Is there a way that we might struggle for autonomy in many spheres, yet also consider the demands that are imposed upon us by living in a world of beings who are, by definition, physically dependent on one another, physically vulnerable to one another? Is this not another way of imagining community, one in which we are alike only in having this condition separately and so having in common a condition that cannot be thought without difference? (2004: 27)

It is a rethinking of community, then, that she hopes for as a result of the insight into our vulnerability. In particular, this rethinking requires the eschewal of violence or revenge and the embracing of our vulnerable condition itself. In other words, this reconceptualisation of community envisages a communal state of

---

1 Grounded as it is in Levinas's ethics of the face-to-face, Butler's concept of vulnerability has its foundation on a pre-social level. Nevertheless, her interest is primarily in the social dimension of the precarious. In Butler's political philosophy, the focus is always on an encounter with several others, who may even remain unknown to us. Precariousness to her is a social condition (see 2004: 20) that demands responsibility on the political level as much as on the personal level. This is a key difference from Levinas, whose ethics is first of all based on the face-to-face encounter with the Other, to which the advent of a third party adds the necessity of consciousness and rules (see Levinas 1996: 168–169).

being open to the world – Butler understands vulnerability as a "way of opening onto the world" (2011: 2) – that acknowledges the vulnerability of the self and the Other and refigures this apparent weakness into a strength. This is, as Watkins rightly points out, a "sombre understanding of community", a community which is "constituted via shared and inescapable, yet ambiguous vulnerability [and] entails not only the possibility for attachment, enrichment, and affection but also detachment, loss, and mourning" (2008: 191). Indeed, the sort of community that is envisioned by Butler is based on the living together of singular beings (in the sense in which this term is used by thinkers such as Jean-Luc Nancy; see 1991: 1–42) whose differences are unconditionally acknowledged. It might perhaps be described, with a nod to Benedict Anderson's (1991) phrase, as a re-imagined community of the precarious – a community that depends on its insight into individual and collective vulnerability and the embracing of this condition.

It is in this context that the potential of the theatre comes into play. Of course, the theatrical space is not exempt from Butler's existential claim of precariousness, for it makes possible "the face-to-face encounter between embodied, vulnerable spectators and Others wherein the former are summoned to respond, to become actively engaged in an exemplary exercise of ethical 'response-ability'" (Aragay 2014: 4–5). That means the theatre is a forum in which questions of vulnerability and 'response-ability'[2] are negotiated, with spectators as, according to Rancière, *per se* active participants in this process (see 2011: 13) – or, as Greig puts it in an interview: "News allows you to look at events but with drama you are inside them" (2014). So the theatre may have its own ways of recalling to us, the always-already involved spectators, our vulnerability, of reminding us of the inevitability of this vulnerability and of asking in its own way the same question Butler asks – how to respond to the vulnerability of the self and the Other?

Greig's *The Events* certainly is a case in point as regards the aesthetic potential of the theatre to address the issue of vulnerability. The play, which was received very positively by most theatre critics (see e.g. Brown 2013; Cavendish 2013; Gardner 2013a; Gardner 2013b), stages the plight of a victim of violence. Claire, a liberal, slightly "hippyish" (thus Greig in an interview; *Herald Scotland* 2013), lesbian priest, is the clearly traumatised survivor of a gunman's attack on her multicultural choir project. The play shows how she tries to come to terms

---

[2] The reference here is to Hans-Thies Lehmann's notion of an *"aesthetic of responsibility (or response-ability)"* with which the theatre aims to reduce the distance implicit in the act of (spectatorial) perception (2006: 185; see Ridout 2009: 56–59).

with 'the events' by looking for answers in increasingly desperate attempts to understand the motives of the shooter. Her efforts, however, remain futile and lead to her "descent into a kind of madness" (Cavendish 2013). Throughout Greig's play, the issue of the vulnerability and precariousness of our lives and the challenges and possibilities that follow from the recognition of this vulnerability are prominent.

This begins with the fragmented structure of *The Events*, which itself creates a sense of precariousness – a feature that has been reinforced in performance practice. The play's setup, which is inspired by ancient Greek tragedy (see Greig 2014), requires only two actors and a choir on stage at all times. There is the actor playing Claire and another actor who plays a number of roles – most notably that of the killer, but also all the other people Claire encounters: her girlfriend Catriona, a psychologist, the killer's father and the leader of a right-wing party, among others. In the playscript, this actor's roles are simply subsumed under the label 'The Boy', although it might perhaps be more fitting to call him 'The Other'. On the one hand, the concentration of multiple roles in the person of one actor leads to the indeterminacy of this 'Other' character. At times The Boy changes characters almost imperceptibly within a dialogue and it is never quite clear in the first place which character Claire is facing at any given moment. For example, there is a scene in which she repeatedly addresses The Boy as 'Catriona', only for her/him to answer with words that can be clearly attributed to the persona of the shooter – "If I'm to leave a mark on the world I have to do it now" (Greig, *The Events*: 48). The play's relative lack of traditional theatrical means such as curtains or entrances that make a clear-cut division into scenes possible – the songs of the choir are the only thing that comes close to such a traditional structural device – makes it difficult to distinguish which of the various personae The Boy is assuming in any particular situation. Thus a feeling of instability or uncertainty is created, which mirrors the unknowability, or the impossibility of making a "content" (Levinas 1985: 86–87), of the face of the Other.[3] On the other hand, from the dramatic minimalism of the face-

---

[3] According to Levinas, "the Other, in the rectitude of his face, is not a character within a context" (1985: 86), i.e. the face is more fundamental than social roles or cognitive categories. It pierces through a character that may be assumed in a social situation and goes beyond that which we can 'know' in a (socially or otherwise) situated context, laying bare the *"meaning"* of the face, namely, its ethical entreaty not to exploit its vulnerability, or, in Levinas's words, the "'thou shalt not kill'" expressed by the face (1985: 87). In *The Events*, then, the instability of the role of The Boy makes it impossible to 'know' which character he represents in any given scene – what remains is precisely this residual ethical core of the face of The Boy, the "thou shalt not kill" expressed by the face of the Other.

to-face constellation on stage an antagonism must ensue. If, as reviewers have pointed out, the omnipresence of The Boy on stage reflects the way the shooter dominates Claire's thoughts (see Burton 2013; Loxton 2013), then it is also a reminder of her injurability. Through the person of the actor, the face of the killer is contained in every Other Claire encounters. It is a reminder that the encounter with the Other is always potentially violent, a reminder of the precariousness and vulnerability of the face – both of the self and the Other.

This prevailing sense of uncertainty is reinforced by the general nature of the descriptive labels employed in Greig's play. Even its eponymous 'events' remain nameless and thus indeterminate. Just like in the role of The Boy, a generic term is used here rather than a proper name that identifies the events or the person of the perpetrator. This has a double function. Firstly, where The Boy is concerned, his radical alterity is emphasised: his anonymity is in line with Derrida's argument that the "absolute other [...] cannot have a name or family name", as such a name would immediately introduce the familiarity of something that is knowable (Derrida and Dufourmantelle 2000: 25). The absence of even a name thus reinforces the otherness of The Boy. Secondly, the vagueness of the descriptive labels points to the universal nature of the events and of the character of the shooter and thus of our vulnerability. The events might happen anywhere and any bo(d)y might turn out to be the shooter. Indeed, although Greig (2014) cites Anders Breivik's shooting spree on the Norwegian island of Utøya as a direct influence in his writing of the play, the events in it have been linked in theatre reviews and interviews to various atrocities past and present, from the 9/11 and 7/7 terror attacks (*Herald Scotland* 2013) to the Boston Marathon bombings (*Glasgow Evening Times* 2013), the Woolwich murder (*Herald Scotland* 2013), the German NSU right-wing terrorist murders (Theaterkompass 2013) or Elliot Rodger's shooting spree in California in May 2014 (Greig 2014; McElroy 2014). Ramin Gray, the director who worked closely with Greig in putting *The Events* on stage, remarked in an interview that the perpetrators of such attacks "have become totally exchangeable" (Gray 2013; my translation).[4] The concrete massacre depicted in Greig's play is thus as exchangeable as the concrete Boy who commits the violence. What is inescapable is the underlying ontological vulnerability.

In performance practice, strategies of contingency have been employed to create an air of uncertainty and perhaps improvisation that reflects the uncertainty, or precariousness, of encountering the Other. Most prominent among these is certainly the choir (see Trueman 2014), whose functions – much like

---

4 The German original reads, "Die Attentäter sind total austauschbar geworden".

those of the chorus in ancient Greek tragedy (see Weiner 1980) – range from being a guiding voice of common sense for Claire (see Greig, *The Events*: 57–59) to providing neo-Brechtian alienation effects (see 52; 41–43) and, ultimately, as will be shown, to supplying the play's vision of an alternative community of the precarious. It has been stressed that in performance practice the choir should not be a professional choir, that the choir members should not be familiar with the play and that it must be a different choir in every performance (see Trueman 2014). Particularly this latter fact again points at the unpredictable inevitability of 'the events' and at the universality of human vulnerability, as the victims might come from any group of people (see Brown 2013). Due to such scripted randomness, the choir is enveloped in an air of improvisation (see Präauer 2013), which is most prominent when Claire uses a spontaneous, unrehearsed answer by a choir member – "the first thing that comes into [the choir member's] head" (Greig, *The Events*: 41) – to make up a chant in the shamanic ritual to retrieve her soul. This is not the only instance where the play or its director aim at this kind of performative indeterminacy, so it seems that creating such a sense of improvised uncertainty is on director Ramin Gray's agenda. It is worth noting, in this connection, that in July 2014 a special trilingual version of *The Events*, a "'live theatrical experiment'" (Gray qtd. in Trueman 2014) involving actors from the play's British, Austrian and Norwegian productions, all of them performing in their respective languages, was staged in London – notably *without* prior rehearsals and hence with a great deal of "uncertainty [...] at the core of the endeavour" (Trueman 2014).[5] As in the other instances where the dramatic form of *The Events* creates such an air of indeterminacy, this is an uncertainty that not only mirrors the openness towards the Other – reinforced by the multiple languages in this particular staging – that is central to Claire's thinking (thus Gray qtd. in Trueman 2014), but also reflects the insecurity that underlies our every encounter with the Other, i.e. what Butler terms the precariousness of our lives.

On the level of content, vulnerability is an obvious topic because of the nature of 'the events'. It is quite telling that the shooting depicted in the play has been linked in theatre reviews and interviews to such a large number of different atrocities past and present, all leading to what Butler calls, with regard to the 9/11 attacks, "conditions of heightened vulnerability and aggression" (2004: xi). Such intensified vulnerability and aggression is certainly what we witness

---

[5] The role of The Boy was played by a different actor from one of the three casts (and hence performed in a different language, albeit surtitled) in every scene, while the actor for Claire only changed from night to night. For a more detailed description of this "[t]ag wrestling in three languages", see Trueman (2014).

in Claire and her encounters with the various Others that are a central topic of *The Events* from the very beginning. In the first scene, The Boy describes an Australian aboriginal boy watching the arrival of the first ships with prisoners without understanding what is going on, and warns of the violent threat these newcomers pose. The Boy asks, "If you could go back in time and speak to that boy, what would you say? You would stand on the rocks and you would point at the ships and you would say – 'Kill them. Kill them all'" (Greig, *The Events*: 12). After a quick change of scene and a song by the choir, this is immediately contrasted with Claire welcoming The Boy as a new arrival into her choir. She extends her hospitality by saying, "Hi. Come in. Don't be shy. Everyone's welcome here. What's your name?" (12). This means she offers her hospitality before she even knows to *whom* she is offering it (the question after The Boy's name remains unanswered). This is close to what Derrida calls the "absolute or unconditional" form of hospitality that precedes any pact or contract (Derrida and Dufourmantelle 2000: 25) – for it is impossible to make a contract with someone who remains entirely unknown – and it marks a stark contrast to The Boy's hostility. The play here seems to mirror Levinas's ethics: the first impulse presented to us is hostility – just like in the invitation to kill that the recognition of the vulnerability of the face of the Other seemingly makes (see Levinas 1985: 86). And in the same way in which this invitation to violence coincides with the imperative of peacefulness, with the 'thou shalt not kill' of the face (see 1985: 86–87), so The Boy's hostility is immediately followed by the vision of Claire's hospitality – by her 'awakeness to the precariousness of the other'. Thus, in their antagonism, The Boy is marked down as taking a stance of hostility towards the Other, whereas Claire offers openness.

The motif of encountering the Other is present throughout the play: from Claire's strained relationship with her girlfriend Catriona, most notably their half violent, half erotic struggle for a kiss (see Greig, *The Events*: 47), to her visit to the representative of a right-wing party with its implication of the wider social complex of problems surrounding immigration and otherness (see 33–36), and her highly unreliable memory of picking up and accommodating a runaway boy (see 43–44) – all the Others, of course, being played by The Boy. Most striking, however, is the play's climactic penultimate scene, in which the strains of encountering the Other and, in them, our own vulnerability can be seen most clearly. As the play progresses, Claire is driven almost to insanity (and to the edge of suicide; see 54–56) in her quest to understand the motives of the killer and to come to terms with her most traumatic memory – the memory of the shooter asking her and another woman of the choir, "I have one bullet. There are two of you – Which one of you do you want me to shoot?" (26; see also 51, 66), a scene that the play comes back to several times and that only gradually becomes clearer to the spectators, as it is retrieved from the foggy mechanisms of sublimation. Ultimately, as she is caught between feelings of hatred and embracing the Other (as in those scenes where the encounter with The Boy is highly sexually charged; see 52–53; see also 47), or perhaps even forgiveness (although this remains entirely a matter of speculation in the play), Claire visits the shooter in his prison cell, because, as she explains to Catriona, "I have to see him. Face to face" (48).

It is in this face-to-face encounter that "the limits of forgiveness" (Wicker 2013) are put to the test and revenge becomes a distinct possibility. When Claire arrives at the prison, she carries a tea bag in her pocket that she has filled with a chopped up poisonous mushroom. The Boy receives Claire hospitably – he even offers her a cup of tea (see Greig, *The Events*: 60), a gesture that is abundant with dramatic irony and again points to the reversibility of roles and the universality of vulnerability. During their conversation, in which Claire again unsuccessfully tries to uncover the shooter's motives, truly personal information about the killer is revealed for the first time. The mask that covers his face – to remain with Levinas's metaphor – gradually peels off and it becomes clear that he, too, is vulnerable, plagued by sleeping troubles since childhood, and that he, too, is capable of empathy for the vulnerable, as becomes clear from his account of how he offered shelter to a girl that had been abused (see Greig, *The Events*: 61; 63–64). The face of the hitherto seemingly faceless, anonymous, or at least impersonal Boy comes to the fore, thus placing him within "the horizon of ethics" (Butler 2012: 140). And yet, Claire is tempted to revenge when she once more recalls the moment of that horrible question, "Which one of you do you want me to shoot?" A cup of – presumably – poisoned tea is placed before The Boy. As he reaches for it, the answer to his inhumane question is finally revealed: "We both said 'Me'" (Greig, *The Events*: 67) – a memory that immediately prompts Claire to smash the cup as The Boy is about to drink from it and thus to forgo her revenge. This is because this memory of the ultimate ethical act of choosing self-sacrifice over self-preservation – an act that is ethical because it places the life of the Other before one's own life and so fully accepts the responsibility that the face of the Other demands from us according to Levinas (see 1986: 24) – makes it impossible to take revenge; to, as it were, *efface* The Boy.

The cup of tea Claire hands to The Boy is thus a poisoned chalice not only in the literal sense: performing her act of revenge – and thus yielding to what Greig in an interview described as "this voice you're trying to suppress, the violence of retribution" (Wicker 2013) – would implicate Claire in a spiral of violence and ultimately make her lose her own humanity, as revenge is always "a refusal of empathy" (Watkins 2008: 197). She would no longer be a mere victim, but also herself a perpetrator, committing an act of violence against the face of The

Boy – the same can of course be said for the other instances where she entertains violent fantasies without acting on them (see Greig, *The Events*: 54). As Butler explains, "it is absolutely ethically necessary, after one has been injured very deeply, that one not respond in kind", for rather than solving the "problem of vulnerability" (2003), revenge only transfers it to the other who may then react in kind. Thus, with her decision to forgo revenge, Claire breaks such a "cycle of revenge" (Butler 2003). It is a decision not to exploit the vulnerability of the imprisoned perpetrator.

So instead of taking revenge, Claire returns to the community of the choir, which emerges as Greig's version of the kind of community Butler imagines as a response to the insight into the human condition of vulnerability. The choir is portrayed as a hospitable, if not quite safe, haven. It does not lay claim to providing safety either, as other communities might perhaps do – indeed, with the attack on the multicultural choir, which embodies the ideal of liberalism, *The Events* brutally recalls to the audience the vulnerability of this kind of community, or indeed of any community. This insight quite literally strikes home because of the practice, in performance, of using choirs that are rooted in the local community and that are thus closely connected to the theatregoers – they "embody what is at stake", as Ramin Gray puts it in his Director's Note to the playscript (Greig, *The Events*; see McElroy 2014). In this sense, the choir in *The Events* represents precariousness. What is more, it also is the theatrical device that most poignantly alerts the audience to the precariousness of their own lives. This is because if "[e]very act of theatre revolves around a transaction between two communities: the performers onstage and the improvised community that constitute what we call an audience" (Gray's Director's Note in Greig, *The Events*), then the choir is situated right between those two communities – it is a part of the onstage community, but at the same time it is as improvised as the audience. In particular, the choir assumes the function of an onstage audience, as its members remain passive observers throughout most scenes, seated at the rear of the stage on a pedestal and looking back at the audience.[6] Such a setup is particularly apt to underline the "situation of mutual spectatorship [that] raises the ethical stakes in theatre" (Ridout 2009: 15). Thus, the choir is an element the audience can identify with and that simultaneously, by emphasising the act of spectatorship, strengthens the audience's involvement in the stage action and so makes the most striking demand upon the spectators' 'response-ability'– an effort that peaks in the closing tableau of the play, where Claire turns directly to the audience

---

[6] This seating arrangement can be seen in the pictures accompanying the reviews by Loxton (2013) and McElroy (2014).

and invites them to join the choir's closing song, because after all, "We're all one big crazy tribe here" (Greig, *The Events*: 68).⁷ The choir thus contributes to the play's own version of what Lehmann describes as an "*aesthetics of risk*", that is, to the diminishing of the "safe distance" between audience and stage (2006: 187). In this fashion, the choir is the aesthetic device that, by implicating the audience, extends the sense of vulnerability beyond the limits of the stage. However, the play's closing scene makes clear that in this respect the choir does not only embody precariousness, but also represents a tentative response to the state of vulnerability Greig's play unmasks. The vision of welcoming openness the choir projects – Claire's "Come in. Don't be shy. Everyone's welcome here" (Greig, *The Events*: 68) echoes at the very end of the play her inviting words at the start (12) – demonstrates the "resistance to the seduction of vengeance" Butler demands (Gutterman and Rushing 2008: 131). Instead, it embraces diversity and, above all, the state of vulnerability the play abounds with – Claire's and The Boy's and therefore that of all the Others Claire encounters. Hence, the choir is symbolic of the kind of community Butler might have in mind in response to the insight into our ontological vulnerability: a community of vulnerable beings, each vulnerable in their own way, but openly embracing both such a shared condition of vulnerability and the Other. In other words, the choir represents a community of the precarious, always at risk, always depending on the Other and their openness and will to peace. Thus the choir is the element of the play that is most strongly charged with the precariousness of life. It is a symbol of vulnerability and, at the same time, also of responding to vulnerability, of the 'response-ability' Greig's play promotes.

In conclusion, *The Events* is a play that negotiates our ontological condition of vulnerability, and thus the precariousness of life, both in the character of Claire and her quest to come to terms with such vulnerability by trying to understand the motives of the shooter, and, where the structure of the play is concerned, in the instability of the character of The Boy as well as through the use of strategies of contingency in performance. With regard to these aesthetic strategies, Lyn Gardner rightly observes that the play is "full of doubt and hon-

---

7 Incidentally, such an invitation to respond is also achieved by the choir through the very different aesthetic mode of alienation, as when the Repetiteur announces a tea break, which is filled with a "short nature documentary about foxes", or when a choir member reads out a text about chimpanzees (Greig, *The Events*: 42–43; 52). Here, the classical Brechtian alienation effect is achieved, which according to Peter Brook "is a call to halt: alienation is cutting, interrupting, holding something up to the light, making us look again. Alienation is above all an appeal to the spectator to work for himself, so to become more responsible for accepting what he sees" (1968: 72; see also Weiner 1980: 211).

esty, about its own function, its own fragmentary aesthetic, about what we mean by society, and our flailing helplessness in the face of unexpected violence" (2013a). In Claire's multiple encounters with the emblematic Other that is The Boy, *The Events* returns in various ways to the topic of vulnerability and reflects on possible responses. Particularly after Claire's eschewal of violent revenge in the climactic penultimate scene, face to face with the Other, the choir emerges as a tentative vision of a community of the precarious that may help to perhaps not accept, but accommodate vulnerability. In this sense, Greig's *The Events* can be seen as a catalyst for necessary ethical considerations in the face of our irrecusable condition of vulnerability. The closing tableau, then, with the choir on stage as a symbol of resistance to violence and its invitation to the audience to join their song as a further emblem of being open to the world, expresses the hope that however deep the scars caused by the violent exploitation of our vulnerability may be, a community of the precarious may emerge after such events and find a peaceful, ethical response to them.

Works Cited

Anderson, Benedict. 1991 [1983]. *Imagined Communities: Reflections on the Origin and Spread of Nationalism*. Rev. ed. London and New York: Verso.

Aragay, Mireia. 2014. "To Begin to Speculate: Theatre Studies, Ethics and Spectatorship". In: Mireia Aragay and Enric Monforte (eds.). *Ethical Speculations in Contemporary British Theatre*. Basingstoke and New York: Palgrave Macmillan. 1–22.

Brook, Peter. 1968. *The Empty Space*. London: MacGibbon & Kee.

Brown, Georgina. 2013. Rev. of *The Events* (Young Vic, London), by David Greig. *The Mail on Sunday*, 20 October. *Theatre Record* 33.21: 958.

Burton, Tara Isabella. 2013. "Litro in Edinburgh: David Greig's *The Events*". Rev. of *The Events* (Traverse Theatre, Edinburgh), by David Greig. litro.co.uk, 19 August. <http://www.litro.co.uk/2013/08/litro-in-edinburgh-david-greigs-the-events/> [accessed 8 September 2014].

Butler, Judith. 2003. "Peace is a Resistance to the Terrible Satisfactions of War". Interview with Jill Stauffer. *The Believer* 1.2. Believermag.com, May 2003. <http://www.believermag.com/issues/200305/?read=interview_butler> [accessed 26 August 2014].

Butler, Judith. 2004. *Precarious Life: The Powers of Mourning and Violence*. London and New York: Verso.

Butler, Judith. 2005. *Giving an Account of Oneself*. New York: Fordham UP.

Butler, Judith. 2011. "Precarious Life, Vulnerability, and the Ethics of Cohabitation". Centre de Cultura Contemporània (CCCB), Barcelona. 11 July. Lecture manuscript.

Butler, Judith. 2012. "Precarious Life, Vulnerability, and the Ethics of Cohabitation". *Journal of Speculative Philosophy* 26.2: 134–151.

Campbell, Charlie. 2013. "Musical Inspired by Norway Massacre to Open in UK". *time.com*, 28 March. <http://newsfeed.time.com/2013/03/28/musical-inspired-by-norway-massacre-to-open-in-u-k/?iid=sr-link1> [accessed 22 November 2014].

Cavendish, Dominic. 2013. Rev. of *The Events* (Traverse Theatre, Edinburgh), by David Greig. *telegraph.co.uk*, 5 August. <http://www.telegraph.co.uk/culture/theatre/edinburgh-festival-reviews/10223230/Edinburgh-Festival-2013-The-Events-Traverse-Theatre.html> [accessed 4 September 2014].

Derrida, Jacques and Anne Dufourmantelle. 2000 [1997]. *Of Hospitality: Anne Dufourmantelle Invites Jacques Derrida to Respond*. Trans. Rachel Bowlby. Stanford: Stanford UP.

Gardner, Lyn. 2013a. "Best Theatre of 2013, No 1: *The Events*". *theguardian.co.uk*, 31 December. <http://www.theguardian.com/stage/2013/dec/31/best-theatre-of-2013-no-1-the-events> [accessed 4 September 2014].

Gardner, Lyn. 2013b. Rev. of *The Events* (Traverse Theatre, Edinburgh), by David Greig. *theguardian.co.uk*, 5 August. <http://www.theguardian.com/stage/2013/aug/05/the-events-edinburgh-festival-review> [accessed 4 September 2014].

Glasgow Evening Times. 2013. "Playwright David Greig Tells why *The Events* Focuses on Aftermath of Atrocities". *eveningtimes.co.uk*, 28 August. <http://www.eveningtimes.co.uk/entertainment/13262514.Playwright_David_Greig_tells_why_The_Events_focuses_on_aftermath_of_atrocities/> [accessed 8 September 2014].

Gray, Ramin. 2013. "Die Attentäter sind total austauschbar geworden". Interview by Margarete Affenzeller. *derstandard.at*, 19 November. <http://derstandard.at/1381373844061/Die-Attentaeter-sind-total-austauschbar-geworden> [accessed 8 September 2014].

Greig, David. 2013. *The Events*. London: Faber.

Greig, David. 2014. "*The Events* – Q&A with Writer, David Greig". *BBC writers room* blog, 4 July. <http://www.bbc.co.uk/blogs/writersroom/posts/The-Events-QA-with-writer-David-Greig> [accessed 6 September 2014].

Gutterman, David. S. and Sara L. Rushing. 2008. "Sovereignty and Suffering: Towards an Ethics of Grief in a Post-9/11 World". In: Terrell Carver and Samuel A. Chambers (eds.). *Judith Butler's Precarious Politics: Critical Encounters*. London and New York: Routledge. 127–141.

Herald Scotland. 2013. "Author David Greig and Director Ramin Gray Discuss a New Play which Deals with the Aftermath of an Atrocity". *heraldscotland.com*, 16 July. <http://www.heraldscotland.com/arts-ents/stage/author-david-greig-and-director-ramin-gray-discuss-a-new-play-which-deals-with-the-aftermath-of-an-atrocity.2161> [accessed 5 September 2014].

Johnson, Samuel. 1968 [1755]. *A Dictionary of the English Language*. London: W. Strahan. Repr. Heidelberg: Olms.

Lehmann, Hans-Thies. 2006 [1999]. *Postdramatic Theatre*. Trans. Karen Jürs-Munby. London and New York: Routledge.

Levinas, Emmanuel. 1985 [1982]. *Ethics and Infinity: Conversations with Philippe Nemo*. Trans. Richard A. Cohen. Pittsburgh: Duquesne UP.

Levinas, Emmanuel. 1986. "Dialogue with Emmanuel Levinas". Interview with Richard Kearney. In: Richard A. Cohen (ed.). *Face to Face with Levinas*. Albany: SUNY Press. 13–33.

Levinas, Emmanuel. 1989 [1984]. "Ethics as First Philosophy". Trans. Seán Hand and Michael Temple. In: Seán Hand (ed.). *The Levinas Reader*. Oxford: Blackwell. 75–87.

Levinas, Emmanuel. 1996 [1984]. "Peace and Proximity". In: Adriaan T. Peperzak, Simon Critchley and Robert Bernasconi (eds.). *Emmanuel Levinas: Basic Philosophical Writings.* Bloomington: Indiana UP. 161–169.

Loxton, Howard. 2013. Rev. of *The Events* (Young Vic, London), by David Greig. *britishtheatreguide.info*, n.d. <http://www.britishtheatreguide.info/reviews/the-events-traverse-1-9095> [accessed 4 September 2014].

McElroy, Steven. 2014. "And a Choir Shall Heal Them: David Greig's 'The Events' Is Coming to New Haven". *nytimes.com*, 13 June. <http://nyti.ms/UBiHfw> [accessed 8 September 2014].

Nancy, Jean-Luc. 1991 [1986]. "The Inoperative Community". Trans. Peter Connor. In: Jean-Luc Nancy. *The Inoperative Community.* Ed. Peter Connor. Theory and History of Literature 76. Minneapolis and London: U of Minnesota P. 1–42.

Pewny, Katharina. 2011. *Das Drama des Prekären: Über die Wiederkehr der Ethik in Theater und Performance.* Bielefeld: transcript.

Präauer, Teresa. 2013. "Vom Jungen, der das Töten lernen will". Rev. of *Die Ereignisse* (*The Events*; Wiener Schauspielhaus), by David Greig. *nachtkritik.de*, 22 November. <http://www.nachtkritik.de/index.php?option=com_content&view=article&id=8781:die-ereignisse-ramin-grays-erstauffuehrung-von-david-greigs-stueck-ueber-anders-behring-breivik-am-wiener-schauspielhaus&catid=38:die-nachtkritik&Itemid=40> [accessed 4 September 2014].

Rancière, Jacques. 2011 [2008]. *The Emancipated Spectator.* Trans. Gregory Elliott. London and New York: Verso.

Ridout, Nicholas. 2009. *Theatre & Ethics.* Basingstoke and New York: Palgrave Macmillan.

Theaterkompass. 2013. "'Die Ereignisse' von David Greig, Schauspielhaus Wien". *theaterkompass.de*, 15 November. <http://www.theaterkompass.de/news-einzelansicht+M5c45516ab59.html> [accessed 8 September 2014].

Trueman, Matt. 2014. "Tag Wrestling in Three Languages: *The Events* Stages a Radical Coup de Theatre". *theguardian.co.uk*, 4 July. <http://www.theguardian.com/stage/2014/jul/04/the-events-play-tag-three-languages-shooting-breivik> [accessed 9 September 2014].

Watkins, Robert E. 2008. "Vulnerability, Vengeance, and Community: Butler's Political Thought and Eastwood's *Mystic River*". In: Terrell Carver and Samuel A. Chambers (eds.). *Judith Butler's Precarious Politics: Critical Encounters.* London and New York: Routledge. 188–203.

Weiner, Albert. 1980. "The Function of the Tragic Greek Chorus". *Theatre Journal* 32.2: 205–212.

Wicker, Tom. 2013. "*The Events:* 'What do we do about evil?'" *telegraph.co.uk*, 2 August. <http://www.telegraph.co.uk/culture/theatre/theatre-features/10190565/The-Events-What-do-we-do-about-evil.html> [accessed 9 September 2014].

Martin Middeke
The Inoperative Community and Death: Ontological Aspects of the Precarious in David Greig's *The Events* and Caryl Churchill's *Here We Go*

> The universe cannot enter into the sphere of life without becoming afraid [...]. The highest living creature is man, who is also the most fearful and the most feared creature. He fears and is feared more than any other because he is the only creature with the idea, the obsession, and the terror of the great gulf of death into which the torrent of life has been pouring ever since the beginning of time. (Ferrero 1942: 30)

> Community is revealed in the death of others; hence it is always revealed to others. (Nancy 1991: 15)

The Inoperative Community and Death

The commonly accepted model of community is built on the foundations of (a) common language, values, signs, laws, institutions, and (religious) beliefs. In contrast to the idea and concept of 'society' – which, as a rule, is fathomed as more abstract, amorphous, anonymous, and governed by instrumental reason – communities rest on their social capital: the proximity of their members, propriety, combined and cooperative work, emotional bonds, pre-existing subjectivities, as it were, and their face-to-face cohabitation (see Miller 2011: 16–18).[1] The idea of community conveys the promise of home, identity, totality, warmth, and a sense of belonging. Roberto Esposito aptly points out that subjects look upon their community as both a property and an attribute that identifies each of them as part of that totality. The substance of community is established by intersubjectivity:

> [C]ommunity is conceived of as a quality that is added to their nature as subjects, making them also subjects of community. *More* subjects, subjects of a larger entity, one, that is senior or even better than simple individual identity, but from which it originates and in the end reflects. Despite the obvious historical, conceptual, and lexical differences, from this perspective the organicistic sociology of *Gemeinschaft*, American neo-communitarianism,

---

[1] For the distinction between *community* and *society* see Tönnies 2005 [1887] and Plessner 1981 [1924]. The traditional concept of community also underlies such well-known and influential studies of community as Anderson 1991 [1983].

DOI 10.1515/9783110548716-015

and the various ethics of communication [...] lie beyond the same line that keeps them within the unthinkability of community. For all these philosophies, in fact, it is a 'fullness' or a 'whole' [...]. It is also, using a seemingly different terminology, a good, a value, an essence, which depending on the case in question, can be lost and then refound as something that once belonged to us and that therefore can once again belong to us; an origin to be mourned or a destiny foreshadowed based on the perfect symmetry that links *arche* and *telos*. In each case, community is what is most properly our 'own' [*il nostro più proprio*]. Whether it needs to appropriate what is common to us (for communisms and communitarianisms) or to communicate what is more properly our own (for the ethics of communication), what is produced doesn't change. (Esposito 2010: 2)

Philosophers like Esposito and, before him, Maurice Blanchot, Georges Bataille, Giorgio Agamben, Alphonso Lingis, and Jean-Luc Nancy have distanced themselves from such a romanticised view of community. Both the essentialism and the politics of 'othering' inherent in the affirmation of community (as an identity- or totality-building framework) have particularly been carped at. David Greig's and Caryl Churchill's notions of community and, especially, their concepts of aesthetic communities generated by literary and performative means very much resemble these latter positions. In order to make these concepts clearer, my analysis of Greig's *The Events* and Churchill's *Here We Go* will focus on the theoretical positions put forward by Roberto Esposito and Jean-Luc Nancy.

Taking his cue from Martin Heidegger, Nancy understands community as 'Being-with' and, concomitantly, no longer looks upon *com*-munication as normative or teleological action in the way it was, for instance, within Aristotle's concept of the *zôon politikon*. Different from Aristotle, Nancy's concept of community is an entirely ontological one. Community, so to speak, always precedes communication, and also precedes individuality and intersubjectivity. Intersubjectivity, Esposito likewise notes, is "always intent on finding otherness in an alter ego similar in everything to the *ipse* that they would like to challenge" (2010: 2). In intersubjective terms, the other and the self are supposed to be the same. In other words, if I live in such a community, every member of this community, in the end, is supposed to be like me. Nancy's community of Being-with, however, as an ontological given, cannot be chosen, we cannot help it: community, understood as Being-with, is the dowry of Being.

While analysing the etymological complexity of the term 'community' in this context, Esposito uncovers the aspect of 'gift' in the Latin origin of the word com-*munus*.[2] Apprehended in this way, 'community' entails a 'duty', an 'office'

---

[2] Lat. munus, muneris, n., 1. *a service; office; post; employment; function; duty. 2. a work; service (to the dead); favour; present; gift; public show; spectacle; public building for the use of the peo-*

to/for the Other that is conferred on us: "What predominates in the *munus* is [...] reciprocity or 'mutuality' [...] of giving that assigns the one to the other in an obligation [*impegno*]" (Esposito 2010: 5). If this is so, it cannot come as a surprise that no worldly (read: related to existence or Dasein rather than to Being), ontical (or 'existentiell' in Heidegger's terminology)[3] community or communal form of organisation can ever do full justice to this ontological 'gift' other than in a practice of sharing or, in Nancy's terminology, in a practice of 'compearing' (see Nancy 1991: 58).[4]

But what is it then that is shared or compeared in Being-with? One could say that the community based on Being-with involves the precarious in each encounter between self and Other. Nancy sees persons not as individualities, but as 'singularities'. Thereby he shifts the viewpoint of what communities are or where the communal must be allocated from the realm of the ontical to the ontological. No singularity can ever accommodate an alterity that can be fully communicated to another singularity. Similar to Judith Butler, who draws on Emmanuel Levinas's opinion that the (singularity of the) Face is "the extreme precariousness of the other" and peace (or ethics in general terms), accordingly, is the "awakeness" to this precariousness (Levinas qtd. in Butler 2004: 134),[5] Nancy accentuates that what singularities share or compear is no longer their nation, their homeland, their language, their race, their gender, their laws and religions, or any particularised individual interests, orientations, or beliefs, but their finitude and their mortality. Each singularity is defined by the simple fact that it will have to die.

---

ple, erected at the expense of an individual; the structure of the universe (see Lewis and Short 1879).

3 Heidegger's fundamental definition of this distinction is this: "Dasein always understands itself in terms of its existence – in terms of a possibility of itself: to be itself or not itself. Dasein has either chosen these possibilities itself, or got itself into them, or grown up in them already. Only the particular Dasein decides its existence, whether it does so by taking hold or by neglecting. The question of existence never gets straightened out except through existing itself. The understanding of oneself which leads *along this way* we call '*existentiell*'. The question of existence is one of Dasein's ontical 'affairs'. This does not require that the ontological structure of existence should be theoretically transparent. The question about that structure aims at the analysis [...] of what constitutes existence. The context [...] of such structures we call '*existentiality*'. Its analytic has the character of an understanding which is not existentiell, but rather *existential*" (Heidegger 1962: 33).

4 For the aesthetic and critical impact of 'compearance' see Miller 2011 and Middeke 2016.

5 For a more Levinasian reading of Greig's *The Events* see the chapter by Martin Riedelsheimer in this volume.

J. Hillis Miller draws attention to the fact that within traditional communities individuals surely perceive themselves as mortal beings too; in fact, they do nothing less than cherish their cemeteries as important spaces and sites of collective experience. However, such collective memorising and such communal consciousness-raising bring about a "constant renewal from generation to generation" and, consequentially, "a kind of collective immortality" (Miller 2011: 14) of the respective community. In contrast to this, in Nancy's and Esposito's concepts of community – and, as we shall see, in Greig's and Churchill's fictional and theatrical ones as well – community and its ontological precariousness derive from the very *imminence of death* on the one hand and from the ultimate indetermination and, hence, 'un-workability' of death on the other:

> The death upon which community is calibrated does not operate the dead being's passage into some communal intimacy, nor does community, for its part, operate the transfiguration of its dead into some substance or subject – be these homeland, native soil or blood, nation, a delivered or fulfilled humanity [...], family, or mystical body. Community is calibrated on death as on that of which it is precisely impossible *to make a work* (other than the work of death, as soon as one tries to make a work of it). Community occurs in order to acknowledge this impossibility, or more exactly – for there is neither function nor finality here – the impossibility of making a work of death is inscribed and acknowledged as 'community'. (Nancy 1991: 14–15)

In what follows, I shall discuss the topical and formal consequences of the various ways in which the community based on this imminence of death is translated into drama and theatre in *The Events* and *Here We Go*. The precarious fact that we are conscious of our own death, but cannot witness or experience it, warrants that death can only be insufficiently 'worked' in likewise precarious ways, that is, in the observation of the death of others. Hence, if the precarious means the failure of the address to the Other, as Judith Butler points out drawing on Levinas, if one singularity can never fully realise other singularities, then drama and theatre that seek to address and discover a representation of the precarious(ness of death) are faced with the paradoxical situation of having to represent failure and, at the same time, strive to go beyond such failure without ever claiming to overcome it completely. Plays that address community via death or compearing singularities cannot be aesthetically based upon causal, coherent, teleological structures. These plays and their aesthetics themselves become literary and theatrical examples of unworkable, inoperative (Nancy), coming (Agamben), or unavowable (Blanchot) communities. These works no longer seek to domesticate time, finitude, mortality, or constant change, but rather highlight the fluidity of the unworkable community of (implied) authors, texts, directors, actors, readers, and spectators, and their respective singularities.

De-Immunising Community and the Fear of Death: David Greig's *The Events*

Greig's *The Events*[6], first performed at the Traverse Theatre, Edinburgh, on 4 August 2013, is a play that centres around the deconstruction of community. In his Director's Note from July 2013, Ramin Gray points out that the case of the Norwegian right-wing extremist, terrorist, and mass murderer Anders Breivik, who killed 77 people in the attacks he perpetrated on 22 July 2011, destroyed "one community while simultaneously and unintentionally galvanising other communities around the world" (Greig, *The Events*). At the same time, Gray continues, this play – like any other play – "revolves around a transaction between two communities: the performers onstage and the improvised community that constitute what we call an audience". In a variation of the events in Norway, Greig's play is about Claire, a priest, who runs a community choir that consists of such "vulnerable people" (Greig, *The Events*: 14) as elderly men and women, asylum-seekers, immigrants, and young mothers. One day, out of the blue, a boy walks into the rehearsal room and randomly shoots some choir members dead. In her review of the Edinburgh premiere, Lyn Gardner wrote that the play was a "quiet, compassionate and restrained" response to what "binds us together as a community, the things that drive us apart, and what it is that makes us human" (Gardner 2013).

The play juxtaposes the character of Claire and her attempt to understand and overcome these events and her trauma by interacting with the character of The Boy, who, successively or in turns, assumes the roles of a narrator, the assassin, a priest, Claire's partner Catriona, a psychologist, the assassin's father, a journalist, a school mate, and a politician – in short, The Boy incorporates the collective Other(s) of Claire's community and the multiplicity of their viewpoints. Co-present on stage is the Choir, who eventually partakes in both action and dialogue. The Choir is meant to be formed by local choirs, a different one for each of the performances. The Choir, therefore, functions as a threshold, a precarious hinge, as it were, between the fictional world on stage and reality, between the fixed lines in the playscript and the differences and contingencies brought about by the changing choirs every night – a fact which is further enhanced in the revised edition of the play from 2014, in which, in comparison to the first edition, the first two scenes of the play are reversed, and thus the play opens and ends on the Choir's singing and Claire's appeal to The Boy at the beginning and to the audience at the end to join in.

---

[6] In the following I quote from the 2014 edition of the play, which contains revisions.

The ontological condition of Being-with and its inherent gift, pledge, or debt has precarious consequences. Esposito underlines that the ineluctability of Being-with is also an exposure to the Other, so that the ontological given can also be felt as an ontical or existential threat: "That which everyone fears in the *munus*. Which is both 'hospitable' and 'hostile', according to the troubling lexical proximity of *hospes-hostis*, is the violent loss of borders, which[,] awarding identity to him, ensures his subsistence" (Esposito 2010: 8). What all community members have in common, Esposito proceeds to explain drawing on Thomas Hobbes and 'Leviathanian' principles, is "the fact that anyone can be killed by anyone else" (Esposito 2010: 13). If Being-with entails an inevitable exposure to the Other at all times in this rationale, then what makes individuals equal to each other is their capacity to be killed by anyone else at all times. What community also denotes, in short, is the gift and the fear of death. Communities and their individuals, for that reason, employ strategies of inclusion and exclusion in order to protect themselves from death.

Greig's *The Events* radically reproduces viewpoints which demonstrate this attempt to immunise oneself from the danger emanating from the Other. At the very beginning of the play an almost programmatic scenario is evoked: an aboriginal boy is imagined, who sees British ships approaching ready to colonise his community. A characteristic piece of advice is supposed to be given to the boy: "You would stand on the rocks and you would point at the ships and you would say – 'Kill them. Kill them all'" (13). – "The first impulse towards the other's vulnerability", Judith Butler writes, "is the desire to kill" (Butler 2004: 137). Killing the other for self-preservation, however, is precarious insofar as it ignores the singularity of the Other and also contradicts the very foundations and ethical impact of the ontological situation of Being-with. The logic of killing for self-preservation underlies the assassin's motives for his terrorist act. He imagines a community of "Viking warrior shamen" (Greig, *The Events*: 16) who would protect their people by working themselves up to delirious states and then "go berserk" (17) amongst their enemies' people. Such trance-like states of violence take place within a narcissistic circuit that, after all, seeks to "make a mark on the world" (18). The narcissistic impulse is directed against strangers and foreigners in a fatal mixture of xenophobia and racism:

> CHOIR: Do you hate foreigners? [...]
> I don't hate foreigners. I hate foreigners being here. There is a difference.
> [...]
> Your actions will be shocking to many people, many people will ask – why do you kill? What will be your answer to such persons?
> I kill to protect my tribe.
> CLAIRE: Really?

THE BOY: I kill to protect my tribe from softness.
CLAIRE: Softness?
THE BOY: A softness born of cheap togetherness – which is an illusion fostered by failed elites who cling on to power and wealth through immigrant labour and globalisation. (19–20)

The immunitary gesture of the assassin, as can be seen quite clearly, has a high price in the end: the assassin eliminates the danger of the Other by eradicating it. Communitarian bonds, thus, are broken; social relations to anything that is "foreign to the vertical exchange of protection-obedience" (Esposito 2010: 14) of the assassin's 'tribe' are crushed. One community, therefore, is paradoxically destroyed in order to preserve the integrity of individuals of another community. Obviously, when life is sacrificed to the preservation of life, then immunisation generates the vicious circle of self-destruction.

The nationalist blood-and-soil ideology of the assassin finds many echoes and variations of immunising strategies in the views uttered by other voices: homophobic fears, acts of victimisation and scapegoating, racism and fear-mongering as populist political tools (see, for example, the view of the politician). Claire's attempt to break this self-destructive cycle of immunisation – "How can I hate him if I don't understand him" (Greig, *The Events:* 21) – even sets her beyond the pale of her partnership. When Claire and her partner engage in a physical fight over Claire's decision to apply for a job as chaplain at the very high-security prison the assassin is an inmate of, Catriona literally uses the same narcissist argument as the assassin himself did before:

THE BOY: [as Catriona; MM] Jesus.
Why don't we both go away?
Just the two of us.
I could learn to make a bomb.
If we could just get up and go
To Somalia
    For guerilla training.
To Iona
    For the festival of spirituality.
We could watch jihadi videos.
We could stay with the community there.
    You could pray,
I could manufacture a bomb with nails and bolts and stones bursting out of the back of a rucksack tearing a hole through everything and everyone.
We could just do it.
What do you think?
Claire?

> Because I'm running out of time
> *If I'm to leave a mark on the world I have to do it now.* (46–47; emphasis added)

Aside from the erratic eclecticism of motives put to use here in order to glue the community of a personal relationship together, the passage reveals that not only does Catriona's fear of death lead to an immunitary exclusion of the Other, but such immunitary reaction also brings forth autoimmunitary effects as Catriona – by trying to save her community – destroys her own 'immune system', as it were, by adopting the very argument that she set out to protect herself from. Not only does she produce antibodies, so to speak, against whatever is foreign, she protects herself against her own self-protection stratagem by destroying her own immune system. Rhetorically, a simple repetition with a difference on Greig's part – "If I'm going to make/If I'm to leave a mark on the world I have to do it now" (18 and 47) – lays bare and deconstructs the self-destructive absurdity of such immunisation tactics (see also Derrida 2003: 73 and, relevantly, Timár 2015).

Greig's ethical appeal, thus, is unequivocal. No community can preserve itself by contradicting or sacrificing the ontological given of Being-with. Immunisation, inclusion, and exclusion sacrifice the aspect of '*cum*' in 'com-munity' as much as they violate the ethical obligation inherent in the '*munus*'. Rather than that, Claire's attempts throughout the play to *understand* the assassin and, hence, to disrupt the paradox circuit of violence and counter-violence as well as her ultimate resolution not to take revenge, but rather spill the poisoned cup of tea on the floor (see Greig, *The Events*: 64), are responses to the Face, the acknowledgement of what is precarious in another life, an insight into the precariousness of life itself and into the unworkable singularity and finitude of each human being. Greig's point, of course, is that his idea of a community is no longer that of pre-established subjectivities. In other words, he works against a community where its members classify as either red, German, Muslims, or activists. His concept of a community no longer has a guarantee of meaning, identity, belonging, or the essence of a unified collectivity. In this, Greig's community echoes Nancy's idea of "community without community" (1991: 71). Greig shares with Nancy, Agamben, and Esposito the critical trajectory in his designation of an inoperative or coming community that is ceaselessly working to produce more democratic, open, and fluid relationships with others that foster a sense of "being with" (Nancy 1991: 33).

Aesthetically, Greig relies on the openness of the Choir, which not only is an instance of performative immanence (see, importantly, Pattie 2016), but whose changing nature in each performance does also remind audiences and readers alike of their singularity, their finitude, their mutability, their creative transformability even, as well as of their precariousness and, ultimately, of their death:

CLAIRE: Come in.
Don't be shy.
Everybody's welcome here.
We're all one big crazy tribe here.
If you feel like singing – sing
And if you don't feel like singing
Well that's OK too.
Nobody feels like singing all the time.
CHOIR: (*sing*) *And we're all here, we're all here.* (65)

The community of the theatre that is envisaged here is a community of singularities, of fragments, a community "mediated not by any condition of belonging [...] nor by the simple absence of conditions [...] but by belonging itself" (Agamben 1993: 85).

Both performance and audience interaction in *The Events* thereby redefine the notion of theatrical community. This community does not force an ideology on anyone; in the final tableau of the play there is an element of contingency and unworkability of the singular attached to every decision to either leave the theatre, be quiet and watch and listen, or to join the Choir. Every audience member is exposed to their sole selves and also to everyone else's in the audience; everyone is singular and plural, immanent and finite at the same time. It remains entirely open if or how a transformative power of the performance is at work. Instead, this community remains unworkable as it is only realised for a short period of time and, eventually, cannot even be sustained completely for the duration of a performance. The performance itself is as finite as the effect it has on its audiences. What is finally offered is the bare, precarious, inoperative community of a liminally transformative experience. The aesthetic community of implied author, readers, directors, audience members, and actors, therefore, is the community of Being-with (see Middeke 2016): a simple sharing or compearing of finitude and singularity that transcends notions of nation, race, gender, class, ideology, religion, or, understood aesthetically, even personal predilection and simple taste. By resisting normative claims for unity, coherence, origins, ends, and closure, and by repealing the fear of death that underlies such claims, the play also resists notorious totalitarian strategies of exclusion and inclusion which remain ineffective here.

Finitude Compearing and the Triumph of Death: Caryl Churchill, *Here We Go*

Churchill's short, minimalist *Here We Go* was first performed on the Lyttleton stage at the National Theatre in London on 27 November 2015, directed by Dominic Cooke. The play is divided into three scenes, the chief topics of which are death, dying, time, and the temporality or, perhaps, absurdity, of human existence. Michael Billington called it "a chilling reminder of our mortality" and "a striking memento mori for an age without faith" (Billington 2015); Andrzej Lukowski's review in *Time Out* hinted at the Beckettian intertext of Churchill's minimalism and prophesied polarised audiences "between those who think Dominic Cooke's production is pretentious wank and those who see something profound haunting at its heart" (Lukowski 2015); Paul Taylor also acknowledged Churchill's debt to Beckett and Dante and called the London production downright "unforgettable". "You feel", he added "as though you've aged a decade as the light gradually fades on a quietly remorseless quarter an hour of this" (Taylor 2015).

Churchill's play is about the unrepresentable void of death which Being-with is constituted by. It is, in fact, about the impossible: the first scene in the play, entitled "Here We Go", is set at a party after a funeral. Nameless characters, the identity, exact number and gender of whom remain opaque – the text suggests "[n]ot fewer than three in the first scene and not more than eight" (Churchill, *Here We Go*: 9) – are engaged in a loose, disjointed conversation in which, accordingly, only fragmentary, incoherent pieces of information about the deceased are given along the way: his wide range of acquaintances, his eventful life, the War, his career as a former MP in the 1950s, three marriages, a love of literature, an interest in physics, a libertine luxury life; for some he seems amiable, others remember him as quarrelsome. Nothing in this, actually, seems worth mentioning if it was not for the ten short speeches at the end of the scene, in which these nameless characters report the circumstances of their own deaths. The conversation at the funeral party is to be interspersed at random with these speeches. There are ten speeches altogether, and in case there are fewer actors than that for the scene, some speeches will have to be omitted provided that each actor has one speech. A closer look at these speeches shows an arbitrary variation of causes of death such as accidents, illnesses, murder and suicide, and likewise arbitrary times of death – while one character remembers he died the next day, others die days, months, years or even decades later. Although there is some remote sense of personal attachment and empathy aroused by these individual fates – a suicide victim reasons s/he should have thought about who would find her, and another regrets not having lived to see an at that time unborn baby alive – Churchill's emphasis is clearly *not* on the individual fates. The sheer contingency of the ten speeches and their arbitrarily meaningless and exchangeable circumstances lay emphasis on the singularity of each case; they shift our attention away from *a* particular death to death as such. Obviously, Churchill's concern is ontological rather than ontical or *existentiell*.

The impression of such contingency is further enhanced by the second scene of the play, entitled "After". This is a character's soliloquy delivered after death from what seems to be some purgatory-like in-between-space. The scene, again, foregrounds the impossible, and, consequently, what the character can actually say about something s/he cannot know in the first place is mostly made up of clichés: the pearly gates, St Peter, the beard, the key, a consciousness of being as transient and insignificant as "a speck of sand in a desert" (Churchill, *Here We Go*: 23); vague lamentations on the injustice of the world that seem almost banal in the face of the fact that life for this consciousness is over; even more banal reflections on an alleged other go at life and what one would prefer to be in this second go: president, king, general or some fancy animal; and a final frantic memento to all of us that "there you all are for a short time" (Churchill, *Here We Go*: 28).

Churchill carefully adheres to the ambiguity, opacity, and singularity of the scenario by obliterating any faint remainder of a traditional causal and teleological plotline. The character in "After", Churchill insists, "can be but needn't be the man whose funeral it is in the first scene" (Churchill, *Here We Go*: 9). By displacing any character continuity or causal connection in the character configuration of the scenes, Churchill deflects from any particularised individual interest and, again, brings singularity into focus. This character can be any character, this character actually *is* any character: everyman. What is brought to the fore are singularities compearing in their finitude. The scene emphasises Nancy's thesis that the community of Being-with "is revealed in the death of others" (Nancy 1991: 15). There can be no experience of one's own death, therefore, the finitude that all singularities have in common can indeed only be felt in the death of others. By fictionally rendering the experience of one's own death as accessible to consciousness in Scenes 1 and 2 of the play, Churchill dramatises the most impossible of all possibilities. What readers and audience members share by witnessing the death of the other is the point of maximum vulnerability, of maximum void, of maximum ontological precariousness – the extreme limit and liminality of our experience. The death of the other confronts us with what we cannot experience ourselves, it also confronts us with our own incapacity to make a work of death by giving expression to its experience.

In this, Churchill's play seems to be entirely consistent with Nancy's and Esposito's positions. As was argued above, for Nancy, community and Being-with are calibrated on death as something that remains altogether unworkable. In fact, community virtually

> *occurs* in order to acknowledge this impossibility, or more exactly – for there is neither function nor finality here – the impossibility of making a work out of death is inscribed and acknowledged as 'community'. (Nancy 1991: 15)

Esposito almost seems to comment on Churchill's play when he argues that we can learn nothing from death because, once dead, we lose any benefit from the lesson it might teach us. We can resort to fiction or to imagination, as Churchill does, to ponder upon the situation, the fears, or simply the experience of someone who sees death, but of course as long as we are alive this remains impossible:

> It's true, therefore, that the death of the other returns us to our own death, but not in the sense of an identification and even less of a reappropriation. The death of the other instead directs us again to the nature of *every* death as incapable of being made properly one's own [*inappropriabile*]: of my death *as* his since death is neither 'mine' nor 'his' because it is a taking away of what is properly one's own, expropriation itself. Here is what man sees in the wide-open eyes of the other who is dying: the solitude that cannot be lessened but only shared. The impenetrable secret that joins us [*ci accomuna*] together as our 'last'[.] (Esposito 2010: 123)

Whereas Scenes 1 and 2 centre on the impossible experience of death and afterlife, Scene 3 reverts back in time to the situation of "Getting There". At the centre of the scene are an old and very ill person and his/her carer. The National Theatre production cast the actor from "After" also in this scene in order to provide both scenes with at least some continuity, yet Churchill's introductory remarks in the text disavow any such disambiguation. Again, the old, diseased person may or may not be the man from the earlier scene, the carer may or may not be a person we have encountered before (see Churchill, *Here We Go*: 9). The short third scene is without words, and in its looping movement of repetitive acts it resembles a piece of performance art or Minimal Art rather than a stage play:

> *A very old or ill person and a carer.*
> *The old/ill person is in nightclothes and is helped by the carer to get dressed, slowly and with difficulty because of pain and restricted movement.*
> *Then to get undressed and back into nightclothes.*
> *Then to get dressed.*
> *Then to get undressed and back into nightclothes.*
> *Then to get dressed ...*
> *for as long as the scene lasts.*
> *End. (29)*

Like the frantic, inconclusive soliloquy of "After", this short scene manifestly resembles the absurdly cyclical and recursive movements of (empty) repetition in Beckett's work all the way from *Waiting for Godot* or *Krapp's Last Tape* to the minimalist pieces from *Footfalls* onwards to *Quad I* and *II* (see also Middeke 2005). Unlike Beckett, however, the scene's shock potential derives from the fact that however reduced and abstract it becomes, it is still visibly, recognisably, and realistically grounded in an intimate everyday situation. And unlike such later Beckett protagonists as, for instance, May in *Footfalls* or the old woman in *Rockaby*, the sick old man here is not alone. The iterative actions of dressing and undressing and their almost geometrical looping movement become structural reflections of the insight that, in the end, we are nothing but time, temporality, and finitude. For the reader and the audience the repetitive action of dressing and undressing becomes a painful image of living-towards-death, perhaps even a sardonic image of life as such which, from an ontological perspective such as Schopenhauer's or Heidegger's, resembles nothing but the meaningless cycle of getting dressed and undressed, getting up and lying down. The moment when we realise that what we see on stage, the singularity of the nameless and wordless character, is a repetition with a difference of our own singularity, and that what we share as singularities is nothing in the end but our finitude – this moment, on the one hand, is a moment of pure immanence in which we become aware of the Other's repeated sufferings and, thus, experience our own. The community that we experience here is no longer the community of egos; the play does not confront us with the drama of individuals. In an ontological as well as in a theatrical sense, what we have in front of us is a community of singularities sharing their finitude, a community of mortal beings. On the other hand, however, the community of singularities that can be experienced here corrodes the pure immanence of the theatrical moment by remorselessly highlighting duration and the relentless flow of time through repetitions which can never be identical, and, thus, lay bare the impossibility of our own immanence as well as of any immanence inherent in performative acts on stage (see Nancy 1991). Moreover, the fact that the last scene is virtually speechless is the perfect final image of the precariousness of the unworkable (or, indeed, un-*word*-able), *in*operative community:

> [I]t is precisely the wordless vocalization of suffering that marks the limits of linguistic translation [...]. The face, if we are to put words to its meaning, will be that for which no words really work; the face seems to be a kind of sound, the sound of language evacuating its sense, the sonorous substratum of vocalization that precedes and limits the delivery of any semantic sense. (Butler 2004: 134)

Conclusion

Both the subject matter and aesthetic structure of Greig's *The Events* and Churchill's *Here We Go* suggest a re-orientation and a deconstruction of the commonly accepted model of community that is based on identity, belonging, communication, inclusion, exclusion, and, ultimately, the triumph over death. Both plays – thematically and aesthetically – assemble inoperative, fluid communities which entirely *accept* the precariousness and vulnerability inherent in human communication, interaction, and, in fact, in human life. The success of this community is no longer dependent upon the premise that ideas or convictions are shared by all its members; instead, what both plays make clear is that, ontologically, the only things that *can* be shared by all singularities are their finitude and, thus, their precariousness – ultimately, we all have to die.

The displacement, or disavowal, of traditional communitarian values such as nation, individuality, subject, teleology, or blood and soil is corroborated in both plays by their experimental and self-reflexive formal structures. Both plays plunge their readers and their audiences into self-reflexive "autopoietic feedback loops" (Fischer-Lichte 2008: 55): The Boy in *The Events* takes over the roles of many characters, opinions, and consciousnesses; the characters' identity and even the deictic references to them in *Here We Go* remain ambiguous; Churchill's play challenges traditional expectations of chronological order, sequence, and frequency. While Churchill's aesthetic strategy mostly rests on ambiguity, Greig relies on the contingency inherent in different choirs, different perspectives. Music and the Choir, hence, also become media of the precarious here (see Pewny 2011: 59–62), with the Choir clearly becoming a link between the realms of the fictitious, the real, and the imaginary. In both plays actors, spectators, and readers experience community as precariousness of the Other. Community and interpretation as much as spectatorship are thus seen as active ideas, as interruptions working from the notion of the impossibility of a lasting, fixed collectivity. In fact, Greig's and Churchill's plays resist collectivity itself as much as they resist the individual (see Nancy 1991: 71).

By placing the sharing, or compearing, of precariousness and finitude, temporality, and death at their centres, both plays present a community of singularities joined in Being-with as a likewise active and interruptive idea, which requires a continuous unworking of the totalising and exclusionary myths of collectivity. Moreover, the community Greig and Churchill have in mind must be open to other possible and potential networks of relations, of living and being with others. Like Nancy's inoperative community, Greig's and Churchill's aesthetic communities in *The Events* and *Here We Go*, which include the interactions of (implied) authors, (implied) readers/spectators, text, performance, reception-processes, and interpretation, demand a resistance to everything that would bring these processes to a halt, let alone to completion.

In the course of the first two decades of the twenty-first century such insistence on the unworkability of art and community is faced by a social reality characterised by the advantages and flipsides of globalisation; by a growing precarity generated by the unjust distribution of wealth; by global financial and economical crises; by wars and global terrorism; by religious fanaticism and radicalism; by a growing disorientation in times of "liquid modernity" (Bauman 2000); by populist pied pipers and their oversimplifications, who seek to ruthlessly capitalise on the insecurity of others; by racism, xenophobia, and scapegoating. Much of this is the result of the inclusion and exclusion strategies deployed in order to stabilise a sense of community and existential belonging which some are yearning for and others are preying upon. In this context, as crucial counter-discourses, plays such as Greig's *The Events* reveal any processes of self-immunising to be deeply paradoxical and self-destructive, and in their insistence on the ontological situation of finitude and precariousness, both *The Events* and *Here We Go* offer an ethical, if not political, stance that can challenge totalitarian tendencies and easy solutions. In their emphasis on the ontological singularity of human beings, on their finitude, and on the incommensurability of death that unites us in our humanity, both plays remind us that there is still community if we give up the community we are used to. Instead of killing the Other for fear of death and its precarious Face, why not be curious about the precarious, interested in and open to it?

> CLAIRE: Isn't it possible, isn't it just possible that – after sixty thousand years of entirely unchanged culture – isn't it just possible that if you asked the aboriginal boy how he felt about seeing those ships in that moment he might say – in an aboriginal language of course – something like 'Thank fuck! Thank fuck something interesting has finally happened round here'. (Greig, *The Events*: 62–63)

Works Cited

Agamben, Giorgio. 1993. *The Coming Community*. Trans. Michael Hardt. Minneapolis and London: University of Minnesota Press.
Anderson, Benedict. 1991 [1983]. *Imagined Communities: Reflections on the Origin and Spread of Nationalism*. London and New York: Verso.
Bauman, Zygmunt. 2000. *Liquid Modernity*. Cambridge: Polity.
Billington, Michael. 2015. Rev. of *Here We Go* (National Theatre, London), by Caryl Churchill. *The Guardian*, 29 November. <https://www.theguardian.com/stage/2015/nov/29/here-we-go-review-a-chilling-reminder-of-our-own-mortality> [accessed 25 April 2017].

Butler, Judith. 2004. *Precarious Life: The Power of Mourning and Violence*. London and New York: Verso.
Churchill, Caryl. 2015. *Here We Go*. London: Nick Hern.
Derrida, Jacques. 2003. "Autoimmunity: Real and Symbolic Suicides – A Dialogue". In: Giovanna Borradori (ed.). *Philosophy in a Time of Terror: Dialogues with Jürgen Habermas and Jacques Derrida*. Chicago and London: U of Chicago P. 85–135.
Esposito, Roberto. 2010. *Communitas: The Origin and Destiny of Community*. Trans. Timothy Campbell. Stanford: Stanford UP.
Ferrero, Guglielmo. 1942. *The Principles of Power: The Great Political Crises of History*. Trans. Theodore R. Jaeckel. New York: G.P. Putnam's Sons.
Fischer-Lichte, Erika. *The Transformative Power of Performance: A New Aesthetics*. Trans. Saskya Iris Jain. London and New York: Routledge.
Gardner, Lyn. 2013. Rev. of *The Events* (Traverse Theatre, Edinburgh), by David Greig. *The Guardian*, 5 August. <https://www.theguardian.com/stage/2013/aug/05/the-events-edinburgh-festival-review> [accessed 25 April 2017].
Greig, David. 2014 [2013]. *The Events*. Rev. ed. London: Faber and Faber.
Heidegger, Martin. 1962. *Being and Time*. Trans. John Macquarrie and Edward Robinson. New York: Harper & Row.
Lewis, Charlton T. and Charles Short (eds.). 1879. *A Latin Dictionary. Founded on Andrews' Edition of Freund's Latin Dictionary*. Rev. ed. Oxford: Clarendon Press. <http://www.perseus.tufts.edu/hopper/text?doc=Perseus%3Atext%3 A1999.04.0059% 3Aentry%3Dmunus> [accessed 24 April 2017].
Lukowski, Andrzej. 2015. Rev. of *Here We Go* (National Theatre, London), by Caryl Churchill. *Time Out*, 15 December. <https://www.timeout.com/london/theatre/here-we-go> [accessed 25 April 2017].
Middeke, Martin. 2005. "Minimal Art: On the Intermedial Aesthetic Context of Samuel Beckett's Late Theatre and Drama". *Anglia: Journal of English Philology* 123.3: 359–380.
Middeke, Martin. 2016. "The Art of Compearance: Ethics, (Reading) Literature, and the Coming Community". In: Martin Middeke and Christoph Reinfandt (eds.). *Theory Matters: The Place of Theory in Literary and Cultural Theory Today*. London: Palgrave Macmillan. 247–263.
Miller, J. Hillis. 2011. *The Conflagration of Community: Fiction Before and After Auschwitz*. Chicago and London: U of Chicago P.
Nancy, Jean-Luc. 1991 [1986]. *The Inoperative Community*. Ed. Peter Connor. Trans. Peter Connor et al. Theory and History of Literature 76. Minneapolis and London: U of Minnesota P.
Pattie, David. 2016. "*The Events*: Immanence and the Audience". In: Mireia Aragay and Enric Monforte (eds.). *Theatre and Spectatorship*. Special issue of *Journal of Contemporary Drama in English* 4.1: 49–60.
Pewny, Katharina. 2011. *Das Drama des Prekären: Über die Wiederkehr der Ethik in Theater und Performance*. Bielefeld: transcript.
Plessner, Helmuth. 1981 [1924]. *Grenzen der Gemeinschaft: Eine Kritik des sozialen Radikalismus*. In: Helmuth Plessner. *Macht und Menschliche Natur*. Vol. 5 of *Gesammelte Schriften*. 10 vols. Frankfurt/M.: Suhrkamp. 7–133. Engl. *The Limits of Community: A Critique of Social Radicalism*. Amherst: Humanity Books, 1999.

Taylor, Paul. 2015. Rev. of *Here We Go* (National Theatre, London), by Caryl Churchill. *The Independent*, 30 November. <http://www.independent.co.uk/arts-entertainment/theatre-dance/reviews/here-we-go-national-theatre-review-this-is-unforgettable-a6754436.html> [accessed 25 April 2017].

Timár, Andrea. 2015. "Derrida and the Immune System". In: *Terror(ism) and the Immune System*. Special issue of *Et al.: Critical Theory Online*. <http://etal.hu/en/archive/terrorism-and-aesthetics-2015/derrida-and-the-immune-system/> [accessed 14 April 2017].

Tönnies, Ferdinand. 2005 [1887]. *Gemeinschaft und Gesellschaft: Grundbegriffe der reinen Soziologie*. Darmstadt: *Wissenschaftliche Buchgesellschaft*. Engl. *Community and Civil Society*. Jose Harris (ed.). Cambridge: Cambridge University Press, 2001.

Notes on Contributors

Mireia Aragay is Professor of English Literature and Theatre Studies at the University of Barcelona, Spain, and Life Fellow of Clare Hall, University of Cambridge, U.K.

Christian Attinger is based at the University of Ulm, Germany, and currently working on his PhD thesis entitled "The Theatre of Philip Ridley: Representations of Globalization, Precariousness, and Communities".

Bettina Auerswald is a doctoral candidate at the University of Augsburg, Germany, where she is writing her PhD thesis on the poetology and ethical aspects of verbatim theatre.

Elżbieta Baraniecka holds a PhD in English Literature and is currently teaching German as a foreign language at Alpha Aktiv Language School in Heidelberg, Germany.

Cristina Delgado-García is Lecturer in Drama at the University of Birmingham, U.K.

Clara Escoda holds a research and teaching postdoctoral position at the University of Barcelona, Spain.

Christoph Henke is Associate Professor of English Literature at the University of Augsburg, Germany.

David Kerler is Assistant Professor of English Literature at the University of Augsburg, Germany.

Martin Middeke is Professor of English Literature at the University of Augsburg, Germany, and Visiting Professor of English at the University of Johannesburg, South Africa.

Enric Monforte is Senior Lecturer in English Literature and Theatre Studies at the University of Barcelona, Spain.

José Ramón Prado is Senior Lecturer in English Literature at Universitat Jaume I, Spain.

Martin Riedelsheimer is Lecturer in English Literature at the University of Augsburg, Germany, and currently working on his PhD thesis on "The Fiction of Infinity: Ethics in the Contemporary Novel".

Verónica Rodríguez recently completed her PhD thesis entitled "Globalisation in David Greig's Theatre: Space, Ethics and the Spectator" (December 2016), is based in London and currently turning her thesis into a book.

Adina Sorian is Lecturer in English Literature at the University of Augsburg, Germany.

Index

7/7   15–16, 22, 31, 34, 37, 39, 208
9/11   2, 6–7, 16, 22, 24, 31, 39, 97, 142, 205, 208–209

Adorno, Theodor W.   26, 196
aesthetics   7–11, 34, 50n, 56–57, 59, 66, 70–71, 74–75, 80–81, 83, 86, 89, 91–92, 97n, 98n, 99, 102, 104–105, 110n, 119, 126, 148–150, 203, 206, 213, 220, 224, 230
affect   21, 26–27, 37, 39, 43, 91, 93, 96, 98n, 101, 125–126, 128, 130, 132, 135–138, 151, 155–159, 166
Agamben, Giorgio   5, 218, 220, 224–225
agency   8, 10–11, 17, 27, 77–79, 81–83, 87–89, 102, 137n, 171
Ahmed, Sara   156
Anderson, Benedict   206, 217n
Anderson, Davey   128
– *True or False*   128
aporia   4–6, 20, 24
Aragay, Mireia   190, 206
Arendt, Hannah   125–126, 188
Aristotle   218
asylum   3, 49, 221
Atkin, Douglas   182
avenir   20–27, 145–151

Bakhtin, Mikhail   57–58, 70–71
Bataille, Georges   218
Baudelaire, Charles   72
Bauman, Zygmunt   5, 16, 65, 130, 138, 141–142, 144, 151, 156, 158, 174, 231
Beckett, Samuel   157–158, 226, 229
– *Footfalls*   229
– *Happy Days*   157
– *Krapp's Last Tape*   229
– *Not I*   158
– *Play*   158
– *Quad I, II*   229
– *Rockaby*   229
– *Waiting For Godot*   157, 229
B/being   3, 5, 11, 20n, 38, 49, 66, 70, 100, 119, 121, 127, 141n, 157, 159–160, 171–173, 176, 178–180, 183, 185, 188–189, 196, 198–199, 203, 205–206, 213, 218–219, 230
Being-with   5, 11, 218–219, 222, 224–227, 230
belonging   5, 116, 120, 173, 181–182, 217, 224–225, 230–231
Benjamin, Walter   163
Berlant, Lauren   31–32
Blanchot, Maurice   218, 220
Bohr, Niels   148
Boll, Julia   94
Bottoms, Stephen   99, 111, 114
Bourdieu, Pierre   127
Bourriaud, Nicolas   158
Brecht, Bertolt   39, 41–43, 86, 161, 163, 209, 213n
Brennan, Clara   128–129, 135–137
– *The Wing*   128–129, 135–137
Brittain, Victoria   111
– *Guantanamo: 'Honor Bound to Defend Freedom': Taken from Spoken Evidence*   111
Butler, Judith   1–4, 6, 9, 17, 26, 31–33, 38, 65, 70n, 83–84, 89, 97, 100–114, 116, 118–120, 128–129, 142, 156–157, 161, 171, 176, 179, 189n, 191, 193, 195, 197–198, 203, 205–206, 209, 212–213, 219–220, 222, 229
Butterworth, Jez   7, 63–75
– *Jerusalem*   7, 63–75

Callender, Emma   128
Cameron, David   104, 191
carnival(esque)   12n, 63, 70–72
Castells, Manuel   126, 131–132
Cavarero, Adriana   38, 187–189, 192–193, 198–199
Chea, Pheng   53
Churchill, Caryl   9, 94, 217–218, 220, 226–231
– *Far Away*   94
– *Here We Go*   9, 217, 220, 226–229, 230–231

Claviez, Thomas   2n, 4n, 6n
cohabit(ation)   31–35, 38, 43, 84–85, 112–113, 116, 120–121, 127, 135–137, 217
Collins, Suzanne   147
– *The Hunger Games*   147
community   4–6, 9–11, 16, 18–19, 32, 40–41, 48, 83n, 84, 86, 91, 101, 103–105, 110, 115, 120, 125–138, 142, 147, 171, 172n, 182, 188–189, 196, 198–199, 203–214, 217–231
– *aesthetic community*   8, 128, 225
– *coming community*   5, 224
– *inoperative community*   5–6, 9, 20n, 157, 188, 217–231
compear(ance)   6n, 20n, 199, 219–220, 225–230
consumer(ism)   7, 9, 33, 88–89, 156–157, 159, 171, 173–174, 181–182, 185, 195–196, 198
Crimp, Martin   7, 9, 16, 22–23, 43, 187, 194–198
– *Fewer Emergencies*   7, 16, 22–24, 27
– *In the Republic of Happiness*   9, 187, 194–198
crisis   3, 64–66, 91, 102, 105, 118, 128, 137, 142, 173, 187, 192
Crouch, Tim   8, 77–90, 91–105
– *The Author*   8, 77–90, 91–105

death   3, 6, 9, 35, 38, 49n, 50, 65, 72, 158–159, 171, 178, 185, 188, 217, 220–231
Deleuze, Gilles   79–80, 82, 125–126
Delgado-García, Cristina   158
Derrida, Jacques   1, 4–5, 7, 16, 20–21, 23–25, 27, 33, 52–53, 68, 70n, 71, 119, 141, 162, 210, 223
Dolan, Jill   21, 150–151
Duchamp, Marcel   115
dystopia   7, 47, 50–51, 55–60, 144, 146, 148, 150–151, 195

ecstasy   9, 17, 20n, 155–167, 172
empathy   35–36, 40–43, 132–133, 137, 183, 190, 211, 226

Esposito, Roberto   217–220, 222–224, 227–228
ethics   3–5, 7–8, 10, 17–19, 31–35, 40, 43–44, 48, 65–66, 70, 72, 75, 77–79, 82–90, 91–103, 112–114, 116, 118–121, 128, 138, 141–142, 148–152, 155–157, 187–199, 203–207, 210–214, 219, 222, 224, 231

face (Levinas)   3, 6–7, 17, 18n, 32, 34, 36, 38, 49, 65, 66n, 70, 72, 75, 99, 142, 188, 190–191, 197, 203–208, 210–211, 214, 219, 224, 229, 231
Felman, Shoshana   196
finitude   5, 20n, 49, 188, 192, 197, 199, 219–220, 224–231
Fischer-Lichte, Erika   21n, 81, 230
Forced Entertainment   8, 141–152
– *Tomorrow's Parties*   8, 141–152
forgiveness   4, 10, 113, 211
Foucault, Michel   138
Fragkou, Marissia   190
Freud, Sigmund   16
Fukuyama, Francis   19n
future/*future*   8, 10, 19–21, 23, 27, 47–48, 50, 56, 59, 98n, 141–152

Gauthier, François   182
Giddens, Anthony   155, 157
gift   4, 23, 218–219, 222
Gilson, Erinn C.   129
globalisation   2, 7–8, 10, 16, 19, 22, 25, 31, 43–44, 49, 65, 73, 79, 91, 114, 116, 120, 127–128, 138, 141, 149, 155–166, 231
Goddard, Lynette   189
Greig, David   7, 9, 16, 24–27, 155–167, 203–214, 217–218, 220–225, 230
– *The American Pilot*   7, 16, 24–27, 163
– *The Architect*   160
– *The Events*   9, 158, 164–167, 203–214, 217, 220, 221–225, 230
– *Fragile*   164, 166
– *Midsummer* (with Gordon McIntyre)   164
– *One Way Street*   160
– *Outlying Islands*   158
– *San Diego*   158, 163

– *The Speculator* 160–161
– *Timeless* 161
guest 7, 11, 21, 23–25, 32, 38, 52–53, 65, 68–71, 74, 133
Gupta, Tanika 128–129, 132–135
– *Project N.I.G.H.T.* 128–129, 132–135

Hare, David 111, 118
– *The Power of Yes: A Dramatist Seeks to Understand the Financial Crisis* 118
– *Stuff Happens* 111n
Harris, Zinnie 94
– *The Wheel* 94
Hegel, Georg Wilhelm Friedrich 142, 145, 148
Heidegger, Martin 5, 218–219, 229
Hendricks, Thomas S. 176
Hobbes, Thomas 7, 47–49, 51, 222
hospitality 4–7, 10, 15–17, 20–27, 31–38, 43–44, 49, 52–53, 68–70, 85, 210–212, 222
host 7, 8, 11, 21–25, 32–33, 52, 65, 68–71, 74–75, 79, 85, 133
hostage 8, 23, 25, 33, 69, 79, 85, 103n, 133
hostility 16, 21–22, 24, 51, 53, 85, 204, 210, 222
Hurley, Kieran 128
– *Amanda* 128

identity 5, 7, 47, 54–56, 63, 65–66, 68n, 69, 72–75, 80, 132, 141n, 145, 157, 166, 182, 198, 217–218, 222, 224, 226, 230
immanence 5, 155, 162, 165–166, 171–172, 224–225, 229
intermediality 10
intertextuality 7, 10, 63, 73–75
intimacy 5, 8, 36, 38, 93, 174, 178, 220

Johnson, Samuel 2, 48, 116, 203

Kane, Sarah 85, 94, 158
– *4:48 Psychosis* 158
– *Blasted* 94, 158
– *Crave* 158

Kaufman, Moisés 110, 118
– *Gross Indecency: The Three Trials of Oscar Wilde* 111
– *The Laramie Project* 110, 118
Kelly, Dennis 9, 171–185
– *Love and Money* 9, 171–185
Korte, Barbara 2n

LaBute, Neil 128
– *Pick One* 128
Lacan, Jacques 17
Lehmann, Hans-Thies 34, 48, 59, 118, 194, 206n
Levinas, Emmanuel 1–4, 6–7, 9, 16–19, 31–32, 38, 43, 48–49, 65–66, 69, 72, 93, 99, 114, 120, 142, 203–205, 206n, 210–211, 219
Lévy, Pierre 80–82, 89
liminal(ity) 11, 16, 49–50, 58, 65, 67–68, 73, 75, 87, 225, 227
Lingis, Alphonso 218
liquid (modernity) 5, 8, 30–31, 130, 141–144, 151, 156, 158, 231
Lorey, Isabell 2
love 9, 16–18, 23, 120, 171–185

Malabou, Catherine 8, 142, 145–150, 152
Mbembe, Achille 38
Megson, Chris 94, 141, 182n
memory 7, 47–48, 50n, 54–58, 75, 141, 152n, 210–211
Middeke, Martin 6n, 194, 219n, 225, 229
migration 3, 22–23, 38, 128–129, 132–136, 163, 210, 221, 223
Miller, J. Hillis 6n, 217, 219n, 220
Monforte, Enric 190
mortality 3, 5, 49, 152n, 171, 219–220

Nancy, Jean-Luc 1, 5, 9, 16, 20n, 93, 125–126, 141, 157, 162, 167, 171–172, 174, 178, 180, 187–189, 198–199, 206, 217–220, 224, 227, 229–230
neighbour 7, 16–27, 32, 35–36, 189
neoliberalism 2, 7, 9, 19, 23, 31–32, 37, 43–44, 59, 126–127, 130, 132, 137, 159, 187–198

Norton-Taylor, Richard   111
– *The Colour of Justice: Based on the Transcripts of the Stephen Lawrence Inquiry*   111
Nussbaum, Martha   125–126, 132

O/other   3–9, 17–19, 23, 25, 32–36, 38–39, 41–44, 48–49, 53, 65–66, 68–70, 72, 74–75, 80, 83, 88, 91, 93, 95, 99–101, 112–114, 116, 118–121, 128–130, 138, 150, 156, 171–185, 187–194, 197–199, 203–214, 217–224, 227–231

Paget, Derek   109
Pattie, David   224
performative   4, 7, 11, 21n, 66, 73–75, 141, 150, 209, 218, 224, 229
Pewny, Katharina   1n, 203, 230
plasticity   8–9, 141–152
postdramatic   7, 10, 158
postmodern(ism)   7–8, 10, 63–75, 79, 88–89, 144, 165n
Price, Hanna   128
Price, Tim   128–132
– *Capitalism is Crisis*   128–132

Rancière, Jacques   8, 58, 78, 83, 121, 128, 206
Ravenhill, Mark   7, 31–43
– *Shoot/Get Treasure/Repeat*   7, 31–43
Rebellato, Dan   100, 155n, 157, 160–162, 195
Regard, Frédéric   2n
Reinhard, Kenneth   16–17
representation   3, 6–8, 10–11, 33–34, 75, 78, 81, 86, 91, 94–105, 110n, 111, 117, 121, 131, 142, 158–162, 191, 220
'response-ability'   34, 48, 59, 119, 206, 212–213
responsibility   4–5, 7, 9–11, 16–18, 23, 32–33, 40, 59, 65–66, 79, 83, 88–89, 91–95, 99, 102–105, 110–116, 117n, 119–121, 130, 133, 138, 149–150, 152n, 165–166, 187, 190–191, 195, 204, 205n, 206n, 211, 213n

Ridley, Philip   7, 47–60
– *Mercury Fur*   7, 47–60
Ridout, Nicholas   33, 99, 187
Rifkin, Jeremy   126–127
Rubik, Margarete   120

Santner, Eric L.   16–17
satire   8, 10–11, 57n, 79, 85, 89, 147, 191, 194
Schopenhauer, Arthur   229
Schwitters, Kurt   115
Shaw, Bernard   125
– *Pygmalion*   125
Sierz, Aleks   194
Simmel, Georg   176
singularity   5, 10–11, 20, 38, 114, 131, 157, 164, 166, 174, 188–189, 198–199, 206, 219–220, 222, 224–225, 227, 229–231
Slovo, Gillian   111
– *Guantanamo: 'Honor Bound to Defend Freedom': Taken from Spoken Evidence*   111
Soans, Robin   8, 109, 113–121
– *Talking to Terrorists*   8, 109, 113–121
Sontag, Susan   26
spectator(ship)   4, 6, 8–10, 21, 24, 26–27, 34, 39–40, 44, 48, 57–59, 77–89, 91–93, 97, 99, 101–105, 111, 113–114, 117–119, 121, 128, 132–135, 151, 157, 159, 164–166, 187, 189–198, 206, 211–212, 213n, 220, 230
Spinoza, Baruch de   125
Standing, Guy   32
Stephens, Simon   7, 15–16, 22, 27, 31, 34–39
– *Pornography*   7, 15–16, 22, 27, 31, 34–39
subject(ivity)   8–10, 16, 18, 33, 66, 79, 89, 98, 102, 143, 158, 171–185, 187–188, 190–199, 217, 224, 230
Suspect Culture   9, 155–167
– *Airport*   161–162
– *Mainstream*   162–163

terror(ism)   31, 34–43, 95–97, 113–121, 142, 144, 208, 221–222, 231
Theatre Uncut   8, 125–138

Thomas, Mark   128
- *Church Forced to Put Up Gates After Font is Used as Wash Basin By Migrants*   128
Thomassen, Bjørn   58
threshold   7, 10, 15–17, 20–27, 48–50, 58, 64, 69–74, 221
Thrift, Nigel   156
Tomlin, Liz   158
trauma   9, 17, 19, 54, 97, 100, 141, 164–165, 203, 206, 210, 221
tucker green, debbie   9, 187, 189–191, 198
- *dirty butterfly*   9, 187, 189–191
Turner, Victor   130

utopia   7, 9, 15, 19–22, 25, 27, 47–48, 50, 59, 104, 131, 144, 147, 151, 195
utopian performative   7, 21, 23, 25n, 26–27, 151

verbatim theatre   8, 94, 109–121
virtual(ity)   8, 10, 77–89, 138, 148
vulnerability   3, 5, 7–11, 20, 31–32, 34–35, 38, 41, 43, 48–49, 51–53, 65–66, 69, 72, 75, 83, 85, 91, 94n, 100–101, 103n, 112–116, 118–119, 127–130, 136, 138, 141–142, 149, 151, 171–185, 187–188, 189n, 190–191, 194n, 195–199, 203–214, 221–222, 227, 230

Wade, Laura   9, 187, 191–194, 198
- *Posh*   9, 187, 191–194
Wallace, Clare   158, 161, 163
war on terror   6–7, 31, 33, 39, 41, 92, 94–95, 97n, 101, 105
Weiss, Peter   118
White, Gareth   82–83, 104
witness(ing)   8, 11, 34, 39, 51, 56, 109, 112, 121, 132–133, 187, 190–196, 220, 227
Wyllie, Andrew   54

Zaroulia, Marilena   25n
Žižek, Slavoj   16–20, 23, 25, 145–146, 149–150, 182

www.ingramcontent.com/pod-product-compliance
Lightning Source LLC
Chambersburg PA
CBHW030619230426
43661CB00053B/2059